SAW-PIT WHARTON

The only portrait of Wharton known to be genuine. It was painted by Van Dyck and shows Wharton at the age of nineteen. This reproduction was taken from the original while it was on loan from Czar Nicholas II to the Royal Academy of Arts, London, for their Van Dyck exhibition of 1900. It is reproduced by permission of the Academy.

SAW-PIT WHARTON

The Political Career from 1640 to 1691
of Philip, fourth Lord Wharton

G. F. TREVALLYN JONES
University of Sydney

SYDNEY UNIVERSITY PRESS
1967

SYDNEY UNIVERSITY PRESS

Press Building, University of Sydney, NSW, Australia

U.S.A.: PENNSYLVANIA STATE UNIVERSITY PRESS
NEW ZEALAND: PRICE MILBURN AND COMPANY LIMITED
ELSEWHERE: METHUEN AND COMPANY LIMITED AND THEIR AGENTS

First published 1967
© G. F. Trevallyn Jones 1967

*This book is supported by funds
from the Eleanor Sophia Wood Bequest*

Registered in Australia for transmission by post as a book
PRINTED AT THE GRIFFIN PRESS, SOUTH AUSTRALIA

TO ANNE WHITEMAN
*who introduced me to Wharton
and who taught me to write*

ACKNOWLEDGEMENTS

It is with love and gratitude that I acknowledge that assistance and support which was essential to the making of this book and which my wife provided in every way during the research and the writing.

For many invaluable suggestions in arrangement and clarification I am also grateful to the editor of the Sydney University Press, Michael Turnbull.

CONTENTS

ACKNOWLEDGEMENTS   vii

ABBREVIATIONS   x

I   THE MAN AND HIS AGE, AND THE SCOPE OF THE STUDY   1

II   THE HOUSE OF WHARTON, 1530-1637   13

III   YORKSHIRE AND THE BISHOPS' WARS   20

IV   OPPOSITION AMONG THE PEERS   29

V   THE REVOLUTIONARY LEADER   39

VI   PURITAN PARLIAMENTARIANS   50

VII   WHARTON IN THE FIELD   58

VIII   BETWEEN THE PEACE PARTY AND THE EXTREMISTS   69

IX   THE 'GODLY PARTY' AND THE WESTMINSTER ASSEMBLY   78

X   THE 'INDEPENDENTS' AND THE SCOTS   90

XI   THE WAR'S END BRINGS NO PEACE   103

XII   A MOST BARBAROUS PLOT   116

XIII   WHARTON AND THE REGICIDES   128

XIV   WHARTON AVOIDS TEMPTATION   138

XV   THE 'JUNTO' AND THE RESTORATION   151

XVI   DANGER AND DELIVERANCE   166

XVII   THE HEAD OF THE PRESBYTERIAN PARTY   174

XVIII   SWIMMING AGAINST THE TIDE   187

XIX   THE GREAT ADVERSARY   201

XX   THE TIDE BEGINS TO TURN   214

XXI   WITH SHAFTESBURY TO THE TOWER   222

XXII   EXCLUSION AND THE POPISH PLOT   237

XXIII   FEAR AND TRIUMPH   252

XXIV   DISILLUSION AND DEATH   260

APPENDIX I   COUNTRY PEERS IN OPPOSITION   269

APPENDIX II   THE OSBORNE AFFAIR   275

SOURCES   283

ON THE USE MADE OF THE SOURCES   287

INDEX   289

ABBREVIATIONS

AHR	American Historical Review
BIHR	Bulletin of the Institute of Historical Research
CJ	Commons' Journals
DNB	Dictionary of National Biography
LJ	Lords' Journals
EHR	English Historical Review
EcHR	Economic History Review
HMC	Historical Manuscripts Commission
TRHS	Transactions of the Royal Historical Society

I

THE MAN AND HIS AGE, AND THE SCOPE OF THE STUDY

'constant opposition to the councils prevailing'

My general aims in this study are to throw light on the political career of one prominent seventeenth-century Englishman and by that illumination to clarify or modify where possible or necessary the political history of England in that century. Some particular aims are to examine that career as it throws light on certain elements of seventeenth-century politics: the role of a peer, the role of the House of Lords itself, the connection between puritanism and political opposition, and the workings of the various oppositions to the Stuart Kings. Others are to consider that one peer's activities in the context of the activities of other peers, his associates; and, in the same context, his attitudes to the great political, constitutional and religious controversies of the century; and, finally, to attempt to evaluate the total effect of that peer's participation in politics.

The 'good Lord Wharton' as he was called by some with affection and respect (or 'Saw-pit' as he was derisively called by others) seemed to me a particularly useful and appropriate subject for a seventeenth-century political biography. First, he was a peer of the realm and seventeenth-century England was aristocratic, as much as or more than sixteenth-century England and almost as much as eighteenth-century England; moreover, in his lifetime, the role of the peerage changed in important ways economically and politically. Secondly, Wharton was a puritan, and one can say that the seventeenth century was for England the century of puritanism: certainly puritanism had no other century in English history. Neither its beginnings in the Elizabethan Church of England nor its survivals in the accepted nonconformity of later centuries affects the truth and importance of the puritans' rise to a climax of power and ambition almost exactly halfway through the seventeenth century, and nearly halfway through Wharton's life. Again— and this is the third point—the seventeenth century was, in spite of the prevalence of aristocracy (within and without the peerage), the first century in English history in which democracy in a number of forms seriously challenged the aristocracy. At the same time, a section of the aristocracy was itself challenging the monarchy. Some opposition lords were ready to ally with democratic factions, and Wharton was one of these.

His life spanned almost all the seventeenth century, and his activity and prominence in politics covered nearly half that century, a period full of revolutions and attempted revolutions, in most of which Wharton was involved, and always on the revolutionary side. The first of these—and perhaps the greatest in English history—was once generally called the *puritan* revolution. One of my aims in this study has been therefore to see if Wharton was typical of those numerous peers who opposed the principles and practices of Charles I and his Ministers before and during the civil wars. Oversimplifications of the 1640s range the King and the peers against the merchants and yeomen, with the bulk of the gentry on one side or the other, according to the taste of the simplifier. In fact the revolution split all ranks of society including the royal family —two of the King's nephews supported him, but a third tried to supplant him—and of the peerage more than half was at one time or another involved in opposition.

Various theories, past and present, would have the opposition lords consist of either the more ancient in nobility (resisting a growing royal absolutism), or a newer, economically more enterprising type of magnate impatient with royal support of an allegedly feudal type of society and economy. The possibility that principles, whether political or religious, could play much part independent of material interests is usually heavily discounted.

Wharton had close political relations with many leaders of various factions, men who attacked or defended the privileges of either one or both of the Houses of Parliament, men who could be called democrats or oligarchs, or tyrants. He also had close relations with many leading puritan divines, and it is certain that he held tenaciously to strong religious beliefs. For a time he was the leading political defender of the puritan religious interest. The connection between religion and politics in Wharton's life is therefore a major theme of this study.

Finally, the seventeenth century was the century *par excellence* of plots. True, there were a few plots against the Tudors, and some Jacobite intrigues against the Hanoverians, but little enough compared with the never-ending stream of conspiracies by, for, or against the Stuarts in their century in England: the Main Plot, the Bye Plot, the Gunpowder Plot; the Army Plots, the Derwentdale Plot, the Grand Design; the Popish Plot, the Meal-Tub Plot, the Rye House Plot; and the countless nameless conspiracies and intrigues by puritan colonisers, Covenanting lairds, Irish chiefs, Cavaliers, republicans, fanatics, soldiers, Whigs and Tories. Even a cursory glance shows that Wharton had an impressive record of involvement one way or another in plots, either as a prosecutor or an intended victim, a framer of the innocent or an innocent trying, in every sense, not to lose his head.

All original research tends to be the result of relatively narrow specialisation. The snare set in the way of the specialist is the temptation, sometimes almost irresistible, to exaggerate the importance of his speciality in order to justify his study. This pitfall is particularly dangerous to a biographer, especially to the biographer of a person admittedly in the second rank. Details of the private life, the family affairs, the household expenses and the like, which tend to nauseate even in the lives of the great, are even less easy to stomach when served with the excuse that they are necessary to present a full picture, or even make a rounded figure, of some not-quite-great person.

Wharton is such a person, and thus I have limited my study to his *political career*, and I deal with his *private life* only when it impinges on his *public* life; for example, when family relationships affected or may have affected political activity, or when political aims may have influenced family arrangements such as marriages. However, even a political biography raises difficulties, and there are special difficulties here because Wharton's political career was particularly long. Properly **to** explain it, a full political history of Britain in the seventeenth century would need to be written around his life, which, since Wharton was seldom the most important political figure on the public stage, would leave the biographical part of the work spread rather thinly. It is essential to keep Wharton in the foreground, yet too great a concentration on Wharton without adequate background would not only mislead the reader; it would also fail to explain the significance of much of his activity. Connected with but distinct from this is the danger of overemphasising the importance of events in which Wharton figured largely, or in which he took great interest, while ignoring or minimising events in which he took little or no interest or part. There are, however, some obvious advantages in studying a political figure whose sentient life spanned most of a century. It is interesting and possibly useful to see how a mind whose attitudes began to form in the last years of James I reacted, undimmed by senility, to the conditions of the first years of William III.

But even if I had not wished to limit the scope of my study, the hard fact remains that many seventeenth-century figures do not and cannot come alive for their biographers. One of the latter has written:

> the men of 1688 and the two Juntos, the founders of our political system—Russell and Montagu, Shrewsbury and Burnet, Somers and Wharton . . . elude us.[1]

The Wharton named was the fourth lord's son and successor, Thomas, Marquess of Wharton, one more noticed in history than Philip, his father.

In the case of Philip Wharton, the arbitrary chances of the survival of evidence as well as his cautious, evasive and retiring nature combine to make it difficult for us to form a clear picture of the man himself. He left no diaries and relatively few letters to speak with his own voice. Where his words survive, they are rather matter-of-fact for a puritan of the early seventeenth century: neither the emotional if obscure religiosity of a Cromwell nor the passionate eloquence of an Eliot garbles or ornaments his usually simple and unrhetorical prose. Neither

1. J. Carswell, *The Old Cause*, London 1954.

was he, unfortunately, enlivened by any of the wit so common among the statesmen who were his contemporaries in the second half of the century. There is no evidence that he had much sense of humour, although—unlike some—he could understand when others were fooling; and once at least, near the end of his life, he rejoined in kind. However, there was little or none of the alleged gloom of the puritans in Philip Wharton at any age. As a young peer he was on easy terms of friendship with his equals and neighbours, not only those who were puritan, swapping news and haunches of venison. He was able to show himself not merely cheerful but even 'merry', whatever that might mean applied to him; but in spite of his excellent physique (an adversary called him a 'Saint of the largest size') he did not display any remarkable fondness for the field sports so beloved by most of the upper classes. His youthful portrait shows a fairly handsome face with some suggestions of both shrewdness and complacence. His early life was simply that of a country gentleman of more than ordinary rank and status— the condition of many Jacobean and Caroline peers.

Wharton's monument in the parish church of Wooburn called him:

> an active supporter of the English Constitution, a loyal observer, advocate and patron of the reformed religion, a model alike of good works and of a true and living faith.[2]

The first of these claims must be examined, and will be examined. The last needs little examination, for it admits of no argument. Wharton's charities were sufficiently numerous and considerable to bear out the claim so far as it concerns good works.[3] We cannot know when his puritan upbringing took root in Wharton, but only a strong and genuinely religious faith could have made him become an inflexible protagonist in the religious struggles of the Restoration, and expose himself to the humiliation of arrest for attending conventicles long after all other peers and most gentlemen had conformed outwardly to the established Church. This judgement is not weakened by

2. E. R. Wharton, *The Whartons of Wharton Hall*, London 1898, 37.
3. B. Dale, *The Good Lord Wharton, His Family, Life and Bible Charity* (London 1906) makes this abundantly clear.

evidence of equivocation, disingenuousness or outright lying, where the end justified the means. To a puritan the honour of God was of infinite importance, and Wharton was seriously affected by his scruples over the unworthiness of some who claimed to be God's instruments and over the (to him) idolatrous kissing of the Bible in taking an oath, whereas the world's concept of a nobleman's honour was of little importance. Thus Wharton might indeed perpetrate pious frauds, but if he did so, they would be quite as pious as fraudulent (like that of the patriarch Jacob) for Wharton was not himself a pious fraud.

By the time Wharton's words and actions enable us to see much more than a name, he is revealed as a middle-aged man of impaired health, patient but stern, businesslike, indefatigable in committees, cautious in most things but stubborn in some, devious in his ways, hard and disingenuous to his opponents though loyal to his friends. My avoidance of his private life, which reduces the incidence of pettiness and prolixity, is no hardship, for his family provided no spectacular scandals and Wharton himself lived a blameless married life with each of his three wives, who were in turn apparently as blameless. Of the first, virtually nothing is known, and of the character and possible influence of the last, very little. Jane Goodwin, the second Lady Wharton, may have had considerable character and intelligence, and therewith some influence on her husband, for Arthur Goodwin wrote to her when he wanted her husband to do something in the House of Lords, and she made some impression on Cromwell. However, Wharton will have been very much the master in his house. The care of his nine children (all that survived of the fifteen he sired) he gave—under close supervision—to four tutors, for each of whom he drew up a time-table and a syllabus. His instructions read in part 'if any of them do amiss' their father, if at home, must 'be acquainted that night' for their swift punishment; if he were abroad, his deputies had power to chastise. Was he harsh or merely strict? It is impossible to be positive. His sons, who were mostly high-spirited, lived in the utmost awe of him even to their own middle-age. It has been claimed that the eldest learned his great art of dissimulation during years of unctuous hypocrisy for his father's deception, while the second son, an unhappy youth who grew up half crazy, thus advised his own (illegitimate) son, if he in turn should be 'blessed with children':

> Prescribe them not so much outward awe of you as may hinder them from freely communicating their thoughts.

When a daughter married against his wishes, Wharton barred her from the sacraments for her sin of disobedience.

Yet there is another side to the problem. The disobedient daughter had chosen a young man who was not merely impecunious but also the brother of her step-mother, thus incurring an unwelcome if vague suggestion of incest. In the interests of his children Wharton was careful and indefatigable. He fought elections for his sons, which he apparently never troubled to do for friends or clients. For the financial security of his eldest daughter and her possible children he gave up his own plans and endured slights. Even his sons' turbulence may have been not so much a reaction against his severity as a result of his mistimed kindness in choosing for the post of their tutor in their education abroad the candidate recommended as 'mild and sweet' rather than the possessor of 'the more authoritative presence'.[4] The speed with which the young Whartons became debauched soon made their father repent and change his decision, but by then the damage may have been done. Also, the sheer violence of the young Whartons' wildness —two of them later desecrated a church with every circumstance of obscenity and blasphemy—suggests an almost uncontrollable devilry which might provoke sternness. Certainly it was always controlled or disguised in Lord Wharton's presence.

Philip Wharton was equally ambiguous in his treatment of political opponents. When he helped to prosecute and condemn victims of political rancour, his knowledge or suspicion that injustice was perpetrated by his own party never inspired him to mercy or fairness. Roman Catholics he could use or contemplate using as allies without ever abating his fear, hatred, contempt and cruelty towards them. Yet, as so often in his days, personal ties could override party hostility. Naturally enough

---

4. The quotations and most of the information in the above account of the upbringing of Wharton's sons are from Carswell, *Old Cause*.

he remained a good friend to Anglican Cavaliers who were closely related to him; more surprising and illuminating is his intercession for an Irish Catholic peer married to a connection of Wharton's mother. It is possible even that Wharton had some reputation for humanity; certainly Charles II appeared to single him out to hear his indignation at the barbarous murder of Archbishop Sharp.

Wharton was *honest* politically, in that he never deserted one party to join with another. His *financial* honesty, another pleasing facet of his character and one even less common in the seventeenth century, seems connected with his apparent complete lack of that extreme greed so rife especially in public figures, often leading to peculation, bribe-taking, extortion and other forms of financial dishonesty and oppression. Wharton's hands were clean in this respect, although he would *give* a bribe in a good cause. Yet in spite of his modest acquisitiveness, or possibly because that modesty was balanced usually by an equal modesty in expense (suitable to puritan morality) or at least by sound and prudent management, he left his heir £8,000 *per annum*[5] in contrast to little more than £2,000 *per annum* enjoyed by his grandfather in 1600. Only part of this increase could have come from the lands of his second heiress wife, and much came from lead-mining interests which he himself built up with care and success.

Some of the things we learn from Wharton's character and career are what might well have been expected without any close study, but other discoveries are more interesting. It is not surprising that for some statesmen growing up in the first half of the seventeenth century, religion should be the mainspring of political activity; but more surprising is the persistence and effectiveness of this motive in one such statesman late in the century. It is hardly surprising that a puritan should tend to oppose the effective use of strong monarchic power; but quite surprising to find a peer by inheritance, even if a puritan, so unaristocratic. The easy assumption that political and religious aims were closely connected with economic and political interests can find little support in Wharton's career. He was a landowner

5. *Memoirs of the Life of the Most Nobel Thomas, Late Marquess of Wharton,* London (printed for J. Roberts), 1715.

whose wealth grew steadily while his puritanism persisted and even became more extreme. After all the upheavals and reversals of the Interregnum, and in spite of his wealth and privileges, he advocated a constitution in some ways more democratic than could be had in England before the twentieth century.

In the struggles that convulsed seventeenth-century England there were two great issues, constitutional and religious. The fears of arbitrary government and of Roman Catholicism were the constant factors in almost every crisis. Religion was always made the first war cry, whether it mattered most to those who raised the cry or because it roused the greatest number of people. To say (as did his monument) that Wharton supported the English constitution, is to beg the question: what was that constitution? To those of his contemporaries who took one view of it, Wharton was a life-long assailant of the constitution. In simple truth, Wharton's century was that in which the development of the constitution took a decisive turn away from personal monarchy towards parliamentary government. It was also a century in which it was harder than ever to find a definite and coherent formulation of the constitution which could achieve even general, let alone universal, acceptance. Wharton served in every Parliament, after 1629 and until 1691, which made or attempted any significant or permanent change in the constitution. He was an ally, lieutenant or opponent of most of the leaders of reform, revolution or reaction, from Strafford, Pym, and Hampden, through Say and Sele, Vane, St John, Haselrig and Cromwell, to Sydney, Shaftesbury, Holles, Halifax and Danby.

Of the two great aims, political liberty and religious reform, it is not certain which most strongly drew Wharton into the thick of the puritan revolution of the 1640s. Some circumstantial evidence suggests that puritanism was the factor which decided a number of reformers to continue into revolution. One thing is certain, that Wharton was not inspired by fear, or pique, by greed for gain or lust for power. Twenty years later, in Restoration England, Wharton's mainspring of activity was very clearly religion. Just before and during the Interregnum, religion was settled by puritans and Erastians in a way especially pleasing to those puritans of Wharton's persuasion, the Independents. Therefore Wharton's withdrawal from politics between Pride's

Purge and the Restoration, so far as it was not on moral grounds, must have been due to political objections. Both that withdrawal, and the later temptation to reverse it, must be regarded as important or even crucial evidence of his political and constitutional beliefs and aims, at least in that period.

Usually opposition leaders (and often government spokesmen), especially before 1648 and after 1660, declared their adherence to the classical theory of 'mixed' government, the combination or interaction of monarchy, aristocracy and democracy. In practice, and even to some extent in theory, most favoured the aristocractic element, and tended towards a Venetian republicanism. Wharton left no evidence whatever of any belief in monarchy, or that the monarchic element was necessary or even useful; nor did he show any practical gratitude to any monarch for those favours from them which he acknowledged. Wharton may have had more loyalty to his own order, the hereditary peerage, but this was at best lukewarm. His republicanism seems to have grown more radical with the passing of time. While no doubt he would not have objected to a figurehead monarch, and to the continuation of the legislative rights of the peerage and the peers' great personal privileges, he was nevertheless willing, in practice in the 1640s and in principle in 1689, to see his own House of Lords dominated by the Commons. He almost seems to have felt a need to apologise for calling the House of Commons the 'lower' House. More, in contrast to the theories and practice of most of his contemporaries, he seems to have wanted the Commons elected more democratically.

However, Wharton did not worship parliament or democracy as necessarily right. In practice, he constantly sided with the more radical groups in the House of Commons, frequently against a majority in his own House, but when the majority in the Commons was immovably opposed to the things he aimed at, he would support outside forces, the army, the mob, or even the King. The insoluble dilemma of puritans interested in political liberty was how to obtain a form of government which would give political rights to the nation and yet ensure a 'godly' rule. Wharton fell between the aristocratic republicanism of a Sydney and the oligarchic theocracy of an Owen. His pragmatic approach to the problem of securing a godly government seems to have been to play on the anti-Catholic prejudices of the masses in order to secure the destruction of any who hindered the religious policies or practices of the puritans.

The sources of this study are mostly Wharton's own papers in the Carte manuscripts in the Bodleian Library. A certain imbalance results from the fact that Wharton's earlier political career, of unobtrusiveness in power and in the work of administration, is much better documented by the *Lords' Journals* and the *Calendars of State Papers* and by Wharton's copies of State papers than are his later years of prominence in largely fruitless opposition. However, this later period is much more fully treated (than are the earlier years) in one important source which needs special mention here. In October 1685, while temporarily and inconspicuously resident in the Rhenish provinces of the Elector of Brandenburg, Wharton thought it good to submit to the Elector's representative, Alexander, Freiherr von Spaen, President of the Government of Cleve and Mark, a long Latin letter.[6] This has been called a 'political testament'.[7] It was in fact a brief autobiography, designed to explain both his recent withdrawal from England and his desire to remain anonymous. With a prudence typical of the writer, it was not left with von Spaen. Like most things about the fourth Lord Wharton the letter is somewhat enigmatic, and notable as much for what it does not say as for what it does say. Nevertheless, a political testament is an obvious beginning, if only as a point of departure, for an examination of its author's political career. I have tried to use it to provide a framework for this study, or at least for such periods of Wharton's life as are at all covered by the document, all of which is embodied piecemeal in the following text.

I begin with its penultimate paragraph. This gives a guarantee of credibility not, regrettably, justified, but it does fairly accurately and succinctly strike the keynote of consistency, which was a characteristic of Wharton's whole career:

> The truth of the above I affirm on the word of a gentleman and as I shall have to answer at the last day. If you read to

6. MS Carte 81, 736-8, endorsed: 'Letter to Baron S. shewn to him but not left with him. October 18, 1685'.
7. By Carswell, *Old Cause*, 62.

the end you will be convinced that the three Kings I have mentioned, from the first to the last, openly showed me all tokens of goodwill despite my constant opposition to the councils prevailing, especially with the late and the present King.

II

THE HOUSE OF WHARTON
I530-I637

'the professed enemy of Popery and profaneness'

PHILIP WHARTON, the future fourth baron, was born in 1613, the heir of a house whose history in the past four generations typified the fortunes of many a family climbing from obscurity, only to fall back again, in the troubled arena of politics and religion of post-Reformation England. His ancestor, Thomas Wharton, whose family had 'always' held Wharton in Westmorland, sat for Appleby in the Reformation Parliament, to the satisfaction of the King, for he was soon made Sheriff of Cumberland.[1] From that position he rose rapidly to be Deputy Warden of the West Marches (to the disgust of the Dacres, Cliffords, Musgraves and others who scorned the 'new man') and won his peerage in 1543 by his great victory over the Scots at Solway Moss. The career of the first baron bore some similarity to that of his descendant, the subject of this study, if only in his longevity and in the number of diverse governments under which he lived. He too was consistent, but only in following and profiting by every government in turn. Although he was conservative in religion (voting against the act allowing priests to marry) he helped suppress the Pilgrimage of Grace, and was enriched with monastic lands.[2] Some of these—the manor of Kirkby Stephen, with rectory and advowson (late of St Mary's Priory, York), the site and demesne of the Abbey of Shap, and the manor of Ravenstonedale (late of Watton Priory)—were in his ancestral Westmorland; but so many more were in the North

1. The details of the first two barons are from *DNB* unless otherwise stated.
2. For the details of their acquisitions, see Dale, *Good Lord Wharton*, 12-14.

Riding—the manors of Healaugh and Catterton and the site, demesne, tithes and advowson of Healaugh Park Priory, the house and site of the priory of Sinningthwaite and some of its lands, and the manor of Muker and other Swaledale lands of Rievaulx Abbey—that he moved his seat to one of them (Healaugh) and the later Whartons were brought up as Yorkshiremen. The first Lord Wharton was promoted by the strongly Protestant Lord Protector Somerset, sat in judgement on him, and was further promoted by Somerset's destroyer, the even more recklessly Protestant (in policy) Protector Northumberland. He served Queen Mary and, in his old age, Queen Elizabeth.

In contrast, his son and heir, also called Thomas, showed consistency of a different kind. He was devoted to the Catholic princess Mary Tudor. He was Steward of her household before her succession and the fall of Northumberland. He escorted her to Framlingham Castle in the crisis of Northumberland's abortive attempt to substitute for her on the throne of England the Protestant Lady Jane Grey, and at once became Queen Mary's Master of the Henchmen, indefatigable Privy Councillor, Sheriff of Cumberland and Warden of the East and Middle Marches. For his services Queen Mary granted him several manors in Essex and made him Steward of many Crown estates in Yorkshire. On Elizabeth's accession Wharton was excluded from Parliament and the Privy Council, and in 1561 was sent to the Tower for a time for hearing Mass in his house. He did nothing for or against the rebellion of the northern earls, and died, in 1572, four years after his father, leaving a minor to succeed him.

Philip, third Lord Wharton, was obviously named by his father in compliment to the Spanish husband of his mistress, but as a royal ward was entrusted to Lord Burleigh and the Earl of Sussex and brought up a Protestant.[3] He married one of the Cliffords, whose family had looked down on his grandfather, and married one of his daughters to the head of the Musgraves; but these social successes brought no great advance-

3. L. Stone, *The Crisis of the Aristocracy, 1558-1641*, Oxford 1965, 739. The other details of the third Lord's career and connections come from Dale; *DNB*; from J. E. Doyle, *The Official Baronage of England*, London 1886; and G. Burton, *The Life of Sir Philip Musgrave, Bart.*, Carlisle 1840.

ment. In 1617 at Wharton Hall he entertained the King on his way to Scotland, and this may account for one of his few and relatively unimportant official appointments, to the Commission for the Peace of the Borders in 1618. His attempts to form Court connections were dogged with ill-success. His daughter Margaret was married to Lord Wotton, Privy Councillor and Treasurer of King James's Household, but that courtier's erratic career faltered long before he was excluded from the Council as a Roman Catholic on the accession of Charles I. Sir George Wharton, the third baron's eldest son, married a daughter of the Earl of Rutland, and might have made a place for himself at Court had he not in a duel in 1609 killed, and been killed by, one of the royal favourites, the King's godson, Sir James Stuart. By the King's order the two young homicides were buried together.

This disaster virtually ended for a century the hopes or at least the attempts of the house of Wharton for advancement at Court. Yet the third lord may have had great need of royal favour. His income at the turn of the century was £2,107, barely reaching the average for an apparently hard-pressed peerage in an age of inflation.[4] It seems agreed that the lavishness of James I brought financial relief to the aristocracy, but this was not true for all, and any efforts by the first Philip Wharton to catch some of this reviving shower of gold must have failed. By 1618, his debts totalled £16,713.[5] To pay them he conveyed to a group of trustees, headed by Humphrey Wharton, his man of business, most of his estates, retaining £500 *per annum* for his surviving son and £600 *per annum* for himself.[6] The manors in Essex, the gift of Queen Mary, were lost in this period, if not before,[7] and when Philip died in 1626 his income had been further reduced to £434 7s 4d.[8]

4. G. E. C., *Peerage*. Stone computed the wealth of the average Elizabethan peer at £2-3,000 *per annum*: 'An Anatomy of the Elizabethan Aristocracy', *EcHR*, XVIII (1948) 38.
5. Dale, *Good Lord Wharton*, 28.
6. Wharton, *The Whartons*, 28.
7. MS Carte 81, 195. Notes on an interview between Philip Wharton and Sir Henry Bennet, 5 December 1663, in which Wharton claimed he had not a pennyworth of land south of Yorkshire before his (second) marriage.
8. G.E.C. *Peerage*.

Philip's second son, Sir Thomas Wharton, married a daughter of that energetic courtier, Robert Carey, who, though only a younger son, ended his life as Earl of Monmouth. Sir Thomas showed, however, no signs of wishing to pursue a Court career, and instead purchased the reversion of Aske Hall in Easby, Richmondshire, which thereafter he shared with its owner, his widowed cousin Lady Bowes, sister-in-law of the wife of John Knox. It has been suggested that economic decline often prompted a religious change to a more extreme, minority faith.[9] Whether he moved to a congenial atmosphere, or whether he was changed by his cousin's deeply Calvinist household, at all events Sir Thomas became, some time during the first or second decade of the century, the first puritan Wharton.[10]

The epithet of puritan was at that time applied by episcopal Anglicans to those who opposed episcopacy and by the more worldly to all whom they deemed excessively religious. It could cover those who accepted the Book of Common Prayer and the institution of episcopacy but who disliked the practices, pretensions and principles of the existing episcopate and who wished for a more fervent preaching ministry; to those who wanted a further reformation of the Church of England on or towards the Geneva model; and to those 'separatists' (then a tiny, impotent minority) who held that the established Church was no true Church. Most puritans were staunchly Calvinist and most disliked as unnecessary much of the ritual and many of the ceremonies and vestments of the Church. Most puritans and many of the gentry—largely anti-clerical gentry in one sense or another—would have liked to see the powers of the Bishops much reduced.

Samuel Wales, the minister of Morley, described Sir Thomas thus:

> He was the professed enemy of Popery and profaneness; a true friend . . . of all godly . . . preachers . . . frequenting God's house not only twice on the Lord's Day, but . . . on Lecture days . . . By profane great ones . . . he was secretly twitted for preciseness and Puritanism.[11]

9. By H. R. Trevor-Roper.
10. *The Diary of Ralph Thoresby [1677-1724]; Letters of eminent men addressed to Ralph Thoresby*, ed J. Hunter, London 1830-2, I, 280.
11. Dale, *Good Lord Wharton*, 31. Wales wrote this in the dedication of his book *Totum Hominis* (1627) to the fourth Baron, who in 1681, with his brother, republished the book.

When the puritan Sir Thomas died in 1622, his eldest son Philip was only nine years old. Three years later the third Lord Wharton died, and his title and reduced income passed to his twelve-year-old grandson and namesake, Philip, fourth Lord Wharton, the Saw-Pit Wharton of this study. To a noble family before the abolition of feudal tenure, the succession by a minor could be a major financial setback, but although the Court of Wards in this period was being used as unscrupulously as ever to enrich those who controlled it, the fourth Lord Wharton reached manhood with his fortunes repaired rather than impaired, at the cost, if it can be called that, of marriage to an heiress.

In 1632 Philip married Elizabeth, sole heiress of Sir Rowland Wandesford, of Pickhill, Yorkshire. The dowry obtained by this marriage may have been considerable, for the Wandesford lands, which were to descend to Wharton and his children by Elizabeth, were sufficient fortune finally to obtain a match for Wharton's daughter with the heir to the Earl of Lindsey. On leaving Oxford University in 1629, Wharton had at least enough revenue to travel for two years with his younger brother and six servants. However, there may have been some measure of economy in this rather prolonged tour, since impoverished peers were likely to go abroad to live cheaply. In 1635, a year after he had come of age, and three years after his marriage, he received a decree by the Court of Wards in his favour and against Humphrey Wharton and his associates, who had claimed the lands under their control.[12] In 1636 Wharton was pleased to hear that Sir Rowland had become Attorney to the Court of Wards, through the agency of Lord Cottington, its Master,[13] and it seems possible that the debt of £1,000 which Wharton owed Sir Rowland as late as 1640, and perhaps even longer, may have been connected with this relatively successful termination of a wardship.

Wharton's childhood in a strictly religious household endowed him (according to a contemporary) with 'the morningstar of early piety'.[14] The influence of his grandfather's impoverished

12. MS Carte 117, 181-92.
13. MS Carte 80, 638.
14. Dale, *Good Lord Wharton*, 61.

state may have confirmed his earliest influences (if there is any substance in the theory that poverty among the gentry fostered dissent—whether recusant or puritan—from the established Church) or possibly his father's example was revived later at Oxford. Wharton matriculated in 1626 at Exeter College, where there was at least one strongly puritan don, and which was the only outpost of the once dominant puritanism of Oxford which Laud failed to reduce to Arminian or High Church episcopalian uniformity.[15]

A few months of warfare in the Low Countries at the age of seventeen or eighteen gave him no taste for a military career, although his younger brother, Thomas, may then have taken the bent which made him a professional soldier. After their return to England, while Thomas took service in the army in Ireland, Philip Wharton lived for several years at Healaugh, the Yorkshire seat of the Lords Wharton. However, soon after the death of his first wife, he moved in 1637 to London, entered Lincoln's Inn to obtain that grounding in legal knowledge so useful to many gentlemen of property who had no intention of practising law, and, in September of the same year, married again.

Wharton's second wife, Jane, was also the sole heiress of a wealthy man, Arthur Goodwin, Esquire,[16] of Winchendon in Buckinghamshire. He was the last of one of the three related families (the others were the Fleetwoods and Dentons) which, in the reigns of the two Stuarts, monopolised the honour of representing the shire in Parliament.[17] John Hampden, although he was cousin, neighbour and life-long friend to Arthur Goodwin, gained that honour only after his Ship-money case made him famous. It was in 1637, the year of Wharton's second marriage, that Hampden's case was heard and decided for the King.

15. Anthony Wood, *Athenae Oxonienses*, ed P. Bliss, London 1813, III, 271; H. R. Trevor-Roper, *Archbishop Laud*, Hamden, Conn. 1963, 113-14.

16. Goodwin contributed nearly twice as much (£1,800) to the Adventure against the Irish rebels of 1640 as did Hampden (£1,000) who was accounted rich. H. R. Williamson, *John Hampden*, London 1933, 293·

17. Lady de Villiers, 'Parliamentary Boroughs restored by the House of Commons, 1621-1641', *EHR*, LXVII (1952) 189.

Of his life from 1629 up to that time, Wharton wrote for von Spaen only this:

> I passed through France as a young man and spent part of a summer as a volunteer under the Prince of Orange. I returned to England at the approach of the winter of 1631 and at that time was commanded by the King to present myself at the customary masque, in which he, like others, always took part.
>
> The following year I married and retired into the country, one hundred and fifty miles from London, living there continuously except when the King commanded me to bear a part in a similar masque, as he did every year till the beginning, I think in 1638, of the troubles in Scotland.

There is a note of apology in the suggestion that the puritan Wharton danced in Court masques only because he was commanded by the King: actually, the handsome young lord was proud of his fine, long legs, and delighted to show them off.[18] However, his mention of this embarrassing youthful levity did serve to bring out the favour with which, he emphasised, Charles I regarded him. His marriage seems to be given as his reason for retiring to the country: perhaps he wished to show that, although a *country* lord as opposed to a *Court* lord, he was no sulking 'country-house conspirator',[19] embittered against the Court. Oddly enough, his second marriage, allying him with an opposition family and faction, and bringing his residence to London or at furthest, Buckinghamshire, receives no mention. Yet it may well have had the same effect on Wharton's life as Mandeville's second marriage had on Mandeville: it may have brought him into the 'opposition'.[20]

---

18. *Memoirs of the Marquess of Wharton*, 5.
19. Phrase used by Professor Trevor-Roper of early seventeenth-century opposition gentry.
20. His second marriage to a daughter of the Earl of Warwick brought Edward Montagu (Viscount Mandeville, as heir to the Earl of Manchester) into the opposition. Clarendon, *History of the Rebellion*, London 1843, §73.

III

YORKSHIRE AND THE
BISHOPS' WARS

*'we desire that this insupportable burthen may be
taken off us'*

SHIP-MONEY was the most promising and productive of the
expedients by which Charles I sought to finance his government without calling Parliament, and thus without Parliamentary grants of taxation. The tax, which negated
Parliament's power of the purse, had provoked opposition,
but this seemed to be crumbling when in this same year of
1637, the King attempted unsuccessfully to force a new
prayer book on the Scots Church and nation. The resistance
of Covenanters led to the two "Bishops' " wars of 1639 and
1640 between the King and his northern kingdom, wars in
which the King's continued failure was to lead him to resort
again to Parliaments.

Wharton's native 'country', Yorkshire, was (for a war with
Scotland) the natural *rendez-vous* for the royal armies; and that
province, the wealthiest in the not very wealthy north, bore a
disproportionate share of the burdens of the wars,[1] culminating
in the exactions of the occupying Scots army that had defeated
the King's forces in the second Bishops' War. Moreover,
although Wharton as a puritan naturally sympathised with
the Presbyterian Covenanters, he was in the winter of 1638-9
summoned with the other lords to appear with horsemen at
York by 1 April 1639, to attend the King in war against the
Scots. Like most of the peers, Wharton was able to take
advantage of the King's willingness to accept money instead of

---

1. Yorkshire petitions of July and August 1640: J. Rushworth, *Historical
   Collections*, London 1659-92, III, 1214-15, 1230-1.

personal service, but his compounding cost him the large sum of £500.[2]

The events of the 1630s wove together many strands of opposition—economic, political and religious. The Scots war involved Wharton directly, as has been seen. He was also involved through his new father-in-law, Arthur Goodwin, and Goodwin's close friend, cousin and staunch political ally, John Hampden. Hampden was—among other things—a member of the Providence Island Company, a puritan group which pursued with religious zeal ventures in privateering against Spain, ventures which fitted ill with the King's recent foreign policy of peace, and possible alliance, with Spain.

The Short Parliament met in April 1640, after the outbreak of the second Bishops' War, and Wharton attended regularly though he played no great part in it. However, he did vote with the minority of peers who agreed with the Commons that the redressing of grievances should precede the granting of supplies.[3] Furthermore, he kept a copy of a speech Pym made at a conference between representatives of the two Houses. John Pym, Hampden's close associate and Secretary of the Providence Island Company, was soon recognised as the craftiest and most effective leader of the opposition.[4]

At this stage in the growing crisis between King and Parliament the most dangerous questions were those involving religion. The hierarchy of the Church of England, led by William Laud, Archbishop of Canterbury, had aroused a considerable opposition in various ways. An Anglican revival combined emphasis on ritual with what was called Arminianism[5] in doctrine, both repugnant to Calvinists and suspiciously suggestive of Roman Catholicism. Not only did most puritans of the 'reformed religion' of Calvin believe that the Church of England from Elizabeth to Charles I was insufficiently reformed, but within that Church, especially among the High Church or Arminian party, and more especially after the rise to power of their leader, Laud, there was a growing reluctance

2. *HMC Buccleuch-Whitehall*, I, 284.
3. *CSP Dom 1640*, 66.
4. MS Carte 80, 30.
5. So called from Arminius, who questioned the rigid belief in predestination of the Calvinists.

to use or accept that description, a dwelling on the evils of the Reformation (especially the plunder of the Church) and an emphasis on the continuity of the catholic Church. Laud's arrogance and harshness in the Courts of Star Chamber and High Commission provoked resentment against those Courts, against the hierarchy and against Laud for his humble birth. The episcopate claimed a kind of divine right to govern the Church by apostolic succession. This clashed not only with the views of puritans like Wharton, but also with both the anti-clericalism common among the literate and with the largely Erastian views of the upper classes, who were in favour of the complete subordination of Church government to secular authority. By this they understood Parliament rather than the Defender of the Faith.

Laud also aroused opposition by his part in attempting to implement what was called the policy of 'Thorough', that is, the strong enforcement of the King's right to govern. In this he supported, and was supported by, Thomas Wentworth, the King's only other great Minister. Wentworth, who became Earl of Strafford in 1640, was President of the Council of the North, and in this his court at York had trodden on many toes among his and Wharton's countrymen before going as Lord Deputy to make even more enemies in Ireland.[6]

Some of the gentry of Yorkshire had early in 1640 made trouble about paying Ship-money, to the displeasure of Strafford, who urged that they should be firmly reprimanded.[7] Now, on 28 July, in the atmosphere of alarm and distrust arising from Strafford's actions, a number of discontented Yorkshire gentry met at the High Sheriff's in York during assize week. Sir Hugh Cholmley and Sir John Hotham arrived with prepared drafts of a petition.[8] Hotham had already fallen foul of the Court. After the dissolution of the Short Parliament he had been examined before the Privy Council in His Majesty's presence and for his undutiful answers sent to the Fleet prison. With him in this misadventure was Cholmley's cousin, Sir

6. S. R. Gardiner, *The Personal Government of Charles I, 1628-1637*, London 1877, I, 275-85.
7. W. Knowler, *The Earl of Strafforde's Letters and Dispatches*, London 1739, II, 393-4.
8. Sir Hugh Cholmley, *The Memoirs of Sir Hugh Cholmley*, Malton 1870, 61.

Henry Bellasis.[9] Bellasis, Cholmley and Hotham were three of the four chosen by the meeting to 'draw up' the petition (as though this had not already been done): the fourth was Lord Wharton.[10]

The affair at once made Wharton an outstanding figure: he was the first to sign the completed petition, and the only peer of England among the forty to fifty signatories.[11] Even Cholmley thought the petition was in 'a pretty high style; for in substance (though not in plain terms) it imported that the country would not lie longer under these pressures.'[12] In fact the petition, which was called that of the gentry of Yorkshire, alleged that the county had spent £100,000 for the King's war last year (1639), complained of the oppression of billeting unruly soldiers (contrary to ancient laws confirmed by the Petition of Right) which tended to the burning of villages and the endangering of wives and children; and the petition contained what might even have been a veiled threat of resistance:

> we desire that this insupportable burthen may be taken off us, lest by their insolencies some sad accident may happen as will much displeasure you and your loyal subjects.

The effect of this petition was very great. As (in Cholmley's words) 'the first action that did with a bare face complain of the King's prerogative which went high in those times', it startled the Council, animated the Scots army which had till then remained in Scotland for fear of the more than 12,000 Yorkshire trained bands, and—without itself asking for a new Parliament—it encouraged a number of peers to gather together to petition the King for one.[13]

9. Rushworth, *Collections*, III, 1167.
10. Cholmley, *Memoirs*, 61.
11. *CSP Dom 1640*, 254, has 47 names; Rushworth, *Collections*, III, 1215, has 41. There are discrepancies, but Wharton heads both lists.
12. Cholmley, *Memoirs*, 62. 'Country' means Yorkshire, in the usage of the period.
13. Ibid. Rushworth corroborates the figures for the Yorkshire militia. C. V. Wedgwood appears to state that this petition asked 'insistently for a new Parliament' (*The King's Peace, 1637-1641*, London 1955, 346); but in neither the *CSP Dom* version quoted, nor in Rushworth's version is there a mention of Parliament. *CSP Dom 1640*, 624-5 gives the tentative date 24 August to the petition dated 11 September below, in which Yorkshire gentry first asked for a Parliament.

Wharton's prominence in this affair is not easy to explain. He was only twenty-seven years of age, of modest estate as yet, and with no experience in affairs of state. He had therefore no weight in national politics and, so far as evidence remains, little interest (in either sense of the word) in local politics. Three of the four ringleaders were closely linked by blood or political outlook. Was Wharton their full confederate, or was he given pride of place as the only peer present? Perhaps, but the name of one peer would add little weight to a document which was still called the petition of the gentry of Yorkshire, and might even emphasise the absence of the names of the other nobles connected with the county; and we know that he was not included among the ringleaders merely in order that, with his peer's right of access to the King, he might present the petition, for another was chosen to take it to the King at Oatlands.[14]

The petition of 28 July 1640 had, as well as its general effects, immediate consequences in Yorkshire. The King received it 30 July, and the next day Strafford wrote to Sir Edward Osborne, Vice-President of the Council of the North, and to the other Deputy Lieutenants of Yorkshire, an indignant letter of which Wharton obtained and kept a copy. Strafford claimed that the petition was 'much misliked of all as well for the matter as the way of expression . . . in such high terms . . . passing by as Cyphers not only the Lord-Lieutenant [Strafford] but my Lords of the Council also.' He had moved the King on behalf of 'the Country' [Yorkshire] and measures would be taken to repress the insolence of the soldiers.[15] Strafford was, after all, himself a Yorkshireman, and one who had once resisted forced loans and billeting, but he thought the figure of £100,000 well out, and held that such complaining when invasion threatened was mutinous.[16]

On 24 August the King was at York. He sent for all the gentlemen in town and pleaded with them to have the trained bands march at the county's expense, promising to repay the

14. *CSP Dom 1640*, 525.
15. MS Carte 80, 32.
16. Rushworth, *Collections*, III, 1215.

outlay.[17] Although a recent history accepts Secretary Vane's optimistic account of the success of the King's persuasive powers as a true forecast,[18] in fact the same gentry who had signed the first petition signed another, denying that the figure of £100,000 quoted in the first petition was wrong. Though glad to hear that the King would personally lead them to the frontiers, they insisted the country was so impoverished that they could not march their men without having received from His Majesty fourteen days' pay in advance.[19]

Four days later, on 28 August 1640, occurred two decisive events, both (according to Cholmley) the result of the first Yorkshire petition. In London, twelve peers signed a petition calling for a Parliament and the 'condign punishment' of the authors of their grievances; at Newburn, the Scots crossed the Tyne, routed the royal army, and brought about the immediate surrender of Newcastle. For a time the King and Strafford, almost alone, believed that the war could still be won with Irish reinforcements and a revived English army; then on 7 September Charles summoned a Great Council of the peers to meet at York on 24 September. But before this took place there came, on 11 September, a further demand for a Parliament, this time from Yorkshire gentry. Only the day before, the King had asked the Yorkshire gentry to advance two months' pay for the county's trained bands: they had offered one month's pay only.

There are several accounts of the manner in which this petition was received: it 'was well taken by His Majesty',[20] but 'the King would not receive it'.[21] Strafford intercepted the petition by asking Wharton, chosen to deliver it, to call on him with the paper, and took exception to the clause about a Parliament. Strafford then called a meeting in the Common Hall, and this meeting voted that he should present the petition to the King but with the last clause, demanding a Parliament, left out. In the course of the debate, some said that they receded

17. Sir Henry Slingsby, *Diary*, ed D. Parsons, London 1836, 56.
18. *CSP Dom 1640*, 630; Wedgwood, *King's Peace*, 346.
19. Rushworth, *Collections*, III, 1230-1; Slingsby, *Diary*, 56.
20. Rushworth, *Collections*, III, 1265.
21. Slingsby, *Diary*, 57.

from the original petition which they had signed, but Wharton was among those 'that thought not fit to have the Petition altered'.[22]

Cholmley has left a vivid account of what followed. Sixteen of the 'principal and most active gentlemen' met together to plan fresh action; but, before anything could be done, someone played informer and the four most active, the same who had been chosen to draw up the first petition (Cholmley, Wharton, Hotham and Bellasis), were sent for by the King. His Majesty told them that their manner of meeting for petitions was unlawful and that he could question them for it in the Star Chamber; he said, however, that he would pass it over this time because he loved them all well, but they must not meddle again in such petitions. The two of them who had drafted the first petition, Hotham and Chomley, still 'the chief cause and promoters of all the petitions', were threatened by the King with hanging if they had a hand in any more.[23]

Much later Gilbert Burnet, the Whig Bishop and historian, claimed that Wharton and Lord Howard of Escrick, for undertaking to deliver petitions urging peace negotiations after the battle of Newburn, were sentenced by a Council of War (urged on by Strafford) to be shot at the head of the army as movers of sedition, and that the King's Scots cousin, Hamilton, averted the execution by prophesying it would cause a general mutiny.[24] Although Burnet gave Wharton as his authority, the tale is not confirmed, nor is it likely to be more than a confusion of several related incidents, such as Strafford's stigmatising of the earliest Yorkshire petition as mutinous; the King's threats to Cholmley and Hotham; the arrest of two puritan peers, Viscount Say and Sele and Lord Brooke, for refusing to take an oath to follow the King into Scotland; and the signing by Wharton and Howard (among others) of copies of the twelve peers' petition, which urged, among other things, the com-

---

22. Rushworth, *Collections*, IV, 603-5, 615-16, the testimony at Strafford's trial of Wharton, Cholmley, and Strafford's witness, Sir Paul Neal. Cholmley (*Memoirs*, 63) says Lord Fairfax was chosen to deliver it, but his evidence at Strafford's trial was that Wharton was chosen.

23. Cholmley, *Memoirs*, 63-4. This evidence concerning the King from a Royalist of 1643 is presumably accurate.

24. G. Burnet, *History of My Own Time*, Oxford 1897, I, 45-6.

posing of the war without blood. We can only guess whether the Bishop or the peer embroidered or garbled the facts, or whether there was some further foundation for the story. Certainly, Wharton was openly hostile to Strafford in the Great Council at York, in the same year as the petition, and his implacable foe later, and at Strafford's trial seemed to bear the fallen Minister a grudge for his alleged overbearing behaviour. Wharton claimed that Strafford not only sent for him to bring the second Yorkshire petition to his lodging, but even appointed a time for Wharton's visit. Strafford strenuously denied that he was ever guilty of such discourtesy even to men far below Wharton in rank.[25]

The twelve peers' petition (which soon bore the signatures of twenty-one peers, including Wharton) had demanded a Parliament; within a week the Scots (in obvious collusion) had humbly asked the King that their grievances might be redressed with the advice of an English Parliament; the obstreperous Yorkshire gentry had finally asked for a Parliament, and so had petitions signed by thousands of London citizens and by numerous clergy. When the Great Council met at York on 24 September, the King, chastened by the loss of his last Scottish fortresses, met the peers with the announcement of writs for a new Parliament. The peers of the Great Council chose sixteen of their number to negotiate with the Scots, and the King appointed these 'popular' lords (who included Wharton) his commissioners. With difficulty and cost they obtained an armistice. That the cost was to the gentry of the north—they had to find £850 a day—would increase Wharton's bitterness. He wrote on 16 October from Ripon to his father-in-law, Goodwin, excusing the commissioners' choice of a solution from among 'many ill ways' for the maintenance of the Scots army:

> The case is lamentable, and the king cannot relieve them nor ... save Yorkshire from contribution ... if the Scotch come on.[26]

Not three weeks later, on 3 November 1640, the Long Parliament met.

25. Rushworth, *Collections*, IV, 618-20.
26. MS Carte 103, 196.

Of these stirring years, Wharton wrote for von Spaen:

> For twelve years past no Parliaments had met in the Kingdom. In the month of April or May, 1640, the King summoned a Parliament so that with its consent he might make war against the Scots, but finding the members opposed to this undertaking, he dissolved it three weeks later and afterwards himself raised an army for the purpose which he led to York about halfway between London and Edinburgh. In the following November he summoned another Parliament.

Wharton omitted not only his unobtrusive opposition in the Short Parliament, but also his large part in the resistance of the Yorkshire gentry, which itself had a large part in making necessary the calling of 'another Parliament'.

IV

OPPOSITION AMONG
THE PEERS

*'Court Lords and country Lords differed: Court
Lords were always biassed.'*[1]

THE twelve peers who, late in August 1640, first petitioned for
a Parliament have received their due meed of praise from
historians. They have also been recognised as providing the
leadership for the opposition within the peerage. However,
Gardiner—who listed the twelve—exaggerated when he wrote:
'Behind these names was England itself.'[2] In 1640, the concept
of the nation against the King was not heard so much as the
terms 'country' and Court.

The first opposition peers of the century were called—in 1621
—'the country lords'.[3] Later, in 1638-9, Manchester, the
King's Minister, distinguished Court lords and country lords.[4]
Later still, Clarendon noticed that Pym 'improved' the
'jealousies and discontents' of 'those lords who were most
strangers to the court, and were believed most averse to it'.[5]
Recently, Professor Trevor-Roper has used 'country party' to

1. Sir Arthur Haselrig (Heselrige), quoted in *Diary of Thomas Burton, Esq.*,
   ed J. T. Rutt, London 1828, IV, 82.
2. S. R. Gardiner, *The Fall of the Monarchy of Charles I*, London 1882, I, 424.
   Behind the twelve were Pym, Hampden and St John (Hampden's
   counsel at his Ship-money trial, and a bitter opponent of the government) who with the leaders of the twelve had drawn up the petition—
   itself apparently a remonstrance originally intended to be presented in
   and by the Short Parliament. In its petition form it gained an additional
   demand—for the punishment of the King's Ministers.
3. C. H. Firth, *The House of Lords during the Civil War*, London 1910, 37.
4. *HMC Buccleuch-Whitehall*, I, 279.
5. Clarendon, *Rebellion*, VII, 410.

describe 'mere' country gentry as opposed to those courtiers, officials, lawyers, entrepreneurs, and monopolists with access to wealth other than from land.[6] Shaftesbury's proto-Whigs of the 1670s were another 'country party'.

Was Wharton, who was to play an increasingly prominent role in the opposition, a typical 'country' lord in an opposition party of 'country' lords? The second part of the question had best be taken first—can the opposition plainly be called 'country'?

The short answer is that, while Wharton was a 'country' lord by any standards, he was not typical of the opposition lords; indeed, if *country* be defined in the only way in which to me seems meaningful, he was almost out of place in the high command of the aristocratic opposition.[7]

At different stages and in different ways from the meeting of the Short Parliament to the outbreak of the Civil War, various but overlapping groups of peers opposed the King. They totalled fifty-five persons, who represented fifty-two permanent peerages, but there were never as many as forty in opposition at the same time, for some ceased to oppose before the meeting of the Long Parliament, and many others ceased to do so during the early sessions of that Parliament. Wharton was not only one of this opposition from first to last; he also soon became one of its leading members.

How *country* were these opposition peers, if we use *country* to describe those peers who lived virtually private lives, not markedly different from those of rich gentlemen, and who were not apparently ambitious or at all assiduous in Court attendance, office-holding, military careers or other great enterprises? It appears that, over a period of two-and-a-half years, an opposition which had been at first predominantly *country* became steadily less *country* as the proportion of courtiers, ex-courtiers, pensioners, failed politicians and the like, grew. By the time war broke out, only one-third of the sixty active Royalist peers were men who had been in 1640 courtiers or officials or even ex-courtiers, while of thirty-one Parliamen-

---

6. H. R. Trevor-Roper, 'The Gentry', *EcHR* (1953 Supplement), 43.
7. See Appendix I, pp. 269-74, for the analyses which are the basis for the conclusions made here and in the following pages.

tarian lords, no fewer than one-third had been in 1640 courtiers, ex-courtiers and ex-officials, not counting a whole group connected with the Providence Island Company, whose significance will be touched on later.

Contrary to suggestions that the Stuart-created peers supported the King while the peers of older creations tended to oppose him, it appears that only those who owed titles to Charles I himself were as a group Royalist, whereas those ennobled or promoted in the peerage by James I tended to become, first, opposition lords then, later, Parliamentarians. The purely Tudor origin of Wharton's rank was not typical of the opposition.

Furthermore, Wharton in 1640-2 owned lands only in the north where he was bred. The opposition and Parliamentarian peers tended to have estates in the south-east, whereas the typical Royalist peer had estates in the north or in the west.[8] However, Wharton was, through his wife, heir-presumptive to large estates in Buckinghamshire.

A constant element in every phase of this opposition by nobles was the group of peers (Essex, Bedford, Warwick, Say and Sele, Mandeville, Brooke and Savile) who wrote to encourage the Scots invasion of the second Bishops' War. In the Long Parliament, as Clarendon recorded, the 'managers' of the House of Lords and the directors of the attack on Strafford were six of those seven lords (all save Savile) assisted by Wharton, Paget 'and such like'.[9] In fact, apart from the conspiratorial six, Wharton was the only peer to rise early and remain high in the leadership of the opposition in the Lords— a leadership which was not only always closely connected with the opposition leadership in the Commons, but at first equal (almost superior) to it in the joint direction of opposition within and without Parliament.

So far, it appears that Wharton was typical neither of the opposition lords in general, though he was more consistent and more forward in this opposition than were most, nor of the

8. An examination of the location of the peers' estates was made by me in a D. Phil. thesis, 1957.
9. Clarendon, *History of the Rebellion*, ed W. D. Macray, Oxford 1888, I, 263n.

peers who were leaders and organisers of the Lords' opposition, although he figured among them with increasing prominence. However, there were other possible links and congruities between Wharton and his fellows. One obvious fact was his puritanism, which is discussed later. Other possibilities were his contacts with members of the Providence Island Company.

No one disputes that in the years before 1640 the directors of this Company, particularly after the dismal failure of their attempts at puritan colonisation, spent much of their time organising opposition to the King's government. It is equally sure that until the outbreak of war the control of the opposition in the House of Lords was firmly in the hands of a group of peers most of whom were connected with the Company. Of the seven who conspired to invite the Scots invasion, four— Warwick, Say and Sele, Brooke and Mandeville—were directors of the Company. So were the two greatest of the leaders of the opposition in the Commons, Hampden and Pym, and the Earl of Bedford was Pym's patron. Essex and Savile had considerable grievances against either the monarchy or its Ministers.

There were at least three ways in which Wharton might well have been brought into contact with this core of opposition, not only before the meeting of the Long Parliament, but even before the Yorkshire petitioning. In the first place, he had acted for some years as co-trustee with Bedford,[10] generally regarded as the chief nobleman in opposition, and business relations may very well have led to political alliance. Secondly, Wharton's second marriage made him the 'son' and heir of Arthur Goodwin, whose cousin and close ally, Hampden, was not only a member of the Company but was also particularly concerned in the organised resistance to Ship-money made by its members. Although there is no evidence that Goodwin was interested in colonisation, he is extremely likely to have taken an interest in this political action.[11] And, thirdly, there was in

10. MS Carte 117, 3-4: Indenture, 6 June 1635. Pembroke and his wife Anne, heiress to the Earl of Cumberland and cousin to Wharton, entrust Westmorland estates to Wharton, Bedford, Sir Gervase Clifton, and Sir John Danvers (another coloniser, later Parliamentarian colonel and regicide).

11. M. Frear Keeler, *The Long Parliament, 1640-1641*, Philadelphia 1954, 190.

the north (and particularly in Yorkshire) a group of Providence Island Company members and gentry interested in colonisation. One Yorkshire member of the Company was Henry Darley, who was a friend and possibly a client of Wharton.[12] Darley became a member of the Long Parliament as a representative of Northallerton in Wharton's part of Yorkshire, a borough whose representation in Parliament was restored in the winter of 1640-1. This restoration may have been the result of aristocratic influence, and certainly most of the restorations by the Long Parliament's House of Commons seem to have favoured strong supporters of the opposition.[13]

If Wharton had become connected with an opposition group based on the Providence Island Company, there is here a possible explanation of his going into the north in June or July 1640,[14] when invasion was imminent. As he was not intending to further the King's affairs, he might have intended to do the opposite. At any rate, at the end of July in that year his cousin Lord Clifford—a future Royalist, though ineffective—thought Wharton very merry for so sad a time.[15]

In the Long Parliament, committees were the main means by which the opposition controlled the Houses and invaded the sphere of government, usurping many powers until then unquestionably the King's. By means of the committees, commands from one House or both Houses were sent to Justices, Mayors and Sheriffs; clergy and laymen were arrested, questioned and imprisoned; common law judges were threatened with the penalties of treason for past decisions in court; prisoners were released and orders were made without process of law to restore to them properties of which they had been deprived by process of law. In particular, the committees of privileges and committees appointed for conferences between the Houses were most important. Almost anything could be

---

12. A. P. Newton, *The Colonising Activities of the English Puritans*, Oxford 1914, 83, 178-9; Gardiner, *Fall of the Monarchy*, II, 17n; MS Carte 103, 78.
13. de Villiers, 'Parliamentary Boroughs', 175, 196 especially.
14. MS Rawlinson Letters 52, 5. A. Heron (summoned by Wharton to attend him into the north) to Sir R. Wandesford, 29 June 1640.
15. Ibid, 1. Clifford (heir to Earldom of Cumberland) to Wharton, 31 July 1640.

deemed a breach of privilege if it annoyed either House,[16] and in almost every case of assumed authority some committee steered the House before a vote was taken. In conferences between the Houses, those who were to manage, or to speak at, the conference were usually named by the House to form a committee, and sometimes a smaller committee was first appointed to draw up what should be offered to the other House at the conference. To estimate the relative worth of Wharton's share of this activity, I have used an analysis of committee appointments.[17] From this his record appears impressive.

When Parliament met on 3 November 1640, Wharton was at once put on all the Lords' standing committees,[18] including the small and important sub-committee of privileges. He also became a member of most of the committees which, being dominated by opposition lords, removed threats to the security of those of their own persuasion and struck terror into the hearts of all who might oppose them. The committee which punished Howes, the Vicar of Banbury, who dared to say that some lords had promised to aid the Scots (which was true, his local magnate Say and Sele being one) had a majority of opposition lords, including three who wrote to the Scots.[19] However, the principal victim was naturally Strafford: in several respects the committees made his defence more difficult.[20] For instance, the committee for the 'speedy and secret' examination of witnesses was solidly opposition, and six of the nine had written to the Scots.[21]

Strafford's innocence of treason gave him no security from the rancour and fear of his assailants. Of the charges against him, one of the most dangerous was that he had planned to use his Irish army to subdue England. The falsity of this charge, Wharton had better reason than most to know since his brother

---

16. For example, Byron, Lieutenant of the Tower, when summoned, refused to leave his post without the King's direction; the Lords voted this a 'high contempt'. *LJ* 4, 508.
17. An analysis of all committees appointed by the Lords 1640-8 is in the author's D. Phil. thesis.
18. *LJ* 4, 83-4.
19. Ibid, 107, 108.
20. Ibid, 189, 191, 99, 103.
21. Ibid, 103.

Sir Thomas Wharton was one of the colonels chosen by Strafford to land with the first regiments in the west of Scotland.[22] Yet Wharton, who signed the twelve peers' petition expressing fears lest the Irish be brought to England, was from the first particularly active against the fallen Minister. Out of the twelve petitioners, only Robartes and Say and Sele exceeded Wharton's total of committee appointments concerning Strafford, and of the rest only Essex and Bath equalled it.

Whatever private animosity Wharton may have felt, his main motives were not merely fear or hatred of the great minister, for his activity for the opposition increased after Strafford's death on 12 May 1641, both relatively and absolutely. Wharton served on great numbers of committees of the kinds already mentioned,[23] especially for conferences, which he sometimes managed but more often prepared or reported. The most active committeemen in the Lords were, until August 1641, Say and Sele and Essex, closely followed by Warwick, Wharton, Robartes and Brooke.[24] From November 1640 to the end of February 1640-1, Wharton was among the first eight or ten opposition lords in committee work, among the first five or seven from March to July 1641, and in August he was the first. Wharton also played a full part in the reaction to the Army Plot which was exploited by Pym and the opposition, long after the crisis was over, to remove support from any attempt by King or Lords to oppose the execution of Strafford.[25] He reported the first conference on the Plot[26] and was one of the

22. Rushworth, *Collections*, IV, 555.
23. For example, on the Star Chamber, Church innovations, and the treaty with the Scots, *LJ* 4, 124, 183, 94.
24. Clarendon did not name Robartes among the leading peers.
25. The Army Plot was a feeble attempt by a few young courtiers to use the unpaid English troops in Yorkshire to counterbalance the pressure of the armed mobs from London which were by May invading Westminster. Firth (*House of Lords*, 91) denies that mob violence affected the voting which condemned Strafford, but his own source for the voting figures—26:19—states Strafford's friends absented themselves because they feared, or said they feared, the multitudes (*A Brief and Perfect Relation of the Answers and Replies of Thomas Earl of Strafford*).
26. *LJ* 4, 236. Gardiner (*Fall of the Monarchy*, II, 167) stated the Lords took matters into their own hands in stopping the ports, but this was what the Commons demanded.

ten lords appointed to examine suspects and witnesses.[27] Similarly, Wharton was active in June 1641 when attacks were made on the Church hierarchy,[28] and in July, when attacks were made on the six judges and the Courts of Star Chamber and High Commission were abolished.

However, by mid-year the Scots army of occupation, the greatest single and only answerable argument the opposition possessed against the King's power, was at last in the process of disbanding. In August 1641 Wharton heard through his wife from her father, Arthur Goodwin, of the withdrawal from Newcastle of the last Scots troops, even before the last of the English army disbanded.[29] By the same month, the King was determined to go to Scotland, hoping perhaps to win enough support there to redress the balance of power in England. The opposition was alarmed, and made strenuous efforts to prevent or delay his journey, or at least to send such commissioners with His Majesty as would foil any such hopes. Wharton was particularly active, explaining to the Scots envoys why the King should stay fourteen days longer in England,[30] helping draft the instructions for the Parliamentary commission to accompany him to Scotland,[31] and reporting a conference[32] which led to the first 'ordinance' of the Long Parliament, giving their commissioners the authority and instructions which the King refused. The ordinance was a device of the Commons' antiquarians, who falsely stated that in emergencies binding decrees could be made by the Houses without the King's consent.[33]

Attendance in the House of Lords had been much reduced during and since the attainder of Strafford.[34] However, with fifteen or twenty more present in August than in May and June, the House was emboldened to treat with scant courtesy

27. *LJ* 4, 235.
28. He reported a conference on restraining Bishops from intermeddling in secular affairs. Ibid, 265.
29. MS Carte 80, 125. A. Goodwin to Jane Wharton, 25 August 1641.
30. *LJ* 4, 350.
31. MS Carte 80, 52.
32. *LJ* 4, 371.
33. Gardiner, *Fall of the Monarchy*, II, 238.
34. See note 25 above.

the demands in church affairs of the majority in the Commons. Wharton, as one of a predominantly puritan and opposition committee, reported in September a conference on the restraining of superstition and innovations and the House agreed with some of the Commons' desires.[35] However, on the following day, 9 September 1641, a thin House of Lords, without consulting the Commons, voted to print an earlier order of their own against any disturbing or altering of the established form of divine service. Against this, six of the seven opposition lords present signed a protest in the Journal Book.[36] Thus they began a practice which was in effect an innovation and almost wholly a form of propaganda or intimidation. The Lords' Journal was open to all, and the signed protests of the minority made clear the identity of their opponents. There was no doubt an element of risk in such a practice.[37]

Although the King's journey north failed to obtain effective support among the Scots, the position of the opposition leaders in Commons and in Lords became weaker as a reaction against them grew. The death, exile or imprisonment of many of the King's Ministers and the legislation of the first session had eased many fears and grievances aroused by the King's misgovernment; new fears and resentments arose from the arbitrary methods and revolutionary aims of the still dominant and still aggressive opposition. This hostility was shown chiefly by placards distributed in London and Yorkshire calling for the expulsion from Parliament of seditious conspirators with the Scots.[38] Arthur Goodwin's letter of 25 August to his daughter Lady Wharton had lumped together (as hostile to the Scots) Catholics, the Universities, the church hierarchy and the 'Riolists'. This is apparently the first use of the term *Royalists* for a party favouring the defence of the King's remaining

35. *LJ* 4, 392. Firth's account (*House of Lords*, 96) suggests the Lords did nothing to satisfy the Commons.
36. *LJ* 4, 395. Two King's Ministers (Manchester and Littleton) also voted against the order.
37. On the practice of protesting, see J. E. Thorold Rogers, *A Complete Collection of the Protests of the Lords, with historical introductions*, Oxford 1875, I, xiii; also the author's 'The Peers' Right of Protest', *BIHR* XXXI (November 1958) 211-15.
38. Gardiner, *Fall of the Monarchy*, II, 271.

powers (as against the earlier use of 'Court party' or 'Straffordians' as labels for those opposing the reformers), and certainly an early piece of evidence for the existence of such a feeling.

The fears of the opposition leaders were reflected in their private meetings. At one of these, attended by Wharton, Newport allegedly proposed that the Queen and her children could if necessary be held as hostages.[39] A more sober and lasting safeguard would be to have all the King's officers appointed only with the approval of the Houses. Pym had indeed brought forward, in June 1641, ten propositions which included the removal of evil councillors, and the altering ('upon reason') by the Houses of the list of chief officers;[40] and the King's vain concessions to his Scots Estates had included allowing them to approve all his appointments in Scotland— as Wharton had heard through his cousin Sir Philip Stapleton, one of the English Parliamentary commissioners in Edinburgh.[41] After the King's return from Scotland, Pym, his hand strengthened by the outbreak of the Irish Rebellion, demanded (in the Grand Remonstrance, voted 23 November 1641) that the King should employ only such councillors and Ministers as Parliament approved.[42]

39. Ibid, 362. Say and Sele, Essex, Mandeville and Pym were also present at this meeting, in Holland's house.
40. *LJ* 4, 285-7.
41. MS Carte 103, 84.
42. *LJ* 4, 432. The Irish rebellion worked against the King in two ways: first, his opponents did not hesitate to accuse the Queen (and sometimes, less openly, the King himself) of encouraging the rebels; secondly, they convinced many that the army needed to suppress the rebels could not be entrusted to the King lest it be used to reverse the reforms of 1641.

V

THE REVOLUTIONARY LEADER

*Lord Lieutenant of Lancashire, Speaker of the
House of Lords, Colonel-General of the Army of
the Adventurers for Ireland, Lord Lieutenant of
Buckinghamshire*

In the second session of 1641, the reforming majority in both
Houses divided. That in the Commons at once split into two
sections, the 'violent' and the moderate. The former were to
become the core of the Parliamentary party in the first Civil
War; the latter were to provide the bulk of the Royalist
Members of Parliament[1] and also the Peace Party at Westminster in the winter of 1642-3. The corresponding split in the
House of Lords was more gradual, partly because so many of
the original moderate *country* lords had left the opposition
earlier.

No historian has analysed the divisions in the Lords beyond
saying that they were divided into three groups: opposition,
middle group, and Court supporters, with the middle group
tending to swing to support one extreme or the other according
to which was more offensive or frightening at the time.[2] In
fact, between September 1641 and July 1642 at least ten peers
left the opposition to protest against its measures or join the
King. Nevertheless, the opposition in the Lords was after
February 1641-2 only once in a minority. This fact makes clear
that the desertion from the Lords opposition were more than
counterbalanced by the desertion—possibly of the timid—

1. Before this, the Court found only 59 to vote against Strafford's
   attainder.
2. For example, Firth, *House of Lords*, 111; B. Wormald, *Clarendon*,
   Cambridge 1951, 14.

from the Royalists, or by the increasing numbers of Royalists leaving Westminster to join the King at York.[3]

Those lords who, like Wharton, continued to protest and vote in support of the Commons in all demands against the King can only be called 'violent'. Wharton was still among their leaders. In general, the opposition in both Houses exploited every possible scare. These included a second 'Army Plot' in which the King was implicated; the 'Incident' in Scotland, by which the King was made to appear as instigating the assassination of his opponents; a plot to kill over a hundred members of Parliament; and even a letter dramatically delivered to Pym on the floor of the House, containing threats and an alleged plague-sore bandage.[4]

Time was on the King's side, as more moderate M.P.s than violent could be expected soon to return to the Commons, but in December 1641 fear (of the impending impeachment of the Queen) provoked Charles into attacking prematurely the leaders of the opposition. Since the King needed the help of the Lords, he originally planned to impeach only five members of the Commons. As an afterthought he transferred Mandeville's name to the list of accused from another list—one that contained the names of seven lords who were to be prevented from sitting on any committees concerning the impeachment on the grounds that the Crown intended to call them as witnesses. The other six were: Essex, three of Mandeville's colleagues of the Providence Island Company (Warwick, Say and Sele and Brooke), their associate Holland—and Wharton. Thus there can be no doubt that Wharton was not only of the 'violent' party in the winter of 1641-2, but even a leading member of it. Furthermore, the seven on the list were almost identical with those seven lords most active in committee work on behalf of the opposition during the first session. Of these, Wharton was the fourth most active,[5] but he was not regularly so. For the first few months of the second session he maintained a comparable activity. In December and January, 1641-2, he

---

3. The largest number of Royalists to protest was eighteen. *LJ* 4, 700.
4. Gardiner, *Fall of the Monarchy*, II, 271; *LJ* 4, 439-40; MS Carte 80, 123.
5. The others (in order) were Say and Sele, Essex, Warwick, Robartes, Brooke and Mandeville.

was the second or third busiest in committee work,[6] but in the next two months his activity declined, absolutely and relatively, to a marked degree. In fact, in the six weeks between 8 February and 19 March there is in the Journal no sign of Wharton's presence in the House.[7]

His absence occurred at a critical time. It was during the months of February and March that the King withdrew to York and the Houses appointed in defiance of him, commanders for the militia of the kingdom. This was the development which made civil war appear for the first time possible; soon it was to appear likely. Wharton's absence from the thick of opposition at this time cannot easily be explained. It may have been due to illness, though there is no notice of his being excused,[8] as were some other lords at this time. Moreover, Wharton in the future was to be punctilious in obtaining leave of absence on the grounds of illness; and although his health does appear to have deteriorated by 1646, neither then nor thereafter does it seem to have kept him from Westminster save when he had other good reasons to be absent.

Alternatively, Wharton's absence may have been due to his having been employed elsewhere on the business of the House. There is no official record of this, but William Montagu wrote to Lord Montagu of Boughton on 29 March 1642, that the Commons had appointed Wharton, Stapleton and 'Mr. Fines' (presumably a son of Say and Sele) to go down to York and there 'lie leiger', to 'agitate' (negotiate) between the King and Parliament.[9] Stapleton was in fact one of those sent on this business in May, but the Lords were at that time represented by Howard of Escrick, not by Wharton.[10] The fact that

---

6. Among other appointments, Wharton and Brooke were to see all Public Orders of the House put into execution. *LJ* 4, 512.

7. All this time the daily roll was not entered.

8. Except that on the actual day on which the list came to the Lords, Wharton and Cumberland were both excused; the latter was not on the list, but neither was the county (Westmorland) of which he later was made Lord Lieutenant. *LJ* 4, 587.

9. *HMC Buccleuch-Whitehall*, I, 295.

10. *The Parliamentary or Constitutional History of England from the earliest times to the restoration of Charles II*, London 1751-62, X, 479, 489. The other Commons' men were Ferdinando Fairfax and Hugh and Henry Cholmley, all of them original Yorkshire petitioners.

Wharton was a likely choice for such a mission suggests that he was during his absence from the House active for the opposition, and makes it possible that he had been sent on some abortive and hitherto unnoticed errand. Another possible explanation is that Wharton's zeal had cooled as the quarrel became more heated. By this time the stream of desertions from the opposition had commenced. Many lords were joining the King in the north, yet the Royalists left in the Upper House were still numerous enough and active enough in the early days of March to protest constantly and even on one occasion to compel the opposition to protest as a minority.[11]

That Wharton shrank from the path of opposition would seem the more likely explanation but for his appointment at about the same time to a militia command, clearly as the candidate of the more extreme opposition. In the first eight days of February 1641-2, Wharton was appointed to no fewer than three conferences on the militia,[12] and in the next two or three days he was voted by the House of Commons to the command of the militia of Lancashire—a position soon made a full Lord-Lieutenancy by the Militia Ordinance. However, when on 12 February the Commons' list of militia commanders reached the Lords, the only appointments not at once accepted were those of Wharton to Lancashire and Strange to Cheshire.[13]

The grounds for these objections are not clear. The objections themselves throw no light on Wharton's absence from the Lords during the critical months of February and March 1641-2, and little if any significance can be seen in them. Strange, soon to be seventh Earl of Derby, held both Cheshire and Lancashire from the King, but on 9 February the House of Commons had begun to debate first, whether each county should have only one Lord Lieutenant, next, whether any one Lord Lieutenant should have more than two counties, and finally whether any one Lord Lieutenant should have more than one county.[14] However, if the last question had been

---

11. *LJ* 4, 622, 627, 628, 631, 645.   12. Ibid, 558, 567, 570.
13. Ibid, 577. Gardiner (*Fall of the Monarchy*, II, 424) stated incorrectly that the list was accepted on 12 February for presenting to the King.
14. The account of the Commons' proceedings is from Sir Simonds D'Ewes' journal, MS Harleian 162, 376-80.

answered in the negative, several prominent opposition lords would be affected—Essex had at one time been Lord Lieutenant of all the counties north of the Trent. Perhaps because of this, the next day the Commons agreed that no Lord Lieutenant should have more than two counties, which should have safeguarded Strange (as well as the opposition pluralists) and when the consideration of the alphabetical list of counties reached—without incident—Cheshire, several M.P.s spoke in favour of Strange, for he had been nominated by all the Knights and Burgesses of Cheshire, as well as by 'the greater number' of Lancashire's M.P.s.

However, Wharton had been named by other Lancashire representatives and Mr [Alexander] Rigby, a lawyer of Grays Inn who sat for a Lancashire borough, made what D'Ewes called 'a long invective malicious speech' apparently against Strange as Lord Lieutenant of *any* county, claiming that he favoured Papists and had opposed the Scots. Others later pointed out that Strange had married his son to the daughter of Cottington, a Minister of the King during the personal rule, but there were also those who defended the heir of Derby against these objections.

Although obviously influenced by a feeling that no one lord should have more than one county, the Commons restricted to that limit only obvious or probable Royalists such as Strange, Carbery, Chandos, Spencer, Littleton and Hertford. Not surprisingly, it was the most committed part of the 'violent' opposition which questioned the appointment of doubtful peers —Hertford's nomination was opposed by Wharton's father-in-law, Goodwin—but the opposition M.P.s sometimes allowed puritan zeal to mislead them, as when Wharton's cousin Stapleton objected to Peterborough as a convert: that former recusant was to be a Parliamentarian commander at Edgehill. Strange was neither an opposition peer nor a puritan, but his wife was a French Calvinist, and he was apparently on very intimate terms with Wharton, who allegedly called him 'father'. To Wharton, Strange wrote on 13 November 1641 a troubled letter saying that Lancashire was never more in need of guarding, for some there were stronger than he; and he asked Wharton to send him some directions which he would obey

'like an honest man'[15]—a significant acknowledgement of
Wharton's place in the councils of the dominant opposition.
Strange obviously feared the Irish rebels, and as the Lords to
whom Wharton read the letter sent it on to the Commons,[16]
some M.P.s may well have felt later that Wharton's appointment to Lancashire would not be unwelcome to Strange.

On the other hand the Lords may have felt less need than
did the Commons to restrict a peer—even a non-puritan peer
—to one county. Possibly many lords knew the extreme pride
and touchiness of Strange, and judged—truly enough—that he
would be offended by the loss of one of his Lieutenancies.
Certainly any chance that Strange would be neutral or lukewarm in the approaching civil war now vanished: he earned
not only the invidious distinction of being the reputed first to
spill blood in the quarrel but also considerable notoriety as
the leader of poorly-disciplined forces containing many
Catholics, with which the former friend of Wharton and enemy
of the Irish made war on the Lancashire puritans with an
alleged ferocity unusual for the campaigns of England.[17]

Perhaps the Lords further hesitated to appoint as Lord
Lieutenant a man who had no property in the county. Indeed
the appointments of men who had no 'interest'—that is,
territorial influence—in their official areas of command was an
anomaly seized on by the King in his declaration against the
Militia Ordinance.[18] However, two days after receiving the
Commons' list, the Lords accepted the appointments of
Wharton and Strange.

A month later, on 15 March 1641-2, the Lords Lieutenant
were ordered to send in the names of their Deputy Lieutenants
to the Knights of the respective shires. A week later the Commons demanded an account from the seven lords who had not
done so, and Wharton, who was one of them, asked 'a few

---

15. *The Journal of Sir Simonds D'Ewes*, ed W. H. Coates, New Haven 1942,
    152-3 and note.

16. *LJ* 4, 442.

17. E. Broxap, *The Great Civil War in Lancashire*, Manchester 1910, passim.
    Strange refused Cheshire from Parliament on 24 March 1641-2.

18. *Constitutional Documents of the Puritan Revolution*, ed S. R. Gardiner,
    Oxford 1906, 259.

Days Time to consider it'.[19] In view of the attitude of the majority of Lancashire's M.P.s he may well have doubted whether he would be acceptable to the county (although a Lancashire petition to the Commons acknowledged him as Lord Lieutenant) and certainly he would be hampered by his lack of knowledge of the county. However, two days later he finally accepted, undertaking to send in a few days the names of his deputies.[20]

Wharton now threw himself into committee work as vigorously as any, and by July 1642 was actually the busiest peer in the House.[21] On 27 May 1642, Wharton was the first opposition lord to hold the office of Speaker;[22] then, by the middle of June 1642—when the 'paper war' of printed messages and justifications by King and Parliament had reached a height of acrimony[23]—he was offered a position of singular honour and trust. The King and the Houses had for some months made a show of co-operation in raising troops for Ireland, but the 'violent' party had never the slightest intention of trusting troops to officers chosen by the King, and it was in fact the Irish crisis that brought to a head the problem of whether the constitutional gains of 1641 would be increased, preserved, or lost. Neither Parliament nor King had much faith in either the loyalty or the abilities of Leicester, the titular Lord Lieutenant of Ireland. Leicester had, in November 1641, scrupled to raise men without the King's commission, though the Houses thought Parliament had power to do so;[24] and it was Wharton who reported to the Lords the Commons' reasons for believing they could raise men without the King's co-operation.[25] This was in May 1642, after the King had offered Leicester a

19. *LJ* 4, 646, 664.
20. Ibid, 666. *Victoria County Histories—Lancashire*, II, 233 mentions the petition; cf *CJ* 2, 476.
21. E.g., committees for commissioning militia officers, keeping the fleet from the King, and moving the King's arms magazine from Hull. *LJ* 4, 646, 697, 707, 724.
22. Six other opposition lords also had this honour in the next few months.
23. The King's 'messages' were now really aimed at the nation, appealing to them from the Houses.
24. *LJ* 4, 429.
25. *LJ* 5, 89.

commission to raise 4,000 troops. Meanwhile the Houses had in February accepted a City scheme to finance the Irish war with a subscription or 'Adventure' of £1,000,000 to be raised on the security of Irish rebels' lands which were to be confiscated; then, in June, the Commons voted the formation of an "Adventurers'" army of 5,000 foot and 500 horse. Its Colonel-General was to be Wharton, who would be independent of the Lord Lieutenant but under the advice of an accompanying committee of both Houses.[26]

Wharton was not himself an 'Adventurer' though his father-in-law, Goodwin, subscribed heavily. In the event no "Adventurers'" army left England, and Wharton saw no service in Ireland, but his appointment as Colonel-General is in itself of some interest. Six months before, in December 1641, men had thought it likely that Essex would command in Ireland.[27] By June 1642, when Wharton was appointed, there was no possibility that the opposition would let its only reputable military leader out of England.[28] The Commons, since they could not look for proved generalship among their noble leaders, presumably chose Wharton for his zeal, honesty, intelligence, or ability to get along with colleagues, or simply because he was the Speaker of the Lords at the time. Perhaps a combination of the more positive reasons was responsible. Wharton was well known to many of the Commons' leaders, and had had opportunities to show his abilities in the many conferences he managed or reported. He was young and presumably active, and had served a campaign in the great Dutch school of war. He was on good terms with the representatives of the Scots,[29] who had already supplied troops for the Irish war.

But it is also possible that the imposing distinction of this military command was offered to Wharton to bind him more firmly to the cause which can by now be called Parliamentarian. Several former opposition lords were finding that when it came to the point they had no stomach for rebellion; and others

---

26. *CJ* 2, 631; *LJ* 5, 153; MS Carte 80, 14-22 (list of Wharton's officers).
27. *HMC Buccleuch-Whitehall*, I, 288.
28. Conway and Holland had been discredited in the Scots wars.
29. R. Baillie, *Letters and Journals*, Edinburgh 1841, I, 290.

wanted to make their peace with the King.[30] 'Many men here I know,' Wharton wrote of his own colleagues in a letter to Sir John Bankes of 14 June 1642, 'and I do seriously profess I dare not in my privatest thoughts suspect or charge any of them for having disloyal hearts'.[31] The word 'dare' is curious and perhaps suggestive. By June 1642 it was becoming dangerous to hesitate, or to falter in unquestioning support of the 'violent' opposition, even, or possibly particularly, for those who, like Wharton, had themselves been identified with the opposition. As early as 11 May, the House of Lords had sent for several of its Royalist members. Three of them (Newport and Savile —who had been prominent in opposition—and Lord Rich, heir to Warwick, that great leader of the opposition) were summoned as delinquents, and Wharton, in a small committee, considered, among other questions, whether any person had ever been judged a traitor for executing the King's verbal commands against the laws of the land. Then, on 20 May, when the Lords voted that the King intended to make war on Parliament, Herbert of Chirbury was committed to prison for saying that he would agree if satisfied that the King would do so without cause; and on 15 June 1642 Portland made the last, lone Royalist protest and within three weeks was imprisoned without charge.

Wharton's letter to Bankes was written on 14 June, just one day before Portland's protest, and that letter has almost a despairing note:

> hath all this kingdom no persons prudent enough . . . to prevent the ruin coming upon us; or is it want of industry, or . . . wantonness of some few interested or unprovided people . . . or . . . a judgement upon us . . . from . . . God?

There was a not very complimentary reference to Parliament's 'old rate of spending many hours and days in doing of a little', and none of the intransigence seen in the letters of Say and Sele and Holles to the same correspondent.[32]

Could Wharton have changed sides, or was he in fact bound by his past record? No record of opposition, however violent

---

30. Waverers included Pembroke, Holland and even Essex. Salisbury went to the King at York, and then fled back to Westminster.
31. G. Bankes, *The Story of Corfe Castle*, London 1853, 133.
32. Ibid, 133, 125, 141.

or unscrupulous, kept a peer from being accepted at Court as a political convert. The examples of Savile and Newport are sufficient. Such deserters might be rewarded (Savile became an earl) though perhaps not trusted. Nor was it ever too late to change. Paget offered ten horses for the service of Parliament on 10 June 1642; soon after, he was in the King's camp[33]— and Paget had been one of the most 'violent' of all the opposition peers, and his soberer colleagues had used him to suggest what they could not openly propose. However, Paget made up for the tardiness of his conversion by denouncing his late colleagues and vilifying their aims.[34] Wharton had perhaps too much honour or too little shamelessness to commit such a *volte-face*.

During July, August and September 1642, while both parties prepared for conflict, Wharton continued to take a full part in committee work, though committees were fewer and of less importance. In mid-July he wrote (in answer to a further letter from Sir John Bankes) politely refusing to give any sense of the 'thoughts and ways' at Westminster until he had heard the result of the last deputation from Parliament to the King, which he thought 'a fair overture'. He expressed no great optimism, but added that he saw 'everybody's expectation so hung upon . . . this petition' that most persons at Westminster would perhaps 'defer their resolutions'.[35] This opinion is curious. Wharton could hardly have thought that there was any chance of war should the King capitulate, or any chance of peace should he not, or that many of those still remaining at Westminster could prove to be moderates and therefore waiting to choose their course of action. Wharton himself was now, whatever he had been before, a trusted Parliamentarian. After the desertion of Paget, he added to his offices on 24 June 1642, the Lord Lieutenancy of Buckinghamshire, another county in which he owned (as yet) no land. Wharton had chosen his side, for what reason or combination of reasons it remains to be seen.

*   *   *   *

33. *LJ* 5, 123.
34. Clarendon, *Rebellion*, ed Macray, II, 181-2.
35. Bankes, *Corfe Castle*, 147. Dated 13 July, 12 o'clock at night.

Of the two years of crisis from May 1640 to June 1642 Wharton was to write only briefly in his autobiographical letter, as follows:

> In the following November he summoned another Parliament in which I joined those members who were anxious to diminish the troubles in the state and innovations in the church occasioned by the infrequency with which Parliament met. In this at first all were in agreement until some grievances were removed but in a few months such disputes arose in either House that the King thought it best to withdraw from Parliament and summon to his side many of either House and in the autumn of this year open war began.

He not only failed to mention his own large share in the direction of reform and revolution, but he actually omitted to say which side he chose! It was also misleading to blame all on the infrequency of Parliaments: the encroachments of Parliament on royal powers which were formerly acknowledged or at least exercised without protest had a share in producing the revolution. More significant, however, is Wharton's omission to say what grievances were removed and what were left to occasion further disputes, an omission the next sentence partly compensated, but—perhaps significantly—the next sentence was deleted by Wharton.

VI

PURITAN PARLIAMENTARIANS

*'In which [war] a hundred to one of the Calvinists
(as it is believed) joined the parliamentarians, and
almost all the Papists fought under the Royal
standard.'*

THE above sentence is the one deleted by Wharton from his
autobiographical letter[1] and referred to in the last chapter.
It is of the greatest interest as the only comment that Wharton
appears to have left on the nature and possible causes of the
Civil War, or on the motives leading Englishmen to choose one
side or the other. Its deletion may be equally significant. One
can make a reasonable guess at the reason for it—a second
thought on the advisability of seeming to identify rebellion
with Calvinism and monarchism with Roman Catholicism.
This second thought might be the more compelling in the year
of Monmouth's rebellion and execution, and in the dominions
of a Calvinist monarch who had triumphed over his own
Parliaments.

For the original comment there can be only one reason.
In 1685, Wharton remembered the Civil War, and in 1642 he
presumably regarded it, as essentially or largely a war of
religion. Although unfashionable now, such a view has some
evidence to support it. Wharton had omitted to say what
grievances were yet unremedied when disputes in Parliament
led to civil war. In fact, the opposition's further aims were of
two kinds—permanent changes and, secondly, *ad hoc* measures
not necessarily producing permanent changes though they

---

1. This deleted passage has not been published before, even in Dale's
little-known work.

were certainly such as would be strong precedents against the monarch's power to resist further changes. The first category, the permanent changes, were religious: *carte blanche* for the reform of the Church and the elimination of Roman Catholicism as a force in England by the Protestant education of the children of upper-class recusants. The second, the *ad hoc* measures, were the conclusion of Protestant alliances and the appointment of Parliament-approved military commanders and Ministers of State.[2] These measures can be seen as designed to further the desired permanent changes; to prevent the reversal of those changes and of the constitutional changes already made by a nearly unanimous Parliament; and, perhaps most of all, to safeguard the leaders of the opposition from the King's possible vengeance. Probably no great support could have been found for these *ad hoc* measures, nor any strong belief in the need for safeguards, had not the Irish rebellion both inflamed the jealous Protestant fears of many M.P.s, and made necessary an army against which safeguards must be demanded. If these political and constitutional measures were the main object of the war, why was the Root and Branch bill brought in to abolish the very institution of episcopacy, and why did the opposition demand a free hand in Church reform? The opposition well knew that on religion and the Church there was none of the near-unanimity shown against the policies, instruments and agents of the "eleven years' tyranny".

Obviously, the control of the Church was important to the whole of the politically active part of the nation, but more than this, the issue of religion was immensely important to a great many people. It had been so long before Laud's accession to power exacerbated religious feelings by 'innovations' or the revival of 'popish' doctrines and ceremonies—this quite apart from Laud's arousing of new antagonisms on social, economic and political grounds. From the accession of James I the declarations of the Commons increasingly revealed the growing difference between them and the Crown on the issue of religion. The first of the revolutionary resolutions of 1628-9 had been against innovations in religion. Thereafter, Laud's systematic

2. Oddly enough, C. V. Wedgwood (*The King's War*, London 1958, 133) mentions only the latter demands as war aims.

enforcement of his innovations, the Scots war which English bishops named *bellum episcopale*, the army of Irish Catholics, the canons of the Convocation of 1640 and, finally, the Irish rebellion all successively and cumulatively inflamed the fears and anger of the puritans. The earliest opposition speeches in the Long Parliament were against innovations. Wharton kept a copy of one by Sir Benjamin Rudyerd, which likened the prayer book to 'the filthiness of the mass' and urged that religion should be the *primum quiete* of Parliament, for all other things were 'but *et ceteras*.'[3] Rudyerd has been called a moderate:[4] what then were extremists like?

Hampden has been quoted, rightly or wrongly, as saying that religion was made the cause since the opposition could not otherwise be sure of the people.[5] Pym to the day of his death was allegedly in favour of a moderate episcopal government in the Church, and Clarendon claims that only the radicalism of Pym's followers, and his need to keep leading them if he were not to be abandoned by them, drove Pym past his hesitations into the more revolutionary activities of the Long Parliament's second session.[6] Yet Clarendon also noted that Pym 'had been most taken note of, for being concerned and passionate in the jealousies of religion.'[7] In any case, any differences in the religious aims of the opposition leaders and those of their most radical followers would be of little importance if in the event the leaders had to adopt their followers' more radical aims in order to retain leadership. The proportion of enthusiastic puritans in the ranks of the opposition would rise as the more conservative left the opposition to join Hyde in defending the existing structure of government in Church and State.

Finally, propagandists are always in danger of falling victims to their own propaganda. Since 1628, and increasingly since 1638, the manifestos of the King's opponents had assumed

3. MS Carte 80, 698 ff.
4. G. E. Aylmer, *The King's Servants*, London 1961, 381.
5. E. Wingfield-Stratford, *Charles, King of England*, London 1949, 317.
6. Quoted G. Huehns, *Clarendon, Selections from the History of the Rebellion*, Oxford 1955, 247.
7. *Rebellion*, VII, 410.

an alliance between Court, Anglican hierarchy and a confederacy of Europe's Catholic powers—this during the Thirty Years War in which Catholic France and to some extent the Papacy opposed the Catholic Hapsburg monarchies! Soon, as Clarendon noted, the Parliamentarians were to persuade their soldiers that the King's forces and councils, though manifestly directed by men 'of whose piety . . . they had received . . . the greatest testimony . . . consisted of no other than papists.'[8] This can help us to understand Wharton's war of Calvinists against Catholics.

Among historians, Gardiner saw the split in the Commons as largely on the issue of religion.[9] Professor Wormald claims that M.P.s tended to be more or less 'violent' in proportion to the extent to which they feared 'Popish' plots.[10] The King's manifestos made a great point of his stand for the Church and the divinely ordained episcopacy.[11] More, long before it broke out, bloody civil war was prophesied (or threatened) by Nathaniel Fiennes as the consequence of the King's defence of the Bishops.[12]

Some further confirmation comes from an analysis of the views of Wharton's colleagues in the opposition in the House of Lords. In late 1642 there were thirty-one Parliamentarian peers, of whom over half—sixteen—had shown no sign of opposition before the Long Parliament met. Of these sixteen, one or two were genuinely puritan, and five or six tinged with puritanism, friendly with puritans or hostile to the episcopal Church. Of the other half of the Parliamentarians—the fifteen survivors of the pre-Long Parliament opposition—two consistently favoured, and were favoured by, puritans, while six were themselves strongly puritan, a total of eight. Among these were the Providence Island Company lords, who had a key position in the collective leadership of the opposition. All the other leading or influential Parliamentarian peers were either strong puritans such as Wharton or allied even before 1640

8. Quoted G. Huehns, *Selections*, 253.
9. *Fall of the Monarchy*, II, 272 ff.
10. *Clarendon*, 14.
11. For example, his reply to the Grand Remonstrance.
12. Clarendon, *Life*, quoted G. Huehns, *Selections*, 26.

with puritans. Of all the many lords who left the opposition to become Royalists, only one—Montagu of Boughton—was a puritan, and he was an Anglican puritan who stood by his Church and its prayer book as well as by his King.

Religion, and the desire for Church reform (for whatever unknowable motives) were the main inspiration for many and a major motive for almost all of those who chose to fight for Parliament. It is no coincidence that a puritan group from the first organised, directed and largely inspired the opposition. Both courtiers and non-puritan *country* lords were less zealous and less persistent in opposition. It is very likely that for some, possibly most of those opposition lords who became Parliamentarian leaders in the Civil War, the decisive factors were religious. Wharton's deleted comment gave a judgement which was basically correct.

What were the Parliamentarians' other possible or alleged motives, of which Wharton left no mention? The thirty-two peers who made the numerically strongest protest did this against the refusal of the House to demand from the King the control of all forts and militia. Were they all equally concerned for the same things, or were some more concerned for public, and some more for selfish private ends? Can one distinguish between public and private ends in this? Limiting the King's powers would allegedly decrease the nation's danger. It would certainly decrease the opposition leaders' danger of exile or execution, and increase the powers of not only those leaders, individually and collectively, but also of their institutions and orders—the Houses of Parliament, the gentry and the peerage. The issue of public safety was inextricably entangled with the religious issue, since the open danger was from Roman Catholic Irish rebels, allegedly encouraged by the Catholic Queen and even by the Arminian King, while the secret danger was from plots made by ex-officers and courtiers, many of them Catholics.

There is no proof that Wharton believed in the danger of Catholic risings in England or of single or wholesale assassinations, but his father-in-law Goodwin accepted as genuine the threats against Pym, and he wanted Wharton and his peers to do something to stop such mischiefs.[13] Similarly there is no

13. MS Carte 80, 123.

evidence that Wharton had any positive political aims after the reforms of the first session of the Long Parliament—in contrast to some of his colleagues. In May, 1642, Northumberland could still write to Bankes:

> It is far from our thoughts to change the form of government...
> if the King please but to grant some few humble desires of
> ours,[14]

(in other words, Parliament's appointment of commanders and ministers and *carte blanche* to reform the Church!). At much the same time Denzil Holles (one of the five M.P.s impeached by the King) explained his dislike of any accommodation in which Parliament made any concessions; and Say and Sele warned that there was no hope of accommodation without the King's accepting the nineteen propositions which embodied Northumberland's 'few humble desires'. Wharton for his part was neither arrogant nor adamant in his attitude, seeming to blame the impending disaster on the lack of prudence or industry of some or the wickedness of others who, from the context, are not necessarily in the King's party.

Northumberland, and presumably others, believed or claimed to believe that: 'those persons . . . most powerful with the King do endeavour to bring Parliaments to be made instruments to execute the commands of the King.'[15] However, the characters of the King's newest councillors, recruited from the original reformers of the Long Parliament, were strong arguments against this, and Northumberland himself later said that twenty to one of the nation were not satisfied whether the King made war on Parliament, or it on him.[16] Wharton as late as June 1642 stated his belief that at York as well as at Westminster, men of great eminence were working for an accommodation.[17] Several of the 'violent' lords (especially courtiers) had reason to believe that the King's capitulation would greatly benefit them, while any compromise which left him the power to choose his own officers of state would be to

14. Bankes, *Corfe Castle*, 133.
15. Ibid, 123.
16. Firth, *House of Lords*, 207.
17. Bankes, *Corfe Castle*, 133.

their great disadvantage.[18] There is no evidence that Wharton stood to gain or lose anything of this nature, for as he told Bankes, he had not 'driven at' any advantage for himself,[19] but life and liberty were precious even to men less fearful than Wharton. 'We shall ever be faithful . . . to [the King's] royal person,' wrote Holles, 'though we . . . provide for our safety.'

Certainly Wharton did not come from a district solid in opposition. The gentry of Yorkshire, although in a 'great distemper' in the summer of 1640,[20] were not unanimous in opposition, for when 140 signed a petition for a Parliament Strafford persuaded two to three hundred to support his amendment. Some even of the 140 changed their opinions.[21] Several of the leaders of the 'distempered' faction—all (save Wharton) men, or relatives of men who had quarrels with Strafford became in time after Strafford's death moderates or Royalists.[22] Wharton and Darley, and the others who did not, were a minority of a minority.

Two explanations seem possible. Either Wharton's most recent associations were by 1642 his strongest, and his new southern connections more important than his old northern ones, or his strong puritanism (or some Providence Island Company connection, itself probably based on common religious ideals) must explain his rapid rise to a leading position in the opposition and also his remaining there so long. It was not simply ability. As well as Wharton, it was noted that Holland, Savile and especially Bristol took a prominent part in the Great Council at York.[23] Hertford, Bristol, Holland, Savile and Wharton were sent from Ripon to give an account to the King.[24] All agree that the indisputably able Bristol was the chief figure at the Great Council and at Ripon, yet when Parliament met he soon lost his influence. With the Commons

---

18. In August 1641, the King had refused the petition of both Houses to make Salisbury Treasurer and Pembroke Lord High Steward. Say and Sele would not long remain Master of the Court of Wards after a Royalist reaction.
19. Bankes, *Corfe Castle*, 133.
20. *CSP Dom 1640*, 630. Secretary Vane's letter.
21. Rushworth, *Collections*, IV, 615-17.
22. E.g. Hotham, Cholmley and Sir John Savile.
23. Lady Burghclere, *Strafford*, London 1931, 221.
24. *CSP Dom 1640-41*, 144.

led by Providence Island Company men, the core of the opposition in the Lords had no further need to put forward moderates as their leaders.

In the spring and summer of 1642, the withdrawal of the King to York was followed by that of a great many moderates of both Houses. Their absence left the extreme puritan minority in a much stronger position. In any case, it seems to be a rule in revolutions that an organised minority of extremists will sooner or later dominate any number of unorganised moderates. The staunch puritans of both Houses were an organised minority, which was openly to assume control as the 'godly party' in the winter of 1643-4.[25]

25. Since this chapter was written, my opinions have been confirmed and strengthened by the publication of Professor L. Stone's, *The Crisis of the Aristocracy, 1558-1641*. In this it is shown (p. 742) that by the early seventeenth century the peerage was split into three district 'clans'—Roman Catholic, Anglican and Puritan—whose members chose wives and friends from within the 'clan'; and that 'it was Puritanism which led so many peers to side with Parliament when war actually broke out'. On the next page (743) Professor Stone notes that all 'the key figures of the parliamentary opposition in 1642' (including Wharton) had shown 'puritan sympathies long before the crisis', and considers that even the professional courtiers who 'ratted on their old master' may have been influenced by this factor.

VII

WHARTON IN THE FIELD

'plaisir en faits d'armes'

ALTHOUGH two-thirds of the peerage joined the King in the summer and autumn of 1642, it was on both sides that peers took the lead in the first months of the Civil War. This was true for the central campaign (between the King's main army and the army led by Parliament's Lord General, Essex) and also for the many local wars throughout the land. Most peers subscribed money and horses, or pledged themselves to maintain troopers for King or Parliament. Wharton offered six horses, the smallest number from any peer on his side (Pembroke gave forty, the greatest number) and £300, almost the lowest amount—Northumberland gave the highest, £2,000. However, most gave only one or the other. In addition, many of the most zealous or most courageous (not necessarily the most youthful) served in person, in which case they were usually commanders of regiments or armies. No fewer than fourteen were Parliamentary colonels.

This noble leadership was the natural effect of a number of causes—the tradition of a fighting feudal nobility (not yet quite dead in England and destined to survive much longer on the continent); the wealth of most, and the great wealth of many of the peers; their hereditary prestige; their local influence with county families and towns; and above all the system by which the militia of each county was placed under a Lord Lieutenant who was normally the local peer most in favour with the government, or whose local influence and lands in that area made him the natural leader of its levies. Both before and after the outbreak of war, many peers attempted to secure the counties assigned to them by the King's Commissions of Array or the Parliament's Militia Ordinance. Bedford and Hertford disputed the west, Stamford and the Earl of Worcester's heir opposed one another in the marches of Wales, Willoughby of Parham raised the Lincolnshire forces for Parliament, the Earl of Newcastle secured Newcastle-on-Tyne for the King, Brooke carried on a local war in Warwickshire.

Wharton was not, according to the practice of the time, ill-equipped for a command. His name carried military prestige, for the barony of Wharton had been the reward of a brilliant feat of arms, and Philip Wharton's brother Thomas was a living proof that his house could still produce good soldiers. Wharton himself was young, and had served the same brief apprenticeship of arms that was all the Earl of Holland had when he was made general of the cavalry in the first Scots war. Wharton no doubt felt qualified to accept the commands of the militia of two counties, as well as that of the proposed army for Ireland. It was natural that he should play an active and prominent part in the field, especially since his charge of Lancashire was the scene of what was believed to be the first bloodshed of the war when Wharton's 'father' the Royalist Lord Strange tried to seize the county magazine. The Parliamentarians of Manchester appealed to the Houses at Westminster to send their appointed defender, Lord Wharton, speedily to their relief.[1] A week later a rumour in Preston that Wharton was advancing with 20,000 men enabled Parliament's partisans there to walk abroad without being abused as Roundheads.[2] The rumour was quite baseless, yet it seems to have inspired a remarkable recent account of manoeuvres in the first half of July between Strange and Wharton, both with local levies.[3]

In July, far from being in the field, Wharton was the busiest peer in the House, and was even Speaker in the second half of June and the first week of July:[4] and apart from these preoccupations, Wharton was in a peculiarly difficult position. In Lancashire he had neither lands nor influence, and it was far from Westminster. In Buckinghamshire he was no more than

1. *HMC 9th Report*, II, 391.
2. E. Broxap, *The Great Civil War in Lancashire*, Manchester 1910, 8.
3. Wedgwood, *King's War*, 106-7.
4. *LJ* 5, 85 ff.

heir presumptive to Arthur Goodwin who, as Knight of the Shire and Colonel of horse in Essex's army, was making full use of his influence and was to prove a more vigorous and capable soldier than his noble son-in-law. Here there was no local war, and when the central campaign reached Buckingham-shire the local forces and garrisons would inevitably fall under the control of the Lord General. Probably Wharton could not in any case have done very much for his two counties. In the event, however, he seems to have done next to nothing. True, after Edgehill three officers went to Lancashire apparently at Wharton's direction,[5] but when his Buckinghamshire Deputy Lieutenants appealed to him for directions and help, Wharton left it to their own judgement whether their newly-raised forces should retire nearer Uxbridge, under the protection of Essex's army.[6] Among their forces was the troop of horse of which Wharton was captain. This would be for him a source of profit without effort, for his father-in-law Goodwin kept an eye on it for him, and all Wharton did was send it an officer to act as cornet.[7]

Wharton's only military service was in the Edghill campaign as Colonel of a regiment of foot, a force, according to a recent work, composed of his own tenants.[8] In fact, all Wharton's lands in 1642 were in Cumberland, Westmorland and the North Riding, areas dominated by the King's partisans or at least inaccessible to Parliamentary recruiting. Wharton's commission from Essex authorised him to beat up his drums in London, Middlesex or any other county,[9] and presumably from London and Middlesex came most of Wharton's infantry.

The war began in the late summer of 1642 with the King's abortive move south from York to Nottingham on the way to Westminster, followed by his march further away from Westminster (and Essex's army at Northampton) through Derby to Shrewsbury in the west. The dilatory parallel march—scarcely a pursuit—by Essex's army to Worcester was regarded

5. MS Carte 80, 80.
6. G. Grenville, Lord Nugent, *Memorials of John Hampden*, London 1854, 306.
7. MS Carte 103, 91; Ibid 80, 80.
8. Carswell, *Good Old Cause*, 28.
9. MS Carte 80, 13.

presumably as a military promenade rather than serious warfare. Clarendon's reasonable explanation of Essex's failure to close with the King is that the Parliamentarians expected an easy and bloodless triumph by wearing out the financial resources of the King's few followers, forcing them to disband and the King to submit. However, after the King's withdrawal to the Welsh marches, his forces became formidable in numbers and morale. At Powicke Bridge near Worcester on 23 September 1642 the Cavaliers made the first successful cavalry charge of the war.

Three weeks later Essex was still slowly fumbling towards Shrewsbury. Whether or not he still thought in terms of a military promenade, he chose Wharton to command the considerable advance guard which on 13 October he sent to Bewdley, about a third of the way from Worcester to Shrewsbury. Essex was to follow with the whole army. It is true that Essex was short of officers possessing both experience and sufficient social status to exert authority over his noble and gentle amateur commanders. Perhaps he was influenced by Wharton's anomalous position as the titular Colonel-General of the Irish Adventurers' Army. Wharton was also a member of the committee of both Houses which accompanied the army, corresponded with the Houses at Westminster and advised (and perhaps to some extent controlled) the Lord General Essex.[10] Whatever the reason for his choice, Wharton had little success in his first and only independent command.

Almost simultaneous with Wharton's advance, the King resumed his march on London, at first to Bridgnorth on the way to Worcester and only sixteen miles from Bewdley. The sluggish approach of Essex caused the King's army to alter its line of march from south-east to east, through Wolverhampton, Kenilworth and Southam to the main road which would lead through Banbury and Oxford to London. The King's march was covered by a screen of horsemen led by the active Prince Rupert. The forces of Essex conformed to the King's movements. Wharton moved east-by-north the few miles from Bewdley to Kidderminster.

Here, as one Parliamentary newspamphlet alleged, Wharton had under him only five troops of horse to face the twenty

10. *HMC Abergavenny*, 88.

commanded by Rupert. Nevertheless, our source continues, Wharton 'valiant and resolute', confronted the enemy for three or four hours before Essex ordered him to withdraw.[11] However, Parliament's hacks were at this period very generous both in their praise of their noble commanders and in their estimates of the numbers in enemy detachments. In September they had credited Stamford and his 600 men with a wholly imaginary victory over Rupert with 1,300.[12] Another newsletter said 'letters came from Lord Wharton that he had made a soldierlike retreat from Kidderminster, excusing his not fighting with Prince Rupert in regard of the inequality of numbers,' but, it continued, it was 'commonly and confidently reported by others that from haste or fear he left some waggons and 3 or 4 pieces of ordnance behind him'.[13] With waggons and artillery, Wharton would certainly have infantry. It seems likely that at Kidderminster he had the whole considerable detachment of Essex's advanced guard, horse, foot and guns. This second source gave as the reason for Wharton's retreat merely his being outnumbered, and made no mention of orders from Essex.

This brief confrontation, more bloodless even than Valmy (having no cannonade) is ignored no doubt rightly by historians of the war. Yet by it the Royalists may have gained several field pieces. At Edgehill, where they still had fewer guns than had Essex, the Royalists derived a quite disproportionate advantage from the moral—if not material—effect of their artillery. Moreover, the withdrawal seems to have seriously weakened the morale of Wharton's men. All armies suffer from desertion, but there seems to be an invidious distinction in the general warrant issued by Essex to all mayors, constables and other officers to apprehend a number of soldiers of Wharton's regiment who had run from the colours and sold or stolen their arms.[14] The discouragement may have persisted until and at the battle of Edgehill, fought little more than a week later. This began with a cannonade. At the first discharge of the Royalists' guns, and before, as Wharton was to report, 'there was any

11. *Exceeding Joyful Newes*, London, 22 October 1642.
12. B.M. Pamphlet, E 118 (44).
13. *HMC 7th Report*, 530.
14. MS Carte 80, 82.

near execution' (casualties) four infantry regiments on the left of the Parliamentary army bolted.[15] Wharton's regiment was one.

After Kidderminster, Essex had tried to parley with the King, who had refused to receive Essex's messenger, and proclaimed Essex a traitor. The tardy and ineffectual attempt to head the King off had brought the outmarched and outgeneralled Parliamentarians at last into contact with their quarry. The King's forces, however, were by then in a good defensive position between Essex and their own objective—and Essex's base—London. Edgehill, fought on 23 October, was the first great battle of the war, and came very near to being the last. A complete victory for either side would have been a political decision as final as anything in history. Essex, better equipped, already superior in numbers and awaiting reinforcements under Hampden, had reason to be confident of such a victory; the Royalists demonstrated their confidence by forgoing their advantage of position to descend the hill and attack. In the event, the King's victory was incomplete, and, because it was not rapidly exploited, indecisive. The Royalist infantry suffered heavily, but Essex's army was driven back and much of it dispersed or demoralised.

It was not until two days after the combat that Essex, now secure from pursuit and making good his retreat to London by a route as far as possible removed from that of the King's advance, sent two of his Parliamentary advisory committee, Wharton and Strode (one of the famous five whom the King had failed to arrest) to give an account to the Houses. It was apparently believed by all, and confidently asserted by Royalist sympathisers, that these two had run away, but they at once gave the minister at St Margaret's, Westminster, a sermon to read giving thanks for a victory. The minister, Mr Case, preached for an hour, 'throwing . . . abominable dirt on private men and making . . . strong expressions to Almighty God.'[16] Whether these offensive words were his own or supplied by Essex or his messengers is not clear.

---

15. *Eight Speeches Spoken in Guild-Hall . . . Oct. 27*, London 1642. Printed elsewhere as well.

16. MS Harleian 3783, 61.

The consternation at Westminster caused by the news of defeat brought by the first fugitives was changed to such relief by the knowledge that Essex still had an army in being, that gratitude and expediency led the Houses to reward their general with £5,000 for the glorious victory which he and they alleged he had won at Kineton—the town through which Rupert had hunted Essex's fleeing cavalry. Strode apparently was so distracted and confused that he had to ask the Commons' permission to confer with Wharton so as to give a better account next day.[17] Wharton next day made two clear and fluent speeches to the City Corporation at Guild-Hall,[18] in his usual unaffected style which compares so favourably with the fervid or unctuous religiosity of so many of his fellow Parliamentarians. His account of the battle was as honest and accurate as most reports on either side of any action in that war—or any war. He claimed that three thousand Royalists died to only three hundred Parliamentarians, but his accuracy in reckoning numbers can be judged from his estimate of the cavalry of his own side at from thirty-five to forty troops. He truthfully reported the disgraceful panic of the four infantry regiments, all of which he identified. He excused the runaways as best he could by saying, truly enough, that they were 'but young soldiers', and stated his belief that they would do better. He accused Rupert's cavalry of ruthless cruelty in pursuit of plunder, alleging they killed harmless countrymen, women and children. 'They aim at . . . pillage . . . and the way . . . is murdering.' Perhaps some personal loss rankled, for Wharton pointed out that officers' baggage was looted, and his own officers claimed they lost everything.[19]

The battle was a turning-point in Wharton's life. Not only did it mark the end of his soldiering, but it was also the beginning of the legend of his physical cowardice. Hostile accounts alleged that he not only ran from the battle, but hid in a saw-pit, 'like a puttock in a marsh.' The war was to see many generals in full flight from stricken fields: Stamford gave his name to the heath from which he fled before a numerically far inferior force; Ferdinando Fairfax, Manchester and Leven

17. Ibid.
18. *Eight Speeches.*
19. MS Carte 80, 84.

aroused mirth by their haste from the battle of Marston Moor which their subordinates won. Yet none seem to have been so indelibly disgraced as Wharton. As late as the 1670s the political jingles of the streets called him simply 'Saw-pitt'.[20] Wharton's officers claimed that some of them had lost blood 'being shot' and that the regiment saved its colours—no mean feat in an army which lost fifty standards. In defence of Wharton's personal courage there is the testimony of two witnesses that he stayed in the field and in the service all the day. Strode in his Guild Hall speech praised Wharton's modesty in omitting mention of his own service. Essex not only sent Wharton to bring up further troops during the night after the battle,[21] and chose Wharton to carry the news to London, both honourable employments, but also referred Wharton's officers, when they petitioned for relief, to their Colonel, who, having served in the battle from beginning to end, could best judge their merits.[22] On the face of it, this should be convincing. It is true that Strode himself had been accused of fleeing and Essex, no doubt, would have been very loath to bring contempt on the peerage by admitting the ill behaviour of one of its members. Indeed, the Lord General was very generous and sparing of reproaches, even when addressing those who deserted at or after Edgehill to hide in or near London:

> I doubt many are gone to visit their friends, but I am confident that those who fought so gallantly will not quit their colours.[23]

The first public jibe against Wharton was made by Prince Rupert in a pamphlet printed to deny Wharton's charges of cruelty. In this the dashing prince said he would have asked Wharton the reason for the statement had he stayed so long as to be asked.[24] Wharton replied in print repudiating the charge of faint-heartedness and daring Rupert, 'bating the reverence' due to the King's nephew, to a personal encounter to prove that a real English baron as much scorned to lie as

20. *HMC Le Fleming*, 143.
21. *Eight Speeches*. This is Wharton's own report.
22. MS Carte 80, 78.
23. Wedgwood, *King's War*, 141.
24. J. Webb, *Memorials of the Civil War in Herefordshire*, ed J. W. Webb, London 1879, I, 170-1, quoting *Prince Rupert his Declaration*, Oxford 1642.

any titular German prince.[25] Yet Wharton could lie, as we shall see, even on his honour as a peer, and in the House of Peers. Moreover, his challenge is less impressive when we remember that there were to be many more fields of encounter in the war, on many of which Prince Rupert could be found. Hampden found him, and his own death. Lord Brooke found his death early in the war. Wharton never again faced a battle: the decision was his own, and the reason for his decision cannot be found in his own words or deduced from his actions. Whether the saw-pit story was true, or simply too good not to remember, or whether some other circumstances now unknown made it seem probable, cannot be determined, for whatever Wharton said, he did nothing to disprove it. It is not surprising that the slur persisted; to avoid a reputation for timidity, though based on only circumstantial evidence, Wharton would not only have had to *possess* physical courage, but also *show* it. Certainly he showed no sign of that 'plaisir en faits d'armes' which was the motto of his house.

Despite the confidence of Wharton and Essex that the soldiers who ran from Edgehill would live to fight again, at least one regiment—Wharton's—ceased to exist. One of Wharton's infantry officers went to his troop of Buckinghamshire horse, others to Lancashire or to other Parliamentary forces; three lived to fight again, but for the King, and one apparently did not live at all, although Wharton's cryptic note on his list ('in a ditch') does not give a clear explanation of this unfortunate man's fate.[26]

The peers who took the field for the King included several who became skilful or at least vigorous soldiers such as Northampton, Capel, Wentworth, Chandos and Arundel of Wardour—and many more who showed courage, constancy and self-sacrifice. Some on both sides proved to be timid, incompetent or defeatist, and their common failings of independence and arrogance led to indiscipline and faction. However, many Royalist peers continued in arms to the closing stages of the war, whereas by 1645 of all the many

25. *An Answer to the scandalous lying pamphlet intituled Prince Rupert his declaration,
    Published in the Vindication of the honour of the High Court of Parliament
    and their Army* . . . G.H., 7 December 1642.
26. MS Carte 80, 80.

Parliamentarian lords who had accepted commissions only four were in active service—Essex, Robartes, Warwick and Manchester. Firth pointed out that the Royalists had no legislative duties, [27] but they had the choice of many responsible though noncombatant posts, as Councillors to the King and to the Prince of Wales, and as Governors raising troops out of the fighting zone. Many quite elderly Royalist peers bore arms. On the other hand, although some of the King's opponents managed to be active in the field as well as in Parliament, nearly half the younger Parliamentarians under forty[28] or in their early forties,[29] and all the young peers who acceded to Parliament during the war,[30] made no attempt to serve as soldiers, although several were so far from being tied down by legislative or administrative duties that they had to be summoned, sometimes repeatedly, to the House,[31] or when present made no great contribution to its work.[32] Lincoln, a trained soldier, apparently never fought for Parliament, though he was to demand his pay as a colonel;[33] and Pembroke, Bolingbroke and Howard of Escrick avoided attempts to put them into military service.[34] Grey of Wark and Willoughby of Parham were soon put out of their military posts, and Fielding did not take an active part in the field until Brooke's death left a vacancy for an independent command.

Thus Wharton's absence from the field was not exceptional in a young Parliamentarian peer. It was also probably best for his party as well as for himself. Had he taken a local command in Lancashire or Buckinghamshire his fate could hardly have been different from that of the other noble commanders— death,[35] disgrace[36] or virulent quarrels.[37] Wharton could and

27. *House of Lords*, 128.
28. Dacres, Suffolk, Hunsdon, Nottingham.
29. Lincoln, Northumberland, Howard, Bruce, Berkeley.
30. Middlesex, Maynard, Montagu of Boughton, de la Warr, Mulgrave.
31. E.g. Dacres, Rutland, Suffolk, Exeter, Bruce, Lincoln, North. *LJ* 5, 350; *LJ* 6, 117, 198, 565.
32. E.g. Maynard, Nottingham.
33. *LJ* 8, 353.
34. *LJ* 6, 145.
35. As in the case of Brooke.
36. As in the cases of Stamford, Grey and Willoughby. Firth, *House of Lords*, 141-2.
37. As in the cases of Fielding (Denbigh) and Manchester. Ibid, 143, 144-6.

did do good war service to his cause in his civilian, parliamentary capacity. Certainly his military service was so slight and its fruits so bitter that Wharton can be excused his not mentioning it in his autobiographical letter. In fact he omitted any reference to any of the events of that eventful struggle.

VIII

BETWEEN THE PEACE PARTY
AND THE EXTREMISTS

*'I am not obliged to swear to the intentions of
others for I think they have other intentions.'*

WHARTON may have shown a lack of physical courage, but he
had soon an opportunity to show moral courage and steadfast-
ness in adversity. Most Parliamentarians had been confident
of an easy and bloodless triumph. The slaughter at Edgehill
was therefore all the greater shock to them. They could continue
to claim that their army had won a victory but their rejoicing
rang hollow as the King's army continued its march on London.
By November 1642 there was, at Westminster, a sufficiently
large Peace Party to make the Houses send overtures to the
King. In the Lords courtiers were its nucleus and with them
acted some mere *country* lords, some of them near-Royalist, and
the few non-'violent' peers who had stayed at Westminster
either from timidity, inertia or because they thought the
King's party the less lawful.

The courtiers stood to gain much from any negotiated peace,
for which they might be able to claim credit. In all the peace
negotiations throughout the war the main noble Parliamentary
envoys were courtiers, Northumberland, Pembroke, Salisbury
and Fielding, but it is true that one reason for their constant
employment as envoys may have been Charles I's weakness for
old friends (however badly they treated him) which made them
sure of a good reception. No doubt some courtiers joined the
Peace Party from timidity; certainly many of them loved
popularity,[1] and when the popular clamour for peace grew

1. E.g. Northumberland and Pembroke. Gardiner, *The Great Civil War*,
   London 1886, I, 92; *A Letter to the Earl of Manchester*, 1648.

greatest in December 1642, the proud and magnificent Northumberland, hat in hand, shouted with the best of the mob. Wharton on the other hand stood his ground when on 8 December he had to face a tumultuous crowd of some hundreds of shouting petitioners for peace. He recommended them to apply to the Houses of Parliament, but when instead they moved on to the Lord Mayor's and to Guild-Hall, cavalry and trained bands were brought up to disperse them.[2]

A few days later, when the Peace Party as a conciliatory gesture omitted some names from a list of Royalist delinquents, Wharton was among the nine who protested. These nine formed in fact a minority War Party which consisted basically of, first, all the lords of the Providence Island Company except Holland (never closely concerned in its affairs) and, secondly, the other serving generals of Parliament.[3] The only War Party lords in neither category were Wharton and the ineffectual Bolingbroke and Nottingham. The generals had most reason to wish, like Pym, to negotiate only from a position of strength: significantly, the courtier Fielding left the Peace Party for the War Party on inheriting Brooke's command. It may be significant also that the War Party lords in the aggregate had the least to lose, and the Peace Party lords the most, in a protracted and expensive war. Of those Parliamentarians whose fortunes are known, nearly four-fifths of the War Party lords had incomes in the two lowest (tax) categories, but two-thirds of the Peace Party had incomes in the four highest categories[4]— which agrees with the contemporary belief that, in the Commons, those with great estates were for an accommodation.[5] Almost certainly of equal or greater significance is the fact that of the Peace Party only Bruce could be called puritan, whereas puritans made up two-thirds of the War Party.

From the analysis of committee appointments referred to in

2. *The Lord Wharton's Speech to the Petitioners for Peace*, London, 12 December 1642.
3. *LJ* 5, 508. J. H. Hexter, in *The Reign of King Pym* (Cambridge Mass. 1941) has in the Commons at this time between the Peace Party and the War Party, a middle group headed by Pym, who was of course for making war. Of the Lords' *two* sections, the War Party seems to have strong affinities with Pym's middle group.
4. According to an analysis in the author's D. Phil. thesis.
5. Gardiner, *Civil War*, I, 116.

Chapter IV, Wharton's record appears impressive, both from the amount of his reporting from committees or from conferences with the representatives of the Commons, and still more from his membership of, regular attendance at, and effective work for such permanent executive bodies as Pym's finance committee and the Committee of Both Kingdoms. From this emerges a picture hitherto unsuspected. Wharton and some other peers played parts more important than those of a number of lords who—whether from their great names, offices, wealth or former intimacy with the King—more easily and more often attracted the attention both of the public in their own day and of historians since. Of the few civilian lords in the War Party, only Wharton and Say and Sele showed notable activity or were capable of it. They thus had a large share in the execution of the financial expedients by which Pym built up the revenue which made victory possible. By December 1642, the unpaid soldiers of Essex had become 'abominable plunderers as bad as Prince Robert', for Parliament's only resources were the greatly reduced customs of London and voluntary contributions.[6] A Committee for the Advance of Money was set up on 26 November. It met at Haberdashers' Hall and comprised ten members of the Commons and five peers—Howard (of the Peace Party), Mandeville and Brooke (generals), Wharton and Say and Sele. It was at Haberdashers' Hall that Wharton faced the peace petitioners, and from Weavers' Hall, where a sub-committee met, Wharton and Say and Sele ordered parish officers to send in the names of those who refused to subscribe for the maintenance of the army. Wharton also signed blank warrants ordering immediate appearance before the Committee. Soon Say and Sele was, with Pym, singled out for the hatred of the war-weary populace in the winter of 1642-3, while the Waller–Tompkins plotters allegedly planned to seize both Wharton and Say and Sele.[7]

6. Hexter, *Pym*, 15; MS Carte 103, 91. Colonel Arthur Goodwin writing to his daughter that he was ashamed to look an honest man in the face. 'Prince Robert' was commonly used for 'Prince Rupert', at least by Parliamentarians.

7. MS Carte 80, 98, 100; *Calendar of the Committee for the Advance of Money*, 3; Gardiner, *Civil War*, I, 186. For the Waller–Tompkins plot, see below p. 72.

In December Wharton was one of the four busiest peers in Lords committees, many or most of them for raising money. Thereafter the Peace Party took more than its share of appointments. Only one of Wharton's committees concerned peace proposals. These were drawn up by the Peace Party, and most War Party lords took little interest.[8] At the 'Treaty' of Oxford, February-March 1642-3, the King rejected these proposals. They included the old arrogant and harsh demands for control of the militia and a free hand with the church and the King's supporters. Nevertheless, they were the best terms offered him during the struggle and the reaction to their rejection reduced the power of the Peace Party. On 23 May 1643, Henry Darley moved the impeachment of the Queen. On the last day of May, Pym disclosed the alleged Waller–Tompkins plot and hastened the ruin of the Peace Party. Two separate designs, a parliamentary campaign for reopening peace negotiations, and a scheme for an armed rising in the City, were represented as a single plan, and several Peace Party lords were implicated.[9] Wharton, a member of the Houses' joint Committee of Safety, an advisory-executive body with limited powers, long dominated by Peace Party lords, had helped investigate the 'plot'. It appears he held evidence dangerous to Fielding. Perhaps that lord's sudden accession to the War Party was a result.[10]

The Royalist victories of the summer of 1643 gave the Peace Party what appeared to be its last chance. Early in August it forced through both Houses peace proposals which were close to capitulation. No War Party lords protested, presumably aware that once again other forces could be used against mere parliamentary majorities. At once the London pulpits were used to incite mobs to march on Westminster, and the Commons revoked their decision.

The Peace Party had hoped to use Essex and his neglected army to compel the acceptance of their terms, and Wharton was informed by his father-in-law, now Colonel Goodwin, of the resentment felt by himself, by his commander Essex and

8. Peace Party lords had far more committee appointments (analysis in author's D. Phil. thesis).
9. Wormald, *Clarendon*, 127-8; *LJ* 6, 90, 115, 117.
10. *CSP Dom 1649-50*, 445-7.

by the officers generally of the pitiful state of their troops—'the very Army . . . laying down itself, only 4 or 5 miles long in Guns, and arms of sick and Runaway men', while the 'baseness' of London and Westminster permitted constant attacks on Essex by the extremists in the Commons. With grim humour Goodwin added that the number of sick, left daily by the way, might be for the best as they still had two or three thousand more than they could pay.[11] Very soon after this letter, Pym procured votes for the payment and recruiting of Essex's army and for a new Council of War, excluding those extremists who had sought to replace Essex with Waller. Heartened by this, Essex rejected the overtures of the Peace Party which finally collapsed. Seven of their lords fled to the King.

Wharton's committee work at once increased both absolutely and relatively despite an obscure charge of disloyalty soon made against him. This arose as follows: late in October 1643 he received a commission as Governor of Portsmouth. This base had been since well before the war of prime strategic importance in the calculations of the King and the opposition, and it was now threatened by the advance of a Royalist army. Wharton claimed that at the first suggestion of his appointment he had obtained the consent of all who had any 'interest' in (or claim to) this office, to which he himself was indifferent.[12] However, as far back as 12 September the town and garrison had petitioned for Sir William Waller to be their governor, and this the Commons had recommended. Now Sir Henry Mildmay, a courtier and a former creature of Warwick who had in the Commons attacked individual members of the Peace Party, asked Pym to support Waller's nomination, for the reason that in August, Wharton had made his peace with the King. Pym expressed his disbelief, but did not inform Wharton of this accusation. Wharton inquired into the state of Portsmouth, sent in ammunition, and freely expressed his resolve to go there himself if he could obtain money to pay the garrison.[13] A few days later, the Commons ordered four Hampshire members to confer with Wharton and then ask Essex to 'take such care of it that some fit man may be put in *whose*

11. MS Carte 103, 86.
12. Ibid 80, 128.
13. Ibid 80, 128, 135.

occasions will give him leave to reside upon the place'. When shown the order, Wharton at first tried to retrieve the position. He made a note to 'Endeavour on Monday to put out these words [those italicised above] and so send it straight to' the Lord General. However, on the same day in an indignant answer which was delivered to the Commons, he wrote: 'I shall think the hours very long till this place be settled in some person's hands . . . *in whom the house may perfectly confide in [sic]. I conceived . . . I had some reason to hope it had been so now, but find my mistake.'* Wharton's answer was read 30 October, and the words to which he objected removed from the original order. Essex, after a delay for considering a matter which concerned 'a great peer of the realm', said he would keep Portsmouth in his own hands. In the event, it remained in the hands of the gentlemen of the county who had held it before.[14]

Two days later Wharton knew of Mildmay's accusation, which had probably been spread about before the Commons made the offending order. At an examination, insisted on by Say and Sele at a conference of the Houses, the Scots Lord Murray (Mildmay's alleged informant) denied saying, and declared that he had no reason to believe, that Wharton had made his peace. Mildmay also denied having made the accusation, and the death of Pym foiled Wharton's attempt to have that statesman examined to prove the contrary.[15]

No evidence supports the allegation of Mildmay; and Say and Sele, the leading peer of the War Party and the only peer at the examination, defended Wharton vigorously, informing the Commons that a great wrong had been done.[16] Presumably the reason for the accusation lies beyond the possibility of its truth. Many of the Commons were probably convinced that Portsmouth needed a resident governor, but Waller, the general of a field army, could have acted only through a deputy. The only reasonable explanation is that the extremists, partisans of Waller's candidacy for the chief command in Parliament's forces, wished to score a prestige victory over the partisans of Essex. Goodwin and Stapleton, the leading

14. Ibid 80, 128, 134; *CJ* 3, 294, 299.
15. *CJ* 3, 323, 333; MS Carte 80, 126, 130, 132, 135. A committee was to examine Pym on his sick-bed.
16. MS Carte 80, 130.

Colonel-M.P.s who supported Essex,[17] were both related to Wharton. Stapleton, Hampden, Pym and Strode were the M.P.s the Waller–Tompkins 'plotters' would have arrested along with Say and Sele and Wharton. Clearly the War Party in the Lords had worked closely with Pym to support Essex. The baffled extremists would vent resentment on a peer because the upper House was more open to attacks as having long harboured a Peace Party majority. At the worst stage of the extremists' attack on Essex, the officer group had temporarily aligned itself with the Peace Party,[18] so that the War Party lords were, perhaps, for a time indistinguishable from the others.

The most remarkable circumstance and the only one that lends any credibility to the charge, is the reference to Murray. If Mildmay's original words were true, Murray later perjured himself rather than maintain an accusation for which he either had no proof or no inclination. If Mildmay invented, then Wharton's dealings with the Scots, or the Scots' dealings with Oxford in mid-1643 must have made the charge seem plausible, and in fact there are two references to such dealings. The King had tried to obtain aid from Scotland, and with this for an excuse, and their danger for a reason, the House of Commons asked the Lords to join in appointing commissioners to go to the Scots and ask their 'brotherly assistance'. A newsletter in May 1643 reported that the Commons had chosen Vane the younger and Armine as their representatives and were planning to induce the Lords to choose as theirs, Wharton and Howard of Escrick who with the other two had already at Leicester met with some Scots lords. These must have been the envoys sent to offer mediation in England. Wharton was sufficiently interested in their affairs to keep a copy of the letter which ordered them home from Oxford, where the King had prevented their going on to London.[19]

Wharton's unofficial journey (with Howard) to intercept the Scots was presumably to put Parliament's point of view. To the Scots, Wharton may have expressed some qualms at the prospect of an alliance whose price would be a church

17. Hexter, *Pym*, 121, 138.
18. Ibid, 134.
19. *Mercurius Aulicus*, Sunday, 14 May 1643; MS Carte 80, 146.

reformation which would make a compromise with the King more difficult, or even impossible. In fact, Wharton soon after recorded his obscure but grave misgivings about the aims of some Parliamentarians. On a copy of the (first) Covenant which all the lords present took on 9 June 1643, against the words 'I believe . . . the forces raised by . . . Parliament are . . . for their just defence', he wrote: 'one's own belief is here intended and so long as I believe the aims are so I will join. I am not obliged to swear to the intentions of others for I think they have other intentions.' Wharton was careful, in an extra note, to say he believed of the Houses as was there said, and hoped others believed so.[20] Marten had already suggested that Parliament should assume sovereign authority, and was soon to propose the extirpation of the royal family.[21] In the event, Howard and Wharton were not chosen to go to Scotland in 1643, and the peers chosen avoided that duty.[22] Vane headed the Commons' delegation which concluded the Scots alliance, sealed by the Solemn League and Covenant. On 5 September the Scots Earl of Loudoun wrote to Wharton explaining that it was to defend the Protestant religion, the privileges of Parliaments, the liberties of subjects, and the King's person and authority and urging the Lords' speedy acceptance of it.[23] This may have been mere courtesy, but possibly Wharton's attitude to the alliance had not been noticeably friendly.

If Mildmay's report had any foundation, the time when Wharton 'made his peace' was either the beginning or the end of August 1643.[24] A royal proclamation at the end of June did not include Wharton among the peers excepted from pardon, but then of that short list (which included Stamford, never a real leader) only one, Say and Sele, was not a general. If he in fact wavered in his allegiance during the summer of Royalist victories, he did not waver for long, for on 22 September

20. MS Carte 81, 533.
21. Gardiner, *Civil War*, I, 154, 238.
22. *LJ* 6, 134-5.
23. MS Carte 103, 80.
24. Ibid 80, 135. Depending on how one reads Wharton's note of 30 October: 'About three weeks since . . . Mildmay . . . told him . . . Wharton . . . made his peace . . . about two months ago.'

Wharton, unlike several peers, neither hesitated nor refused to take the new Covenant. However, by then Essex had raised the siege of Gloucester, and beaten off the King's army at Newbury, breaking the King's run of successes and gaining a respite for Parliament.

IX

THE 'GODLY PARTY' AND THE
WESTMINSTER ASSEMBLY

'learned and godly men may and do differ'

WHARTON was soon one of the committee to treat with the Scots commissioners, and make the alliance more effective for the prosecution of the war. Vane had pressed the Scots to send permanent representatives to Westminster with power to conclude with a similar delegation from the English Houses of Parliament all that was needed for the three kingdoms. The 'godly party', a combination of all the fiery puritans,[1] controlled the Commons after Pym's death in December 1643. Led by Vane and the other former chief 'extremists', and backed by the Scots, it pressed for an Anglo-Scots executive to direct the war with more effect than was possible when the votes of the Houses interfered with, rather than controlled, a number of un-concerted campaigns. The surviving Peace Party lords opposed a policy which would destroy the Committee of Safety and weaken the House of Lords, both of which they had controlled. Also opposed were some of the noble commanders, in particular Essex, who, as Lord General, had a particularly elevated position and who was very sensitive to criticism, slights or restraint. Thus the House of Lords' wing of the War Party fell to pieces. As supporters in the Upper House the 'godly' leaders of the Commons had now only the staunchest civilians of the War Party lords, of whom the most notable were Say and Sele and Wharton. Significantly, the first introduction of a bill for a Committee of Both Kingdoms was by Say and Sele in the Lords on 1 February 1643-4.

1. J. H. Hexter, 'The Problem of the Presbyterian Independents', *AHR*, XLIV (1938) 42.

Meanwhile Wharton, with Vane and Say and Sele, had been sedulous in furthering the designs of the Scots representatives in the Westminster Assembly of Divines (of which more hereafter) seconding a motion, suggested by the Scots, for full conformity in religion between the two countries. Wharton, at the Scots' request, contrived to have 'the relics of the Prayer Book' banished from both Houses,[2] and with Vane and St John (another 'godly party' leader) he was engaged in detecting and exploiting the crop of Royalist plots of the winter of 1643-4. One of these was the scheme of an obscure prisoner, Ogle, to use the Independents and moderates against Scots and Presbyterians for a compromise peace with a moderate episcopacy. Little had so far been heard of the Independents, formerly and later called Congregationalists. These puritans, though as Calvinist in doctrine as Presbyterians, wished to substitute for episcopacy the congregational church system as seen in New England rather than the Geneva-Scots model favoured by Presbyterians. As a proof of their power and goodwill, the King's new auxiliaries were to betray to his troops the town of Aylesbury. The Governor of that town, Mosely, instead betrayed the plot to some leading Parliamentarians. By 11 December 1643, Wharton and two or three of the Commons were examining documents sent from Oxford. After the Lords gave him liberty to walk abroad, Ogle was allowed to escape.

Presumably Wharton arranged this. He was in correspondence with Mosely, and after the Royalists' advance on and disastrous retreat from Aylesbury, he related the whole affair to the Lords. Meanwhile, Vane corresponded with Lovelace, who had left the Peace Party to join the King. Lovelace hoped to obtain information but gave more than he got. Hearing of another design, to have influential citizens move the City Corporation to send peace proposals, Vane at once called in Wharton and St John. They were to help interrogate Riley, the City's 'Scoutmaster' (military intelligence chief) who was a key man in the plot.[3]

2. Baillie, *Letters and Journals*, I, 117, 130.
3. Ibid, II, 133; B. M. Gardiner, 'A secret Negociation with Charles the First, 1643-1644', *Camden Miscellany*, N.S. VIII, 1883; B. Whitelocke, *Memorials*, London 1732, 80.

Wharton was thus a leading man in the 'godly party' in the winter of 1643-4, one of those responsible for internal security. However, in the House of Lords the active supporters of the 'godly party' were outnumbered by two to one. The majority—composed of surviving Peace Party lords, of other moderates returned to the House, and of various generals, active or dismissed—particularly opposed the establishment of the new executive proposed by a second bill for a Committee of Both Kingdoms. Very few of them had been named in the bill as members of the Committee. Hence they struggled in the first place to avoid giving it powers which would greatly and permanently decrease their own influence, or, failing that, to put themselves on the Committee.[4]

Wharton of course had been named from the first a member of the Committee, even in Say and Sele's original bill, and it was this bill (accepted unthinkingly at the time by the Lords) which finally became the ordinance establishing the Committee. The seven peers among its twenty-one members were Essex, Warwick, Robartes, Manchester, Northumberland, Say and Sele and Wharton. Only the last three were civilians and thus regularly available to provide the two lords necessary for the quorum. It has not been recognised sufficiently (if at all) that in the campaigning season, the Committee's direction of strategy and decisions of policy fell to a great extent into the hands of the least military members, meeting regularly at Derby House.[5] This circumstance could explain much of the lack of success of the Parliamentarian forces, despite their superior numbers and resources, up to and even for a time after the raising of the New Model Army.

Wharton was a diligent worker for the new executive, drafting and considering letters to and from the King, and listing Parliament's stores, the disposition of all forces on both sides, and persons on whose credit £300,000 might be borrowed from the Dutch.[6] He continued to work with the finance

---

4. *LJ* 6, 542; Pembroke, Salisbury, Howard, Grey of Wark and Lincoln proposed as extra members.
5. Gardiner (*Civil War*, III, 306) did not draw this conclusion, although mentioning the frequent absence of the military peers; he names only one non-military peer, Northumberland.
6. *CSP Dom 1644*, 18, 36, 37, 44, 68.

committee at Haberdashers' Hall, as a Commissioner for Plantations, and in the Committee for Sequestrations (of the income of 'delinquent' Royalists).[7] Presumably as the result of their commitments to 'Derby House' (as the Committee of Both Kingdoms was commonly called) Wharton, Say and Sele and Northumberland had fewer House of Lords committee appointments. In any case, the upper House was declining in importance. It continued to lose ground in its frequent bickering with the Commons, who were supported by the Derby House Committee. The civilian lords in the new executive had never hesitated to support the Commons against the majority of their fellow peers. The Lords reluctantly agreed on 13 April that negotiations with the King should be left to the Derby House Committee, but insisted that propositions must be presented within six days, before Essex was due to march on his new campaign. In fact, Essex was late in starting, but the Committee, more interested in prosecuting the war than in seeking peace, did not present its propositions before 29 April. Wharton, for England, signed the articles—including the notorious seventeenth, which settled all forces on parliamentary commissioners and against which four peers protested. Soon after, the Lords were supporting Essex when he ignored the spirit of his instructions from Derby House, and the Committee was insolently refusing information to the Lords except at the request of both Houses.[8]

Among Wharton's duties and activities outside the House after the autumn of 1643 was his attendance in the Westminster Assembly of Divines. The Grand Remonstrance of November 1641, which had split the House of Commons, had demanded an assembly of divines to reform the liturgy and government of the church, but the King had rejected a constant succession of bills to authorise this step. The sixth bill became an ordinance in June 1643, after the Lords had amended it so that the assembly should contain ten of the Peers and twenty of the Commons. The Assembly met at the time of the Solemn League and Covenant, and from the first the delegates from the Scots Kirk had little difficulty in persuading the mass of the divines

7. *LJ* 6, 195; *CSP Col 1574-1660*, 324.
8. *LJ* 6, 543; Gardiner, *Civil War*, I, 417-18.

to take Scotland as their model for the new reformation. Also from the beginning, a small group of Congregationalists, never more than ten or eleven but including some highly respected men, opposed this.[9] The newer name of Independents, possibly suggested by their demands, emphasised for their opponents the menace to the unity of the national Church.

Some distinction must be made between a group in religion and a group in politics, even though contemporaries often called both by the same name, and even though the connection between religion and politics was never stronger than in the seventeenth century. To use the terms Independent and Presbyterian for church affiliation only, and 'Independent' and 'Presbyterian' for political affiliation, is the barrier 'between us and nonsense'.[10] There was a small group of true Independent puritans (Congregationalists in religion) in the House of Commons, important largely because it contained many of the ablest politicians including the younger Vane and St John. Until December 1644, it was thought that Say and Sele was the only Independent in the Lords. Vane and St John were among the eleven Commons members who took an effective part in the Assembly and Say and Sele, Manchester and Wharton were the only peers who did so, the other seven all being of the Peace Party.[11] Of the three active peers, Wharton was the only one who was not a member of the Providence Island Company (the Congregational model was universal in the puritan colonies). Vane, St John, Say and Sele and Wharton all worked together in the Assembly and elsewhere. In time, they were all to become leading 'Independents' (political allies of the Independents, whether or not Independent themselves). Even Manchester was not consistently 'Presbyterian' and whatever his beliefs on church government, he appointed the Independent Nye as minister at Kimbolton. It is impossible

9. W. A. Shaw, *The History of the English Church during the Civil War and under the Protectorate*, London 1900, I, 122, 124, 124n, 142-55.

10. Hexter, 'Presbyterian Independents', 37-8; quoting a contemporary reference to 'real' and 'royal' Presbyterians (Ibid, 39, n35).

11. Clarendon, *Rebellion*, ed Macray, III, 507; D. Masson, *Life of John Milton*, London 1873, II, 523-4; W. Notestein, 'The Establishment of the Committee of Both Kingdoms', *AHR*, XVII (1911-12), 485n, 27, labelled Wharton 'a deeply-dyed Independent' in 1643, which seems improbable.

to say at what stage Wharton became an Independent in religion, but no doubt the debates in the Assembly and his simultaneous close association with the leading Independents of both Houses, hastened the change in his beliefs.

The lay members of the Assembly and the Scots delegates did most of their work in a standing committee, consisting of themselves and elected representatives of the Divines. This, called the 'Treaty Committee' by the Houses of Parliament, kept Parliament in touch with the Assembly and normally had great influence on the latter's debates, the divines being inexperienced and long-winded.[12] The Scots representative Baillie thought the Independents were putting off debates because time was on their side,[13] but whether this was so or not, certainly at first those lay members of the Assembly who were later 'Independents' for some time acted in the closest conjunction with the Scots,[14] and neither Vane and St John nor their allies Wharton and Say and Sele at first supported the Independents. In February 1643-4 Say and Sele successfully urged the Assembly to lay aside a question on which a deadlock had been reached, and, against Independent opposition, go on to consider the crucial question of whether many churches might be under one presbytery.[15] Wharton, Vane and St John were present later at a private conference between the Scots ministers and three each of the English Presbyterians and Independents. This meeting came to nought eventually, by which time Say and Sele for one was regarded by the Scots as a supporter of the Independents.[16]

Wharton had been brought into close contact with the leading Independents over Ogle's plot. He told the House of Lords that Philip Nye and Thomas Goodwin had refused to meddle in the business, pretending (with permission) to consent

12. Shaw, *English Church*, I, 151-2, 158.
13. Ibid, 158, 164.
14. Hexter, 'Presbyterian Independents', 45.
15. Shaw, *English Church*, I, 168, 170; W. M. Hetherington, *The History of the Westminster Assembly of Divines*, Edinburgh 1843, 180. The shelved question (whether the London ministers could ordain others) was urgent because of the shortage of ministers, and important because the Independents held that a *congregation* could choose, and its elders ordain, a minister.
16. Baillie, *Letters and Journals*, II, 145-6.

to Ogle's plan in order to find out more. However, the Scot Baillie was not wholly convinced of their innocence, and Ogle's own letters to them mention their 'endeavours . . . always bent this way', and a very 'high and daring' petition (of which Nye informed Ogle) in which the Independents threatened to lay down arms if the Scots Covenant were forced on them. Still, there is no evidence that even the Royalists thought Wharton sympathetic to the plot, although Bristol included 'L. Say, etc.' in his Heads of Instructions for Ogle to approach.[17]

The fact that Parliament concealed the matter of the Independents' petition and gave no publicity to the details of the plot is some evidence of the gravity of the situation. Ogle's main inducement to the Independents was toleration under a reformed episcopacy. This was once their aim, and it was this aim which allegedly first brought them a numerous following. For the common aim of toleration Nye in late 1643 had begun to co-operate even with the fanatic and schismatic sects now proliferating in London and in some Parliamentary forces, whose opposition and numbers, and those of the Independents increased greatly in 1644 in reaction against Presbyterian intolerance.[18]

Wharton was to be much influenced by the ideal of liberty of conscience or toleration. However, in early 1644 the arms of the intolerant Covenanters were desperately needed. The Scots invasion overran the northern counties and lifted the Royalist threat to Lincolnshire and East Anglia. Wharton, regularly present at Derby House, signed instructions from the Committee of Both Kingdoms for his fellow-peer Manchester commanding a Parliamentary army co-operating with the Scots, and (late in June) a request to the Scots for yet more assistance.[19] At such a crisis the restless Vane thought fit to alarm the conservative Scots and Parliamentary generals (then besieging York) by suggesting the deposition of the King.[20] Fortunately for him, a few days later, in the climax of the war, the allies'

---

17. B. M. Gardiner, 'Secret Negociation', iv, 5, 8-9, 29, 33; Hexter, 'Presbyterian Independents', 46; Baillie, *Letters and Journals*, II, 130.
18. Gardiner, 'Secret Negociation', i; W. K. Jordan, *The Development of Religious Toleration in England*, London 1938, III, 60-1.
19. E.g. *HMC 8th Report*, II, 60; *CSP Dom 1644*, 283.
20. Gardiner, *Civil War*, I, 368-9.

victory at Marston Moor put an end to the struggle in the north and to Parliament's pressing need for Scots assistance.

The 'puritan' revolution so far had merely wrecked the Laudian–Elizabethan Church of England; it had provided nothing to replace that church as an enforcer of uniformity in worship. Now, immediately after their decisive victory, the three conservative allied generals wrote to Derby House urging the speedy settlement of church government, while soon after the General Assembly of the Kirk of Scotland passionately demanded complete religious uniformity between the two countries—the aim which had induced the Covenanters to enter the war. The House of Commons did urge the Westminster Assembly to debate church government, but when the Divines followed the Scots' urgings instead of the Treaty Committee's on the terms of the debate, the Commons ordered the Committee to consider the difference of opinion in the Assembly, to try to bring about a 'union' and, if that failed, to find out how to bear with 'tender consciences who cannot in all things submit to the common rule.'[21] In this they were prompted by Oliver Cromwell, then Manchester's Lieutenant-General, Independent in religion, and apparently the one senior officer who listened favourably to Vane's proposal to dethrone the King. By a happy chance for Vane and the Independents, Cromwell had gained as much in credit at Marston Moor as his seniors had lost by premature flight. Later—by 16 September at latest—Baillie recognised as adversaries Cromwell's civilian allies (and Baillie's former close colleagues) Vane, St John, Say and Sele and Wharton.[22]

Wharton made a brief note on the Treaty Committee's long debate on Cromwell's Accommodation Order. Although a Sub-Committee of Agreements was appointed, Wharton noted that the Scots and Presbyterians carried their point—that (failing an agreement) the matter of bearing with those who could not submit to the common rule should be deferred until after the rule itself should be 'found out and resolved upon'.[23]

21. MS Carte 80, 178, 196 (Wharton's copies); Shaw, *English Church*, I, 175, 177.
22. Baillie, *Letters and Journals*, II, 230.
23. MS Carte 80, 195; Gardiner (*Civil War*, II, 75) claims that 'no single step was taken' to give effect to Cromwell's Accommodation Order.

This resolve largely stultified the Accommodation Order.[24]

From the mass of papers on church government (as argued in the Assembly and its committees) which Wharton kept (beginning with the note mentioned above) it is clear that he began to take a close interest in the decisions of the Divines at the time when the issue of toleration for Independents became important. Very likely Wharton like Vane was moved by the ideal of liberty of conscience (however limited) as much as by political radicalism. When Henry Masy, the minister of Kendal, in February 1646-7 called that ideal 'a fancy of two or three years' standing' *partly* entertained by Wharton,[25] the rigidly Presbyterian divine probably underrated its importance to his patron.

In late September and early October 1644 a fierce debate in the Assembly brought rapid gains to the Presbyterian divines. The great particularity with which Wharton noted the qualifications and explanations made by the Independents when they agreed to any propositions indicates how much he sympathised with them, and also suggests that his sympathy was on religious grounds. In all his notes Wharton seemed to accept the Independents' views on the powers of the congregation as opposed to those of the church officers and the power and independence of the congregation with its officers as opposed to presbyteries and synods.[26]

Nevertheless it is not certain that Erastian grounds had no part in leading Wharton to support the Independents. It has been claimed that in the strongly puritan Commons relatively few wanted either a loose confederation of congregations (offering ample opportunity for schism) or a powerful, largely clerical hierarchy of presbyteries: most held the Erastian position of wanting the state to rule the church.[27] The same was no doubt true of the Lords. Wharton kept a copy of the Sub-Committee's report embodying most of the Independents'

---

24. MS Carte 80, 195, 197. The Commons made no protest; perhaps the surrender to the King of Essex's army made their leaders realise that the Scots might be needed yet again.
25. B. Nightingale, *The Ejected of 1662 in Cumberland and Westmorland*, Manchester 1911, II, 909.
26. MS Carte 80, 189.
27. Hexter, 'Presbyterian Independents', 44.

qualifications and stating that an accommodation was not probable. The only suggested compromise was that perhaps an individual whose parish minister could not give him the sacrament might obtain it from the minister of a neighbouring parish. The Independents felt that 'a considerable number' of such individuals should be free to become a distinct church.[28] The fragmenting tendency of such a demand is obvious. Wharton seems never to have faced squarely the dilemma of what to do when puritans fell out. He showed none of the rigidity of the true Presbyterian, and none of the fervent religiosity, verging on fanaticism, which was common with those numerous Independents who, like Cromwell, bordered on the 'seekers' and who suffered such agonising (if temporary) fears for their souls. Wharton's adherence to Independency seems to have been more the result of a rather negative view—that a congregation and its minister should not be ruled, though they should be advised, by a higher church body—than the result of the more positive but somewhat anarchic belief that a gathering of Christians and their chosen pastor constitute a church. Wharton had at least noted that at the 'Committee of Religion' (his term for the Treaty Committee) there was made on 30 September 1644 a plain statement of the most important practical grounds for a strict hierarchy of powers in a centralised national church, and the denial of freedom to congregations: it was impossible to allow all churches in England to send, as in Scotland, officers to vote in a presbytery, for 'ill people and ministers would rebel'.[29] In fact, over much of England puritanism did not have the allegiance of the majority.

Wharton reported to the Lords a further Scots demand sent to the Committee of Both Kingdoms, on 23 October 1644, by the Committee of the Estates of Scotland. In this letter (copied in Wharton's hand) the Covenanters urgently pressed Derby House to take to heart as a first priority the settling of religion, and to influence Parliament and the Assembly towards this.[30] Before the arrival of this demand, Wharton, with Say and Sele, Vane and St John, had pressed vehemently to have the

28. MS Carte 80, 191.
29. Ibid 80, 189.
30. Ibid 80, 198, 200.

Independents' propositions debated in the Treaty Committee, feeling (the Scots thought) that whatever the Committee decided, the Commons would grant the Independents all they wanted.[31] Certainly most leaders of the 'godly party' were now supporters of the Independents against the Scots. The settlement of the Church could no longer be delayed and the 'godly party' split on this issue, but in such a way as to give neither of the resulting factions clear control. It has been claimed that in late 1644 and early 1645—a time of Presbyterian dominance in Parliament—uncommitted puritans and Erastians helped enact a Presbyterian form of church government and directory of worship, and that thereafter the same middle groups prevented the establishment of the Scots–Genevan disciplinary power of excommunication—a period of 'Independent' predominance.[32] In fact, even the directory of worship was not Presbyterian enough for the Scots: Wharton was among those chosen to ask the Commissioners if they had power to give way over it.[33] On the vital issue of excommunication the decision was still less Presbyterian, though more Erastian than Independent. Although the Presbyterian Assembly made the considerable concession that excommunication should not be inflicted for errors in judgement on 'points wherein learned and godly men may and do differ',[34] yet the Houses would not accede to the constant demands of the divines and their allies for an unlimited power to the church in deciding exactly what would entail suspension from the sacrament. Wharton and Say and Sele were put on a committee in November 1645 to answer one such petition from the City and the London ministers. On 13 March 1645-6 they and the other 'Independent' lords mustered a bare majority of eleven votes to pass a provision for provincial lay commissioners to allow excommunication.[35]

Meanwhile, in January 1645-6 Wharton and Say and Sele

31. Baillie, *Letters and Journals*, II, 236 (25 October).
32. Hexter, 'Presbyterian Independents', 44.
33. *LJ* 7, 129.
34. MS Carte 80, 214.
35. *LJ* 8, 208. The ten 'Presbyterians' asked leave to protest, and four actually did so. The 'Presbyterian' party in the Lords, unlike that of the Commons, did not have the former Peace Party as its nucleus; most of the ex-courtier Peace Party lords were now 'Independents'.

had moved in the Lords to adjourn the Assembly of Divines. Baillie wrote that this was really to dissolve it,[36] and in fact the Assembly soon lost all importance. Like the Scots army after Marston Moor, it had outlived its usefulness.

---

36. *Letters and Journals*, II, 344.

X

THE 'INDEPENDENTS' AND THE SCOTS

*'you know his metal. He is as fully as ever for
that party, who daily grows in hopes and
insolency.'*

WHEN Wharton and his 'godly party' associates in the Assembly
openly opposed the Scots, this was for Wharton at least only
the latest exchange in a long and increasingly acrimonious
series. Wharton had been closely concerned with Scots affairs
before and during the making of the Solemn League and
Covenant and thereafter, especially (apart from the Scots' aims
in religion) with the economic problem of supplying the Scots
armies in England and Ireland (acute as early as February
1643-4[1]); with the political problem of differing attitudes to
the King and, hence, peace terms (obvious in March 1643-4[2]);
and the military problem of Scots garrisons and army movements in England virtually outside the control of the English
Parliamentarians—an issue which appeared as early as
October 1644[3]. The first and third combined to produce a
fourth still uglier cause of recrimination in the Scots' maintaining themselves on free-quarter and on their own arbitrary
assessments of the English population.

Wharton came of a Marcher house which gained its peerage
in war against the Scots. Many of his inherited lands and all
his expanding lead-mining interests were in Yorkshire, and in
that province's welfare he had the keenest interest. By treaty

1. MS Carte 80, 136-40, 154, 156; *LJ* 6, 458; *CSP Dom 1644*, 38.
2. MS Carte 80, 208.
3. Ibid 80, 184.

the Scots army was to have £31,000 *per mensem*, and when Wharton drafted a scheme to assure this payment 'in a solid way' from *Parliamentary* assessments, excise, royal revenues, sequestrations and 'all other means whatsoever' in the six northern counties—in return for the Scots' concurrence in a joint declaration against *Scots* assessments—he inserted a clause which would have forbidden the alteration of Yorkshire's contribution under any pretext. This he had to strike out, but he substituted another to the effect that the north should not be burdened by the raising of new troops or the quartering of any forces which could be used in the south.[4]

All these problems, as well as the clash on religion, were exacerbated during 1644 and 1645, and Wharton, often the only English peer at Derby House and serving there on many sub-committees, became increasingly involved. When Derby House and Parliament tried unsuccessfully from October to December 1644 to regain control of the northern fortresses, Wharton summarised the negotiations and noted the unsatisfactory compromise which followed.[5] Yet another area of conflict appeared—the form and the command of Parliament's own English forces. That the Scots should express concern about and seek to influence matters so clearly outside their province was the result of a development which confused all the issues— political and religious—producing two great factions. The split in the 'godly party' had been partly on the cognate issues of more efficient war-making and more extreme war aims. Of Parliament's three chief generals, Manchester and Waller were strongly inclined to a negotiated peace, and Essex—who had misgivings on the social results of prolonged war—was discredited by his shameful fiasco in the west. Vane and St John, when the breakdown of the 'godly party' was imminent, determined to reform the armies so as to give commands to a group of officers of their ideals. By this they drove the Scots and those English who followed their church policy into alliance with the more moderate Parliamentarians, and to accept a

4. Ibid 80, 202. The original provision for the Scots had been the sequestered estates of Catholics and delinquents, which proved quite inadequate.
5. *CSP Dom 1644-45*, 183, 205. The Scots Governor of Newcastle was given a temporary English commission.

more conservative political programme, whereas those who disliked the rigours of Scots Presbyterianism allied with those who wished for a complete military victory which would enable them to dictate whatever terms they pleased.[6] At the end of November 1644 the militarily sluggish Manchester and his fiery subordinate Cromwell quarrelled openly, with charges and counter-charges in either House. Essex and some moderate lords even contemplated impeaching Cromwell, and were dissuaded only because he was 'of great favour and interest with the House of Commons, and with some of the Peers likewise.'[7]

Was Wharton so much an 'Independent' as to favour Cromwell at the very time of his savage attack on Manchester, so long a colleague of Wharton? To some extent Manchester's cause was that of the House of Lords. Wharton served on a committee for Manchester's grievances against Cromwell, and on one to meet the King's envoys, a meeting insisted on by the moderates. More, unlike Say and Sele and even Northumberland—the *quondam* Peace Party leader now 'Independent'—Wharton did not protest when the House rejected Cromwell's famous 'self-denying' ordinance, by which all members of either House would lose all offices, civil and military. A curious incident on 20 January 1644-5 suggests the possibility that Wharton was even hostile to Cromwell. With the Commons members of their Committee absent, six Derby House peers resolved to consider next day the 'opinion of some' in Cromwell's regiment 'against fighting in any cause whatsoever'. Nothing more came of the matter, but that it was a jest seems unlikely.[8] Essex and Manchester were Cromwell's open enemies; Warwick, also threatened by the ordinance, usually followed a line similar to Manchester's; Say and Sele was the original 'Independent'. Therefore it would seem that either Wharton or Northumberland or both failed to oppose the resolution; and Northumberland had a week before protested against the rejection of Cromwell's ordinance. However, Northumberland's

---

6. Hexter, 'Presbyterian Independents', 44-5; Clarendon, *Rebellion*, ed Macray, III, 507.
7. Gardiner, *Civil War*, II, 8; W. C. Abbott, *The Writings and Speeches of Oliver Cromwell*, Cambridge Mass. 1937, I, 312-13.
8. Abbott (Ibid, I, 327) is of the opinion it was 'probably as a jest'.

changes of opinion were numerous, and he may have seen real danger in a 'mutiny' which merely proved that Cromwell's men would not easily accept another commander.

Wharton, on the other hand, was usually a consistent supporter of whatever party he happened to grace, and all his parties so far had been the more extreme of every choice within the House of Lords. He was also a natural 'Independent', and not only on religious grounds; he was always for security rather than trusting the King. Wharton took little interest in the 'Treaty' of Uxbridge of January-February 1644-5, devoting in a letter to Lord Fairfax barely a line to the negotiation, which (he said) the commissioners 'intend . . . very earnestly, but as yet there is not any one step gained'.[9] Most 'Independents' expected it to fail, but the ex-courtier Parliamentarians desperately tried to make it succeed.[10]

Once the 'Independents' had obtained the appointment (as commander of the projected New Model Army) of Sir Thomas Fairfax—an uncommittedly puritan semi-professional soldier, so apolitical as to be not even a member of Parliament, and a good friend of Cromwell—there was little point in further resistance to the 'self-denying' ordinance, which the Lords therefore accepted in April 1645. Before the New Model was tested in battle, its Lieutenant-General was Cromwell, whose 'self-denying' ordinance in its effects denied military rank to all members of either House *except* himself. In May and June, Wharton's committee work for the House decreased, but his activity in the Committee of Both Kingdoms rose to a peak. Wharton, Say and Sele, Essex and Manchester were the lords regularly attending. Unfortunately, the success of Derby House in directing the new campaign did not correspond with its industry in spite of the presence of the two former generals. Say and Sele, believing a story of Savile's that the Governor of Oxford was ready to surrender his charge, persuaded the Committee of Both Kingdoms to send Fairfax on the fruitless errand of besieging the Royalist capital. However, on 14 June the New Model and the King's main army blundered on one

9. *Fairfax Correspondence*, ed R. Bell, London 1849, I, 157-9. The letter, dated 25 January [1644-5] is largely concerned with providing a minister for Grinton in Mardale (inhabited by Wharton's tenants).
10. Gardiner, *Civil War*, II, 65; Clarendon, *Rebellion*, ed Macray, III, 494

another at Naseby and the two-fold Parliamentary superiority in numbers confirmed the verdict of Marston Moor. Almost at once, Derby House named a sub-committee to consider a Westmorland petition against the Scots and to prepare letters from Parliament to the Estates of Scotland.[11]

The English Parliamentarians had ample reason for dissatisfaction. Their new army had been in the field since the beginning of May, whereas Leven's veteran Scots had done little or no serious campaigning since Marston Moor, nearly a year before. They had gone into winter quarters in October 1644 and in spite of many requests did not move south till June, the month of the final verdict of Naseby. Meanwhile towns in the north such as Carlisle, captured by the joint efforts of the Scots and local Parliamentarians, were garrisoned exclusively by the former, who carefully kept their English allies out of the terms of surrender. Wharton accumulated masses of papers about the Scots, which he frequently reported to the Lords from Derby House.[12] He had become an expert in Scots affairs, and was naturally appointed to the Lords committee for instructions to the commissioners who were to go to 'treat' in Scotland.

It is not surprising that Wharton was himself one of the commissioners. What is surprising is that he actually performed the duty laid upon him. His fellow-commissioner from the Lords, Rutland, excused himself as he had before in 1643, and to substitute for him the House insisted on Stamford, an impossible choice, for he was under impeachment by the Commons.[13] The main ostensible subject for the negotiation was the Scots hold on Carlisle. Baillie hoped a 'friendly debate' about it would lead to a stricter union between the nations, and remedy for Scots grievances. However, he had to warn his correspondent, Lauderdale, of 'the leader of the negotiation', Wharton, of whom Baillie wrote:

> you know his metal. He is as fully as ever for that party, who daily grows in hopes and insolency.

11. *CSP Dom 1644-45*, 602.
12. E.g. *LJ* 7, 152, 162, passim.
13. Ibid, 494, 499. Stamford had had his footmen stone Haselrig, an eminent leader of the Commons.

Baillie still believed the only hope of the Scots' prevailing in the Church was the success of their army. The instructions of the English commissioners were concerned with English, not Scots, grievances. Though they were to give the 'best satisfaction' in all that seemed to cause difference, they were to demand the withdrawal of garrisons not only from Carlisle but also from Newcastle and five other places, the end of all oppressions and of the protection given by the Scots to delinquents. This embassy may have been intended in good faith to remove difficulties between the allies. On the other hand, Baillie, who hoped for a 'friendly debate', also wrote that those who sought division between the nations 'blows much at this coal' of the Scots garrison in Carlisle.[14]

This mission, apparently hitherto unnoticed by historians, occupied Wharton and his four fellow-commissioners from the Commons—Vane the elder, Armine, Robert Goodwin and Thomas Hatcher—from early August until 10 November 1645. It involved Wharton in a dubious financial expedient of a type common to Parliament during the Civil War. An ordinance gave him £4,000 from the estate of the late Sir William Savile, Royalist Governor of York.[15] This was later a source of trouble to Wharton, but at the time necessary for the expenses of the embassy, which were not small. The envoys' 'family' or household was very large: ten gentlemen at the commissioners' table, and a total of thirty at the other two tables. On the way to Berwick the commissioners 'treated' with the committees of York and the other northern counties to hasten the completion of the forces of the new Northern Association. Wharton left the others at Raby and went on to Appleby to meet the committees of Westmorland and Cumberland.[16] He was a member of five of the committees of the Northern Association: the only other lords to equal this number were Northumberland and Dacres. At Berwick they learned of the battle of Kilsyth, the final and most crushing victory won in his *annus mirabilis* of revolt (against the Covenanters) by the Royalist Montrose, who was reported

14. Baillie, *Letters and Journals*, II, 230, 298-9; MS Carte 80, 240. Dated wrongly 28 July 1644, presumably for same day of 1645.
15. *LJ* 7, 498-9; cf Ibid, 662.
16. MS Carte 80, 290; *LJ* 7, 552.

to have orders to move south into England. Berwick now seemed the fittest place to treat.

A week after the English arrived, those of the leading Covenanters who were at Berwick appealed to them for English aid against Montrose, but the next day the Scots changed their tune. They apologised for withdrawing Lieutenant-General David Leslie and the mounted troops from the army in England, and now wanted the English merely to watch the King's army—a small force of broken cavalry, the floating wreckage of Naseby—lest it move north and threaten the rest of Leven's army. Wharton and his fellows apparently suggested that the Scots garrisons in northern England would make a considerable force, but they saw no willingness 'to make Use of those Forces in that Way'. The Lords took up the suggestion, and requested the Commons to put it to the Scots commissioners.[17]

The English commissioners doubtless felt they had a golden opportunity to wring concessions from the Scots, but despite constant urging they obtained none. Wharton and the others spent their time asking the Houses to send arms to the Northern Association and directories of worship to replace the Book of Common Prayer, which was used to keep the people Royalist. They reported David Leslie's progress north with mounted infantry, eight regiments of cavalry and one of dragoons, a total of five to six thousand horsemen. On 13 September Wharton wrote of Leslie's triumph, 'God in His Great Mercy appeared mightily for us. They . . . put all the Irish to the Sword.'

Revolting as this sanctimonious cruelty may seem in this age, it was common, almost normal, in that one. Perhaps— we can only hope—Wharton was not fully aware of the manner in which God mercifully appeared: that the Irish soldiers who surrendered on unequivocal promise of quarter were massacred in cold blood on the insistence of the ministers of the Kirk. Even now the English commissioners could get no certain time set for a meeting. They even withdrew for some time to Newcastle, and when they returned to Berwick a complicated muddle by the Scots over the powers of their Committee of the Estates held up negotiations. After indignantly recapitulating

17. *LJ* 7, 566, 568.

the delays they had endured, Wharton and the others finally agreed to go to St Andrews where the long delayed 'treaty' lasted four days, 14 to 18 October 1645.[18]

Two matters were settled amicably enough: the Scots agreed to make up the accounts of their army and the northern counties, and to cease protecting Royalists. However, they would not give up their garrisons, ingenuously suggesting that Carlisle should be left to them because if they had asked for it in 1643 it would have been granted. They asked if the English commissioners had power to agree to the Scots garrisons' remaining, but were answered that the instructions were expressly to demand the garrisons' withdrawal. In the draft of their last paper the English commissioners at first claimed that their demands were agreeable to 'reason and justice'; Wharton, among the many alterations he made, substituted for these vaguer standards 'the Treaties'. There was no reply from the Scots.[19]

The more outspoken Parliamentarians had seen some good in Montrose's victories if the scene of war moved to Scotland and rid England of those 'brethren, who otherwise might not so easily be got out of England'. The chief grievance of even their best friends was the Scots' failure to aid in the war.[20] Leven's army, which sent all its horse and a third of its foot to oppose Montrose, abandoned the siege of Hereford, fleeing back to Yorkshire from the tiny army of the King at a speed which made nonsense of the excuse (lack of transport) for its slowness to advance. Not surprisingly, three days after the last unanswered English paper at St Andrews, the Houses voted that 'the Scots army not engaging against the enemy according to the desires of both Houses, and their continuance in the Northern parts contrary to those desires, is . . . prejudicial to those ends for which their assistance was desired, and destructive to those parts of the Kingdom . . .'[21] On 11 November 1645, the day after his return to Westminster, Wharton received the thanks of the House. He and his colleagues had obeyed

18. Ibid, 573, 581-2, 584, 605; MS Carte 80, 242-77; *CSP Dom 1645-47*, 107, 114.
19. MS Carte 80, 269, 273, 275; *LJ* 7, 689-95.
20. *CSP Dom 1645-47*, 130.
21. Ibid, 200.

instructions which left little latitude, and the Scots and English were now openly and inflexibly opposed on all major fronts, political and religious.

Soon after his return to Westminster, Wharton was again one of the most regularly attending peers in the Committee of Both Kingdoms. The most important and urgent quarrel between the victorious allies was the issue of what terms of peace to offer to the King. Even before Wharton's embassy, the Scots noticed that some at Westminster thought 'only of a bare paper to be accepted or refused, not only without any treaty but without any words'.[22] By April 1646, the Scots commissioners had been for nine months demanding the preparation of peace propositions, and now at Derby House Wharton was chiefly concerned with various propositions, and the remonstrances thereon of the Scots. These last, in December and January 1645-6, he constantly reported to the House of Lords. There he was also remarkably active, his committees covering not only public finance, war and peace terms, but also, contrary to his usual custom, less vital and even private bills.

The first draft by Derby House of an answer to the King's request for safe-conduct for his peace envoys amounted to a rude refusal. The Scots doubted whether 'full and express charges of His Majesty' would conduce to a pacification, and objected to the implication that Parliament would receive no propositions from the King and that the King must assent, without any negotiation, to every particular of the smallest importance. This, of course, was exactly what the 'Independents', of Derby House and the Houses, intended. For weeks the English vainly urged the Scots to give way, but their allies objected to the novel wording of votes by the Houses in which the Scots were included despite their prior dissent. The ingenious explanation of the Derby House Committee that the votes were only 'in order to' the Scots' consent was offset by its plea that the votes could not be rescinded because of the inconvenience. Unmoved, the Scots successfully insisted that the words 'without any treaty' be left out.[23]

One draft answer to the King reproached him for all the

22. Baillie, *Letters and Journals*, II, 298.
23. MS Carte 80, 283, 313, 314, 315, 317-8, 324, 320, 330-6, 341; *LJ* 8, 53-9, 64, 66, 91.

bloodshed and for bringing Irish rebels into both kingdoms. Wharton personally altered one sentence to meet the Scots' demands. The propositions 'which being assented unto by your Majesty will be the only means whereby you can give [satisfaction]', became 'which we conceive to be the only way for the attaining a happy and well grounded peace, and your majesty's assent unto these propositions will be an effectual means for giving [satisfaction]'. Of the peace propositions finally sent them in February, the Scots accepted fifteen articles almost as they stood. However, they found that, contrary to the allies' agreed terms at the time of the Uxbridge 'treaty', the militia now was settled not on the Committee of Both Kingdoms for seven years but on the separate Parliaments indefinitely. This not only entrenched further on the King's prerogative, but gave the Scots no security from their now hostile neighbour. Wharton took part in a conference where the Scots found that the English had no power to discuss alterations. As the Houses also refused to make any but minor concessions, the Scots were driven to publish their case in a pamphlet which the Houses ordered to be burned. Wharton was on the Lords' committee on this.[24]

In December 1645, a committee of both Houses arrived at the camp of the allies besieging Newark. Wharton filed the correspondence between them and the Scots, and from both to Derby House. Because of reports of false musters the English commissioners mustered the army of the Covenant. They found at Newark only 7,000 of whom 4,000 were horsemen, far more expensive than infantry, though far less useful in a siege. The treaty had stipulated 18,000 infantry and 3,000 horsemen. The Commons voted that the Scots had now too many horsemen, and Wharton was employed in having the Lords accept this vote. Only one 'Presbyterian', Lincoln, protested. Both the Lords' commissioners at Newark were unwavering 'Presbyterians', yet they showed considerable hostility to the Scots. Willoughby, a Royalist-'Presbyterian' in 1648, returned to the House only to impress the Lords with the miseries which their allies inflicted on Nottinghamshire.[25]

24. MS Carte 80, 293v, 294, 395-6, 377-82, 383-4; *LJ* 8, 258, 237, 239.
25. *LJ* 8, 28-9, 95-6, 118-9, 137, 143, 344-50; MS Carte 80, 346-7, 385-439; *CSP Dom 1645-47*, 361. For the significance of the number of horsemen,

Gardiner wrote that 'complaints against the cruelty and extortions of the Scottish soldiers were greedily welcomed' at Westminster.[26] It seems far more true that the very real sufferings of their countrymen moved to anger many whose political and religious convictions should have made them allies of the Scots. Wharton was particularly concerned with the case of Tickhill, in his native county of Yorkshire. The inhabitants petitioned Poyntz, General of the Northern Association, claiming they had been forced by Frazer's regiment to pay £1,500 *per mensem*, although Parliament assessed them at only £200, and begging for English troops to protect their wives and daughters. After many requests, the Scots generals agreed to a court-martial. It was put off from time to time and place to place until the witnesses could not be expected to attend. When it sat, it was composed solely of officers from the accused regiment. Naturally, all the charges of wounding, robbery and rape were dismissed.[27]

The House had long suspected the Scots of secret negotiations with the King. St John first opened the matter in the Committee of Both Kingdoms, supported by the allegedly 'Presbyterian' Warwick. Although the Commons could prove nothing, they gave no satisfaction to the Scots, not even naming the source of the accusation, and Wharton noted that the Lords also did nothing in the matter. The Scots' stealthy invitations to the King, though unaccompanied by any written guarantees, nevertheless succeeded. Presumably the King felt that the rift between the Scots and the 'Independents' was so great that he must profit from it. Surrender of some kind was almost the King's only alternative to flight overseas. After the destruction of his last army at Stow-on-the-Wold, the Derby House Committee resolved to sit only three days a week. On 5 May

---

see the author's note *EHR* (July 1958) 464. To raise these horsemen the Scots enlisted so many ex-cavaliers (Parliament named 60 officers) that when they were finally dismissed one cavalry regiment (which had included French and Irish) commanded by one Van Druske, had to be disbanded. MS Carte 80, 421; *LJ* 8, 349; *CJ* 4, 577.

26. *Civil War*, II, 489.
27. MS Carte 80, 360, 423; *LJ* 8, 344-50.

1646, the King entered the Scots camp before Newark. The first Civil War was virtually over.[28]

By this time the Parliamentarians had drawn up a list of honours and more substantial rewards for their chosen leaders or outstanding personalities.[29] While there was a nice balance between 'Independents' and 'Presbyterians', there was obviously little attempt to make each reward fit the deserts of the recipient. Say and Sele was to be given a step in the peerage, to an earldom, and from the Parliamentarian point of view this was possibly deserved, but Wharton, less prominent, was to receive two steps, to the same eminence. Nothing much can be deduced from the honour intended for Wharton, since the well-deserved peerages of some hard-fighting generals were mingled with the great promotions (to dukedoms) of timid and shifty ex-courtiers. All consistent moderates were ignored, as were some leaders of energy and stature who had offended the leaders of the Commons.

After four years of war, Wharton was still a member of the more extreme group of the King's opponents in Parliament, who seemed certain to have their way. The war had merely delayed their triumph. But there had been a time when the King seemed likely to win; a time when Parliament purchased a Scots alliance at what seemed to many an excessive price; times when the need for military or executive efficiency conflicted with the interests of the House of Lords; and a time when the bulk of the clergy, and the City of London (the essential purse of Parliament) pressed hard for a type of church government distasteful to most of the nation. In all these crises Wharton stood firm. He was throughout the war a member of whichever party was in the Lords more energetic in making war. Of those of the original opposition lords still surviving, only Say and Sele could say the same. Throughout the war Wharton was a tenacious and indefatigable worker for its prosecution to a swift and decisive end. Only once, when defeat seemed very near, was there any hint of faltering.

28. Ibid, 123, 182 ff; *CSP Dom 1645-47*, 188, 388; J. G. Fotheringham, *de Montereul Correspondence*, Edinburgh (Scottish Historical Society), 1898-9, II, 565, Appendix, Note C; MS Carte 80, 348-51, 354-8, 359v.
29. MS Carte 80, 72 (Wharton's copy); *CJ* 4, 360.

Like most peers and great landowners, Wharton suffered heavy financial loss during the war, nearly £10,000, he claimed, probably with some exaggeration.[30] Unlike other Parliamentarian lords he did not on that account beg assistance from the House. Many of his colleagues obtained grants of money, lucrative posts or other advantages, but Wharton's £4,000 seemed to have been unasked and most probably used to finance an embassy laid on him. His restraint was in sharp contrast to the greed of Say and Sele and of many other lords of both parties, displayed on many pages of the Lords' Journals.

Firth wrote that after Edgehill, Wharton 'seems to have ceased to take an active part in the war'. If he had meant no further campaigning in the fields, that statement would be correct. But in fact Firth meant no such thing, for he described Northumberland as typical of the lords who 'fought' for Parliament.[31] Firth was far from the truth. Wharton played a considerable part and a markedly effective and consistent part, in the first Civil War. Many Parliamentarians wavered, and showed inconsistency or selfishness. Although many moderates were both consistent and disinterested, only a handful of the extremist lords were consistent and of these only Wharton and Montagu could not be accused of selfish motives. But whereas Montagu was an uninfluential newcomer to the House, Wharton was from 1640 one of its leading members. Thus not only had Wharton an important role in the war: his career was in some respects unique.

Nothing of Wharton's war career, or of the division among the 'Calvinists' with whom Wharton originally identified the Parliamentarians, appears in his political testament. This may be no more than our misfortune, rather than a deliberate (and hence significant) suppression: the matters in dispute were complex, obscure and so far in the past as to be of no great relevance in such an apologia.

---

30. MS Carte 80, 558. He was still able to gain possession, during the height of the war, of Aske (near Richmond) and could boast that he now owned most of the lead-bearing Swaledale (Carswell, *Old Cause*, 28).
31. *House of Lords*, 142.

XI

THE WAR'S END BRINGS
NO PEACE

'the times and I grow worse and worse'

BETWEEN the King's surrender to the Scots and the end of his
reign and life, almost three years passed: the first in efforts by
the Scots to make a Covenanter of the King and by Parliament
to obtain control of the King's person; the second in quarrels
between Parliament, as dominated by the 'Presbyterians', and
the New Model Army, supported in Parliament by
'Independents'; and the third in the preliminaries, outbreak and
aftermath of the second Civil War. In these struggles Wharton
became as deeply 'Independent' as could any peer who still
valued his hereditary rank, power and privileges, but as the
rift so widened that bloodshed within the ranks of the original
Parliamentarians became possible, he was increasingly assailed
by misgivings. The last few months of the existence of the
Parliamentary House of Lords saw, apparently, the realisation
by Wharton and others of his party that the allies they had
so staunchly supported pursued aims incompatible with the
existence of hereditary rank, or even of free parliamentary
government.

Throughout this period there was an almost uninterrupted
decline in the importance and prestige of the House of Lords.
Concurrently there was the growth of the struggle between an
Army which included men hostile as much to aristocracy as to
monarchy and a numerically predominant faction in the
Commons which (whatever its politics) was in religion
sufficiently Presbyterian to abhor the toleration needed by
Independents. These factors may be enough to explain the
simultaneous decline of Wharton's political career and his

diminishing prominence in affairs of state despite his apparently close relations with Cromwell the chief 'Independent' leader of the Army. Certainly, Wharton seemed to fluctuate between despondency at the worst and usually mere conscientious committee work at the best. He would have had to be either little concerned with the fate of Congregational puritanism or little concerned with the fate of his own order to have retained for long any optimism, and with it vigour and enthusiasm for the politics of the years between the two Civil Wars.

The first reaction at Westminster to the King's arrival in the Scots camp was the despatch, apparently by the English members of the Derby House Committee, of 5,000 mounted troops towards Newark. Warned in time, despite the arrest of Scots messengers, the Covenanters moved north at great speed, fearing a conflict 'upon a mistake'. At the Scots' request, the pursuit was halted, apparently by the Lords, but not before the troops reached Banbury.[1] The Commons merely voted without a division that there was no further use for the Scots army in England. Against a 'Presbyterian' majority, the 'Independent' lords tried to second the 'Independent'-led Commons. Twice in May 1646, Wharton and nine or ten others thought fit to protest. The first protest was in support of a Commons' vote that the King should be removed to Warwick Castle (a place within Fairfax's quarters), but the Lords refused to agree even to a different destination; the second was made because the Lords highly commended a City petition against the employment of persons disaffected to Presbyterianism, and for a 'union' with the Scots. This petition (inspired by a letter from the King) the Commons met with veiled hostility.[2]

The Scots now pressed their own terms upon the King. Openly agreeing with the English Parliamentarians to present the Newcastle Propositions, they privately offered the King milder political terms and military support in return for a rigid Presbyterianism in England. Fearing such a bargain the

---

1. *LJ* 8, 308, 316, 538; MS Carte 80, 437; *Papers lately delivered into the Honourable Houses . . . by the Commissioners of the Kingdom of Scotland* (9 June 1646); Gardiner (*Civil War*, II, 479) wrote only of the possibility of such an attempt.
2. Gardiner, Ibid, I, 480, 483, 489; *LJ* 8, 309, 332.

Houses compromised on the power of excommunication. The 'Presbyterian' majority in the House of Lords subsequently, and no doubt consequently, decreased.[3] Wharton kept numerous papers on the negotiations at Newcastle. Among these the curt six lines of the English message to the King contrasted significantly with the eloquent and passionate avowals of loyalty in the appeals of the Scots leaders and officers. At a time when his committees were relatively few, Wharton was active on several for quartering and paying English forces in the north; and, with Say and Sele, he protested when the Lords refused to continue the Northern Association. Clearly the 'Independents', by moving English troops ever closer to the Scots, applied a deliberate pressure either for political purposes or from ill-will.[4]

Ill-will towards the Scots was now rampant, extending even to peers who consistently voted 'Presbyterian'. Such a one was Dacres who as early as October 1645 asked Wharton whether he should use the friendship of a Scots commander to get possession of a disputed estate. Dacres even then saw a likelihood of war, from which he did not shrink, for he wrote that all Cumberland 'as one man' would engage against the Scots.[5]

After the King's answer of 1 August, the Scots gave up hope of his yielding and offered to remove their army on receiving their arrears of pay. After much haggling with absurdly exaggerated claims and counter-claims, a compromise was reached on 1 September. By now, partly as the result of the tension between the former allies, the 'Presbyterians' no longer had a majority in the Lords.[6] In September Wharton was the most active committeeman in the House.

No doubt Dacres asked Wharton's advice on the theory that if a staunch 'Independent' allowed collaboration with a particular Scot, there could be no harm in it. Wharton's inclination towards church Independency, which we can

---

3. Gardiner saw it otherwise, noting only the transfer of Mulgrave's proxy (Ibid, II, 481 and n 2).
4. MS Carte 80, 441, 447-8, 477, 479-80, 481-2, 484.
5. Ibid 80, 165. Wharton must have reassured Dacres, who did so use the Scot (*LJ* 8, 143).
6. Gardiner, *Civil War*, II, 518-19; *CJ* 4, 644; my note, *EHR* (July, 1958), 'Payment of Arrears to the Army of the Covenant'.

deduce from his papers of 1644, must have been obvious to his fellow-peers soon after. By the winter of 1645-6 it had become apparent to the world in general, and in particular to one of his clerical protégés, the strictly Presbyterian Masy. The latter warned him to be sure of his footing before stepping further into the stream, for though the Independents' (Congregationalists') doctrines then seemed orthodox, they would perhaps later appear otherwise. By December 1646, Masy was complaining of the errors and schism beginning in Westmorland and Cumberland, in which Wharton had the chief hand by his protection and encouragement of Mr Taylor and even of the formerly scandalous new convert, Antrobus, once a 'young gallant' who had offered to serve as a Royalist officer. He feared lest Wharton should present an Independent as minister at Kirkby Stephen. Only one draft survives of any answer from Wharton to Masy. It is curt, on business only, and with no mention of religion.[7]

Nevertheless, Masy's disquiet had some basis. The Independents (Congregationalists) were allied with schismatic sects, with whose followers the 'Independent'-led Army teemed. As early as July 1646 Wharton served at a conference on disorders in the New Model. In the following October the Army became a major issue, on which (alone) the 'Presbyterians' at first dominated the Lords. Nevertheless, Fairfax, supported by the Commons, successfully defied the Lords and disbanded 'Presbyterian'-led local troops. More peers left the 'Independents', yet the House voted abjectly to honour Fairfax by waiting on him. Soon only two or three 'Presbyterians' troubled to protest, even against such measures as making a new Great Seal or refusing negotiations with the King.[8]

In November and December 1646, Wharton was one of the busiest committeemen in the House. However, in January, the committee appointments of the 'Independents' in general, and

---

7. Masy wanted his own son to have Kirkby Stephen. In 1650 he took the Engagement which so many Presbyterians refused on principle. A William Taylor later, as Wharton's chaplain, helped collect the names of those ejected at the Restoration: Nightingale, *Ejected of 1662*, II, 821-5, 906-7, 910, 928, where are printed many of the letters to and the draft from Wharton, which are found in MS Rawlinson Letters 52.

8. *LJ* 8, 531, 543, 576, 581, 611, 630.

of Wharton in particular, declined in number, and the tendency was accelerated in the following months. The reason was plain. With the King in English hands (after 3 February 1646-7) and the danger of war with the Scots gone with their army, the anxiety and exasperation which had added so many supporters to the 'Independents' had also gone. Outside Parliament there were riots against taxes and petitions for establishing Presbyterianism, suppressing toleration and disbanding the Army. The Lords, sensitive to change, hastened to make new advances to the King. 'Presbyterian' lords protested in greater numbers, and at last in a majority rejected an ordinance for continuing assessments for the Army. Wharton was among the protesting 'Independents', but the Commons also were now dominated by 'Presbyterians', and it was no longer simply a matter of supporting the pressure of the lower House on an irresolute majority in the upper House. On 9 March 1646-7, after the Commons voted, in effect, to exclude Cromwell from the Army,[9] Wharton wrote of it to Denbigh, now a fellow-'Independent' and a commissioner with the King at Holdenby. He ended his letter:

> My lord, the times and I grow worse and worse, and particularly my arm which must plead my excuse for using another pen.[10]

There is no further clue to the nature of the malady which made it expedient for Wharton to use a secretary, as he normally did from this time on. He was relatively healthy for most of the remainder of his long life, and was even able to make notes in his own hand, though with more than his former illegibility. However, the word 'particularly' indicates that there was something else amiss, perhaps a malady of the spirit rather than of the body. In such times, truly growing 'worse and worse', even the staunchest 'Independent' might well feel discouraged.

Parliament now set about reducing the Army. The Committee of Both Houses for Irish affairs sent a sub-committee

---

9. Ibid, 708; *LJ* 9, 57; Gardiner, *Civil War*, III, 29, 33. Presumably the 'Independents' lost control of the Commons as soon as the Scots ceased to be an irritant. Gardiner gave no explanation for the 'Presbyterians' having a majority in measures against the Army.

10. *HMC 4th Report*, 274.

to Fairfax's headquarters to confer about sending eleven regiments to Ireland. Wharton was the only peer in the group, whose most distinguished members, according to Gardiner, were two 'Presbyterians'.[11] It is not clear why Wharton was chosen, but he was active on the Committee for Irish Affairs. This Committee had recently employed, among others, Wharton's brother, Sir Thomas, to negotiate with his old commander, Ormond, for the surrender to Parliament of the remaining Royal garrisons in Ireland.[12] Perhaps it was thought a confirmed 'Independent' could deal well with the Army or possibly no trouble was expected.

If so, Parliament was soon undeceived. The officers wanted guarantees of pay for the troops for Ireland, and of arrears, and an indemnity for actions in the last war. The soldiery took up these demands, added others, and embodied them in a petition intended for Parliament. When next Wharton wrote to Denbigh, he enclosed without comment a copy of this petition. He gave the unwelcome news of further petitions in the country for disbanding the Army, but this time with no expression of discouragement.[13]

Both Houses declared against the soldiers' petition. No lord protested then, nor when the Lords pushed through a bill under which the City appointed an exclusively 'Presbyterian' committee to control its militia. Despite growing disorder in the Army, Derby House again sent a sub-committee, in which Wharton was replaced by the more 'Presbyterian' Warwick, to enlist volunteers for Ireland. Organised resistance thwarted their efforts.[14] In April and May 1647, Wharton's committee work in the House dwindled to almost nothing, though his attendance was regular. While the Commons tried to appease the troops, the Lords, with growing suspicion of the Army, moved that the King should be invited to Oatlands, near London. On the next day (21 May) five 'Independent' lords

---

11. *CSP Dom 1645-47*, 540; Gardiner, *Civil War*, III, 37.
12. E. R. Wharton, *The Whartons*, 30; *Severall papers of the treatie between . . . Ormond . . . and Sir Thomas Wharton etc.* (Dublin 1646). Ormond later wrote to Wharton (*LJ* 9, 442) who did his best for Ormond's affairs (*HMC Ormonde NS*, I, 118).
13. *HMC 4th Report*, 274.
14. *CSP Dom 1645-47*, 547; Gardiner, *Civil War*, III, 49.

ventured a protest on a minor point. Cromwell this day declared the Army would disband. However, in the first days of June, Cornet Joyce on Cromwell's instructions carried off the King from Parliament's guards and commissioners.[15]

Wharton had leave of absence from the House during the latter part of May, but in June he slightly increased his amount of committee work, although he was erratic in attendance. On 10 June he was appointed (presumably as a leading opponent) to a committee to draft an ordinance granting a City petition for power to raise cavalry in its own defence and for paying off the Army. He was absent next day when Hunsdon introduced an ordinance (for the safety of the kingdom and collaboration with the London militia committee) against which protested several 'Independents' including a recent convert. The day after this Wharton had a pass to go into the country with his family.[16] Presumably it was fear of violence which led him to take such a precaution, though it is conceivable that he was becoming again, and more deeply, discouraged. In fact, it appears he did not leave Westminster, where the pressure of the Army's power soon put the 'Independents' in control again. The Army, full of Independents and sects and fearing religious persecution, offered the King concessions in both church and state in return for religious toleration; the 'Presbyterians', desiring uniformity and fearing religious and social anarchy offered only concessions in civil affairs. The Army's opponents found that no combination of City militia, ex-soldiers, country partisans and a possible Scots army over the border could in fact maintain the independence of the Houses against the Army, which on 16 June formally charged eleven of the Commons, including Wharton's neighbour and cousin Stapleton, with threatening another civil war. Ten days later the eleven withdrew. In the Lords, the 'Presbyterian' majority began to break up, Warwick and Manchester being now among the 'Independents'.[17] On 27 June 1647, the Houses sent three additional commissioners to the Army, with 'so large instructions and so great a power' that some believed they would achieve 'a reconcilement in all things' between King,

15. Ibid, 86-91; *LJ* 9, 202.
16. Ibid, 251, 255, 260.
17. Ibid, 267, 270, 272, 289.

Parliament, City and Army.[18] Wharton was the only peer among them. The next day he wrote to the House from Uxbridge, whence the Army now menaced Westminster. He enclosed the demands which would have to be granted before the Army withdrew to Reading, and urged a speedy assent.[19] On 3 July he wrote that negotiations had begun at Reading, but on 5 July he had to inform the House that the officers had 'several weighty things' to propose for the peace and safety of the kingdom. The Council of War of the Army, despite Wharton's urging, took its time in discussing these propositions.[20]

The Army on 19 July demanded among other things the restoration of the old, largely 'Independent' parliamentary committee for the London militia.[21] Two days later the indignant apprentices, with many ex-soldiers, made the Solemn Engagement of the City. This was to maintain the Covenant and restore the King, who had offered to establish Presbyterianism for three years and give up the control of the militia for ten. The Houses merely denounced this Engagement, and restored the old militia committee.

There were nine peers, six of them 'Independents' in the House on 26 July when, as so often before, a mob of Londoners poured into Westminster. They compelled both Houses to revoke their recent votes. Thereafter the two Speakers—Manchester and Lenthall—led a 'secession', a surreptitious nocturnal flight of 'Independents' (half-a-dozen lords and half-a-hundred of the Commons) to their friends in the Army. In the upper House, the 'Presbyterians' then ordered the absent lords and all who were qualified, to attend but the only answer was a smoothly insolent letter of excuse from Warwick.[22] The Army naturally marched on London accompanied by the seceders, who returned to Westminster on 6 August under the Army's protection.

18. *CSP Dom 1645-47*, 593. One commissioner, Widdrington, was the husband of Fairfax's sister.
19. *LJ* 9, 299. Nottingham, also present, also signed letters as a commissioner of the Lords, but there is no shred of evidence that he had any capacity for any kind of employment.
20. Ibid, 312, 317, 319, 328; Add MS 34, 253, folios 71, 73.
21. Ibid, folio 77; *LJ* 9, 70, 309, 334, 336.
22. Ibid, 358-74.

Manchester has been described both as one of the instigators of the riots, and as an object of hatred to the rioters because he had played a large part in the recent concessions to the Army. The Army's leaders persuaded the Commons' Speaker to go to them, and an understanding existed between Army and 'Independent' lords after the 'violence' which probably existed before.[23] Is it possible that the riots were provoked by 'Independents' and the Army to give the latter the opportunity and excuse for finally crushing its enemies? In any such plot, Wharton, the chief 'Independent' Lords' commissioner with the Army, must have had a part. He was apparently not with the Army at Bedford when Nottingham alone wrote from there on 25 July, but he was again at headquarters on 29 July. It is likely he was at Westminster in the interval, which covers both the famous 'violence' and the secession. He had personally brought the Army's proposals of 19 July to Westminster for the Lords' 'more perfect knowledge' in anything relating to the Commissioners' earlier despatches, and other Lords' commissioners frequently came back to the House.[24] Wharton was present at Fairfax's Hounslow review on 3 August, and among the lords who consulted with the leaders of the Army and of the Commons' 'Independents' that night.[25] Though he did not sign the seceders declaration published next day, that might be because, being officially with the Army, he was not personally affected by the 'violence'.[26]

There is no proof of any secret dealing here by either Wharton or Manchester. However, Manchester's reputation for moderation and 'Presbyterian' politics seems undeserved in the light of his leading the flight to an Army directed by the 'Independent' with whom he had so bitterly quarrelled, who had used dangerous phrases against King and nobles, and whose soldiers had carried off the King from Parliament's custody. Moreover, he later protected Wharton when the latter

23. Firth, *House of Lords*, 170, 172; Gardiner, *Civil War*, III, 166 n 2 (quoting Bamfield's *Apology*); *Selections from the Papers of William Clarke*, London (Camden Society), 1891, I, 219n.
24. Add MS 34, 253, folio 75; *LJ* 9, 282 ff, 308, 339-40, 353, 355-6, 359.
25. *Memoirs of Ludlow*, ed Firth, Oxford 1894, I, 162; C. R. Markham, *Life of Fairfax*, London 1870, 295.
26. *LJ* 9, 385.

was accused of complicity in a more serious plot, and guilty at least of great duplicity.

On 21 September Wharton reported to the House some proposals from the Army, with explanations. The next day he asked leave of absence for ten or twelve days. This may have been on the grounds of illness, but in fact he attended the House in the days which followed, although his attendance soon became irregular.[27] It may be he found his position as protégé of the Army unpalatable. There were now few committees in the Lords and—since seven 'Presbyterians' who sat after the 'secession' had been impeached—no party conflicts. The Army now openly and alone sought its own constitutional settlement, and many soldiers began to express opinions opposed to monarchy and to the House of Lords.[28] Wharton reported further propositions in October, as well as papers intended for the Scots who demanded the King be allowed to treat in London out of the Army's power. Apart from those who had marched with the Army on London, most lords stayed away from the House until, or even after, commanded to attend on pain of £100 fine.[29] The uneasy and degraded 'Independents' clearly wished to make their isolation less obvious and to break a spontaneous boycott. With the most active and courageous 'Presbyterian' lords in the Tower, the 'Independents' would be in no danger from the presence of some moderate but unforceful peers.

Whether from discouragement, disillusionment or ill-health, Wharton in November 1647, served on only a third as many committees as did most of the 'Independent' peers. There is no concrete evidence of ill-health, but the events of September, October and November could induce discouragement. In September and the first half of October the direct negotiations between the Army and the King failed. In the second half of October and the first half of November the Army seemed likely to split into monarchist and republican factions. Urged by the Scots commissioners, the King escaped from the Army's

---

27. Ibid 441, 444 ff.

28. Gardiner, *Civil War*, III, 213; Firth, *House of Lords*, 172.

29. *LJ* 9, 460, 483-4, 486, 494, 499, 504, 512, 515-16, 519. Four came easily enough, five pleaded illness, or were fined for not coming.

custody. Everything pointed to the likelihood of a second civil war, with aims far different from those of the combatants of the first. The triumph of one party seemed to augur a Royalist reaction or a rigid intolerant Presbyterianism, or both; that of the other, the King's deposition and a revolutionary new constitution which would have little place for the peerage.[30]

In December and January 1647-8, Wharton had as many committees as an average 'Independent', and in February and March he became second and first respectively in such work. Again the reasons must be sought in the contemporary events. On 15 November 1647, Cromwell suppressed a mutiny of the Levellers or extreme democrats. For a time the Army was united and under his control, but the King could no longer hope for any help from the Army. The 'Independent' Lords drew up four propositions giving Parliament control of the militia but ignoring the church question. In December the King rejected them, signing instead the Engagement by which the Scots were to support him in regaining control of the militia in return for the establishment of Presbyterianism for three years.[31] Of the Commons' vote on 3 January 1647-8, that no further addresses should be made to the King, Cromwell wrote exultingly:

> this business hath been ... a mighty providence ... to us all.
> The House of Commons is very sensible of the King's dealings,
> and of our brethren's in this late transaction.

Presumably Wharton shared Cromwell's feelings, for it was from Wharton's house that Cromwell wrote.[32] An 'Independent' might well think it was for the best to exclude the King permanently from all real power and to defy the Scots and the English moderates. In this way, at least four of the forces in the political arena, that is, the King, Scotland, the City and the parliamentary 'Presbyterians' could be ignored, and the opinions of only two forces, the Army and the parliamentary 'Independents', need be reconciled. Wharton was ready to

30. Gardiner, *Civil War*, III, 207-11, 236; Firth, *House of Lords*, 173-87.
31. Gardiner, *Civil War*, III, 272-5.
32. Abbott, *Cromwell*, I, 577-8; Add MS 4186, folio 14. Written 'near ten at night'.

punish the 'Presbyterians' by finding precedents in the case of the impeached seven lords, and to guard against Scots invasion or English revolt by raising fresh forces in England and Wales.[33]

The Lords neglected the Vote of No Addresses for some time. When it was debated, the surviving 'Presbyterians' and some who had become again 'Presbyterians' resisted it fiercely, and only yielded when two thousand troops surrounded Westminster palace. Four days after the vote, six of the impeached lords, on their petitions, received their liberty.[34] Perhaps they had received a hint from their late colleagues and more recent persecutors. Although on this issue five or six lords temporarily changed sides, Wharton apparently still followed the official 'Independent' line. Yet he was very slow in taking up his duties at Derby House, where the English members of the dissolved Committee of Both Kingdoms were now again established as a still more predominantly 'Independent' Committee of Both Houses. Wharton apparently was not present before 27 January although appointed to a subcommittee on 20 January. In February he attended the Committee only three times.[35] Nor was he a regular attender of the House, although appointed to a relatively large number of committees. On the last day of January the Commons brought articles of impeachment against the seven imprisoned peers, but by now several former 'Independents' were willing to bail them,[36] and possibly to have them back in the House.

The Scots declared the Treaty was broken and refused to expel English Royalists; late in February a 'Presbyterian' military revolt began in Pembrokeshire; in April, there were tumults in London, and in Ireland the Royalists, Catholics and Inchiquin's private army became allies; in May, part of the navy revolted to join the Prince of Wales and a rising broke out in Kent. The strong 'Independent' line could succeed only with a great deal of bloodshed, and in this second Civil War, which reached its peak in June 1648, the original Parliamentarians were divided.

---

33. *LJ* 9, 600.
34. Ibid, 667. Hunsdon followed them successfully in three days (Ibid, 672).
35. *CSP Dom 1648-49*, 12-22.
36. *LJ* 10, 5, 10, 15, 33.

What was Wharton's attitude to this new struggle? He left no statement, and there is no unambiguous evidence. In August 1651, Cromwell wrote to him:

> Do not say, you are now satisfied because it is the old quarrel; as if it had not been so, all this while.[37]

But from this we cannot tell whether Wharton's dissatisfaction arose in 1648 or later, when the regicide republic made war on a Covenanted King of Scots. Whatever his reasons, however, Wharton seldom attended the House in April and May, and in June scarcely at all until there arose an urgent danger to himself.

37. Abbott, *Cromwell*, II, 453.

XII

A MOST BARBAROUS PLOT

'it were Treason in the highest degree even to
(know it, and) conceale it.'

WHEN in November 1647, the King escaped from Hampton
Court and reached the Isle of Wight, the Governor of that
island, Colonel Robert Hammond, made him prisoner in
Carisbrooke Castle. After the Vote of No Addresses, the King's
imprisonment was more close. Parliament removed his Royalist
attendants and new servants were appointed, many of them
recommended by peers—Henry Firebrace by Denbigh;
Abraham Dowcett by Holland; Francis Cresset by Pembroke;
and Richard Osborne by Wharton. However, the King soon
made Royalists of several of his new household, including the
four named. This is not altogether surprising in Dowcett and
Firebrace, who had been in his service before the war, nor in
Cresset, whose father and brother had been killed in the
King's forces, and who had obtained his appointment at the
King's request. Even Osborne, who allegedly had been
educated by Wharton, and who was apparently a nephew of
Pembroke's Master of the Horse, had also a Cavalier uncle in
Sir Peter Osborne, Governor of Guernsey.[1] Throughout February, March and April there were plots, largely managed by
the King's new servants, for the King's escape. They were all
betrayed, usually in good time, to Derby House. Osborne had
a leading part in another such plot, by which the King was to
escape on 28 May. It was betrayed, and on that day Osborne
himself barely escaped, while Dowcett was arrested.

1. P. Barwick, *The Life of the Reverend Dr. John Barwick, D.D.*, London
   1724, 1, 66; MS Carte 79, 1; G. Hillier, *A Narrative of the Attempted
   Escapes of Charles the First from Carisbrook Castle*, London 1852, 86;
   C. W. Firebrace, *Honest Harry*, London 1932, 29, 36, 81.

By 17 June, Osborne had made his way to London, and had also written three letters. One, dated 1 June and sent to his former patron, Wharton, excused his own part in the escape plot by alleging a plot to murder the King. He claimed that letters to Hammond from the Army urged the removal of the King by poison or any other means, and that Captain (or Major) Edmund Rolph, Hammond's second-in-command, had proposed to Osborne the King's removal to a place of secrecy where they might dispose of his person as they thought fit. The other letters, dated 10 June, were to the two Speakers. To them Osborne sent copies of his letter to Wharton, pointing out the latter's failure to inform Parliament.[2]

On 19 June, Manchester as Speaker read to a House of eighteen lords Osborne's letter and enclosure. Wharton declared, according to the Journal,

> upon his Honour, the Narrative concerning Mr. Osborne's Letter . . . and that he sent it to the Governor of the Isle of Wight, . . .

and the House resolved that it was satisfied with what he said. The House voted safe-conduct to Osborne to make good his charges and ordered the Speaker to draft by next morning a letter desiring Hammond to guard against danger to the King's person. The letter and enclosure were sealed up, and it seems Manchester, Warwick, and Say and Sele moved that the affair be not made public, but the letters were in print next day.[3]

The breaking of this affair at the height of the second Civil War, during a popular reaction in favour of the King, on whom all hopes of a permanent settlement and peace seemed to depend, had a great effect on the public, and this was reflected in the contemporary newspapers and pamphlets for the next three months. Overnight, Wharton changed in Royalist eyes from a ridiculous to a sinister figure. He had been the last and least abused of the 'Independent' lords savaged by *Mercurius Pragmaticus* the week before, merely called

---

2. MS Carte 80, 563. For a further consideration of some aspects of the Osborne affair, see Appendix II, pp. 275-82.

3. *LJ* 10, 332; *Mercurius Elencticus*, 14-21 June 1648; *The Kingdomes Weekly Intelligencer*, 20 June 1648.

a 'tall trencherman' fit only to be 'great Porter to the Junto',
with the ribald suggestion that he should 'board Mrs. Cromwell
and her Female-State-Committee at Windsor'. In the first
issue after the breaking of the affair, Wharton appeared as the
'Saint of the largest size who stands Sentinell betwixt both
Houses in the behalf of the Faction', while *Naked Truth* on
21 June accused only Say and Sele and Wharton among the
lords of having 'Jesuitical Principles'. In that age, the chief
reproach against Jesuits was their advocacy and practice of
tyrannicide. Soon Wharton was called 'the great plotter', and,
with Lenthall, Speaker of the Commons, the engineer of an
attempt to kill the King. As for Rolph, he was soon in danger
of being torn to pieces.[4] There is no proof that Wharton was
an accessory before an attempt on the King's life. However,
he was guilty of placing in the royal household one who spoke
with extreme violence against the King; of doing nothing for
over a week when informed of an attempted regicide, although
as he said, concealment was treason; and finally he was guilty
of innumerable 'evasions', prevarications and plain lies to
confuse the issue, deny and cover up his delay, and discredit
his former *protégé* who informed him of the plot.

Two days after the Lords accepted his explanation, Wharton
published a pamphlet, full of abuse and anti-Royalism, to
counter the publication of Osborne's letters. In this and in
another account of the affair made at the time, Wharton
claimed that Osborne wished to vindicate his 'foul perfidious'
betraying of the trust placed in him by the Parliament, the
Lord General, and the Governor, and to obtain safety; that
Osborne intended to rescue the King 'from the power of the
Parliament, and to have done with him what the Cavaliers
had pleased', although both the King's person and the
kingdom were safer by Parliament's protection; that Osborne
wrote to the Speakers before his first letter reached Wharton;
that before the delivery of Osborne's letters to the Houses
'or the least notice thereof' Wharton had sent the first letter to
Hammond, giving 'timely notice' by 'the proper steps' to the
most proper person, who was able, fit and trusted by
Parliament to safeguard the King; and that a report from

4. *Mercurius Melancholicus*, 26 June 1648; MS Carte 80, 553.

Wharton to Parliament was unnecessary anyway, since Osborne's information was 'single from a person fled, . . . and . . . held out . . . as a thing not to be acted, but past.' Wharton further claimed that Osborne's charges were so improbable as to prove his levity, and in 1660 he was to claim that before Osborne's letters there was 'never the least inkling of such a design'.[5]

Hammond wrote to Wharton on 22 June, flatly denying he had heard any word of any such purpose as Osborne alleged. He sent up to London both Dowcett and Rolph. On 23 June, the Commons heard Rolph and, by their order, his testimonial from Hammond was printed on 26 June, but the same day the newspaper *Mercurius Melancholicus* accused Lenthall, the Speaker of the Commons, and 'Saw-pitt' Wharton of principal parts in the attempted regicide, and the next day the Lords examined Osborne and ordered Rolph's arrest and early trial. A printed declaration (by allegedly 4,736 persons) of 30 June threatened vengeance on members of Parliament should the King die before his freedom and return to his capital. The Lords on 3 July published Osborne's formal charges against Rolph, and examined Dowcett and next day printed Dowcett's statement. This was that Osborne had told Dowcett that the King was in danger; that Rolph planned to take the King to where he could be disposed of as his escort thought fit; and that Rolph betrayed himself in jeering at Dowcett.

> The said Rolph came to me, [said Dowcett] when I was a prisoner and in a jeering manner asked me why the King came not down according to his appointment. And then in a great indignation and fury said, he waited three hours . . . with a good pistol ready charged, to have received him.

Also on 4 July Hammond wrote to the Lords on Rolph's behalf, and about this time he attempted to 'screw out' of the King an 'examination' exculpating Rolph. A pamphlet of 11 July accused the Army of wishing to murder the King and remove a hundred members from the Commons (but it was not

5. *Two Letters sent by Mr. Richard Osburn . . . With an Answer . . . and a Narrative*, London, 21 June 1648; MS Carte 80, 589. A paper, all in Wharton's hand, headed 'Short narrative of proceedings upon Mr. Osbornes letter June 1648', written after 23 June, but probably before 27 June. MS Carte 80, 553, 557.

until the winter that more than that number of M.P.s were purged so that the King might be openly executed). The next day an attack on Hammond was published while by 13 July a scathing attack on Wharton appeared in a pamphlet called *The Independents' Loyalty, or the Most Barbarous Plot (to Murther his sacred Majestie)* . . . *With a cleer and perfect Answer to the Lord Wharton's Evasions.*[6]

Wharton's 'evasions', or (more bluntly) prevarications, lend strength to the suspicions that his behaviour provoked. In 1660 he was prepared to claim that he sent Osborne's letter on to Hammond 'speedily' or 'within a few hours' or 'within a day or 2' of receiving it; specifically, on 17 June, two days (as he pointed out) 'before the letters . . . to the Houses was [sic] communicated'. To explain the gap between 17 June and 1 June (the date on the letter) Wharton was ready to 'prove' that the letter was not written before 11 or 12 June, and that the date was deliberately falsified. The only reason he suggested for such a falsification—that Osborne wanted the letter to seem long in coming, as from overseas, to 'enflame the people' —makes no sense. The Lords noted that there was nothing in Osborne's letters to show where he was. Wharton's 'proof' consisted of the evidence of servants and relatives, who would testify that they heard Osborne say he was eight days in the Isle, four on the road, and two or three in London before writing to Wharton, and that the letter was two or three days in the hands of a servant before reaching Wharton's hands.[7]

This evidence is unconvincing. At Rolph's trial Osborne said he was three days 'or thereabouts' in the Isle after his escape on 28 May. Wharton himself could lie roundly at need. In 1660 he was ready ('If the other plea give no satisfaction') to insist on his honour as a peer that he had never read Osborne's letter. It is far more likely that Osborne's letter was correctly dated, and that whether he parted with it in the Isle,

6. *CJ* 5, 611; *The Resolution, Vow and Covenant of 4736 Persons in . . . London; The charge of High Treason . . . against Captain Rolph*; *A Declaration Delivered into the House of Lords, by Mr. . . . Dowcet, on . . . 3 of July, 1648; LJ* 10, 369; Hillier, *Attempted Escapes*, 209–10; *A Discovery of the Intentions of the Army*; *An Answer to a scandalous Letter Written by Hammond by a Friend of Master Osbornes*, 12 July 1648.

7. MS Carte 80, 560.

on the road, or in London, it reached Wharton by 4 or 5 June.
Wharton did nothing with the letter for nearly a fortnight,
then sent it by his own servant, travelling post, to Hammond,
who merely sent it back to London immediately to the Derby
House Committee of which Wharton was a member. What
are we to make of this extraordinary behaviour? Why should
Wharton do nothing for so long, when (as he himself wrote,
reflecting on Osborne):

> It were Treason in the highest degree even to (know it, and)
> conceale it.[8]

and then act so oddly and in such haste?

The latter question is closely bound up with the sequence of
events between 10 June and 19 June, not only the vicissitudes
of Osborne's correspondence, but also those of Parliament and
especially the House of Lords. Wharton himself claimed that
the letters to the Speakers were written before Wharton received
the first letter. He admitted having that letter 'a day or two'
before he sent it away, that is, by 15 or 16 June; (the two or
three days during which Wharton's servant is so improbably
alleged to have kept it from his lord would be presumably
12-15 June). Yet Wharton also claimed that before the delivery
of Osborne's letters to the Houses 'or the least notice thereof'
Wharton had sent on Osborne's first letter.[9] This could be true
only if letters written in London on 10 June did not reach their
destinations in Westminster till 18 or 19 June. Nowhere in
the mass of his written papers dealing with the Osborne affair
did Wharton use any date other than 10 June for Osborne's
letters to the Speakers, nor did he ever claim (as he did
repeatedly in the case of his own letter) that Osborne had
ante-dated them.

Two slips by Wharton make clear what happened. In his
pamphlet, *Two Letters . . . With an Answer . . . and a Narrative*,
Wharton gave the date for Osborne's letters to the Speakers
as 16 June. Had this been true (as it certainly was not) there
was just time for Wharton to send off, on 17 June, Osborne's
original letter before the Speakers received their letters. But
even this falsehood if believed could not explain why letters to

8. Wharton's pamphlet, *Two Letters . . . by . . . Osburn.*
9. MS Carte 80, 553-8, 570-3, 589.

the Speakers written on 16 June were not communicated to the Houses before 19 June. Wharton's second slip explains why. He was careful to write that his sending away of the first letter was before the other letters' delivery (not to the *Speakers*, but) to the *Houses*, 'or the least notice thereof'. The Speakers had the letters long before they communicated their contents to the Houses, and conferred together about them.[10] Wharton may even have been out of town, but by 17 June he had been advised by the Speakers of Osborne's persistence, and was able to take steps to confuse the issue by sending the letter to Carisbrooke (instead of taking it in person to Derby House or the House of Lords), to appear himself in the House on the same day, and to be ready in his place on the next (sitting) day, Monday 19 June, when after the further delay of a weekend the Speaker, Manchester, at last read to the House the letter he must have had for over a week. That same day both Speakers were active on Wharton's behalf, urging that Osborne's allegations be ignored. Similarly, Hammond wrote to the Houses on 21 June to say that he had sent to Derby House Osborne's first letter which he had 'lately received' from Wharton: it had arrived that day.[11]

This brings us naturally to consider the possible connections between the affair and the politics of the Houses, especially the Lords. Is it merely a coincidence that on 10 June five of the six remaining formerly imprisoned 'Presbyterian' peers resumed their seats in the House, or that on 17 June the Lords rejected *nemine contradicente*, a Commons declaration against those in arms for the King?

In this affair, Wharton's cause was the cause of the Army. Those who tried in Parliament to dismiss Osborne's charges included the two Speakers who had led the 'secession' to the Army of July 1647; Say and Sele, the original and dyed-in-the-wool 'Independent'; and Skippon, Major-General of the

10. This can be deduced from the Lords' ordering Osborne forty days' safe-conduct. It was in his letter to Lenthall that Osborne asked for that precise period; in his letter to Manchester he asked only 'that freedom and security' fit for 'any Gentleman and Christian'.

11. *Colonel Hammond's Letter to William Lenthall Esq., Speaker*, Published by Authority, 26 June 1648; *The Case of Major Edmund Rolph truly stated*, 28 August 1648.

New Model Army, and father-in-law to Rolph, who himself was an officer whose importance in the political higher command of the Army Osborne pointed out. He was one of the three officers to sign the petition of 16 July 1647, for an immediate march on London.[12] Clearly in this time of crisis, the friends of the Army were seeking to preserve the precarious supremacy of the 'Independents' in Parliament, or good relations between Parliament and the Army, which came to the same thing. With the return of five—later six—impeached 'Presbyterians', that faction was very likely to control (in the Army's absence and given the assistance of the majority of the waverers) a House of Lords whose attendance varied from four to twenty. However, the Osborne affair may well have affected the form and completeness of that control, and the relations between the Houses.

Manchester was Speaker for practically the whole of the period 1646-8, and his office had been renewed for a further term of six months as recently as 27 March 1648. *The Independent's Loyalty* alleged that on 19 June Wharton narrowly escaped imprisonment. The fact that Manchester shielded him must have been obvious. At any rate on 22 June Manchester ceased to be Speaker, being replaced almost at once by the arch-'Presbyterian' Hunsdon: though neither absent nor excused, Manchester was seldom Speaker in the following three months. Thereafter only four of the consistent 'Independents' had any considerable number of committees, averaging nine in three months. Wharton and Say and Sele, with no more than four and two appointments respectively, were utterly overshadowed by the four leading 'Presbyterians' who averaged twenty committees.[13]

In these three months the Lords had serious differences of opinion with the Commons, and in some cases had their own way, reviving an independence and initiative which had been almost forgotten. In particular they vigorously pursued Osborne's charges, examining him in a House from which, significantly, all consistent 'Independents' were absent. It was Hunsdon who conducted the examination of Rolph. The Lords

12. *Clarke Papers*, ed C. H. Firth, London (Camden Society), 1891-1901, I, 170.
13. *LJ* 10, 341-534.

kept Rolph in close confinement for two months (during which his prisoner Dowcett had liberty) and did their best to try him at their own bar. The Lords also insisted on an appearance of liberty for the King, and therefore would not let the Commons insist that he accept three propositions before a negotiation could begin. It is even possible that Osborne's charges were intended to enflame not only the people but also the 'Presbyterians' (especially that group in the Lords which had shown concern for the King's liberty in 1646) so that the King might be allowed at last to come to his capital, but for this the only evidence is inconclusive. In his account to the Prince of Wales, Osborne described how he and Dowcett, after their prosecution of Rolph at Winchester, returned to London 'to give the Lords account of our success'.[14]

However, if Osborne's motives were not those of political expediency, what was the point of his accusations if they were untrue? Wharton suggested Osborne sought exoneration and safety, but, as many pamphleteers were quick to point out, no one was likely to obtain safety by accusing the Army. Had he malice towards Rolph, or Wharton, or both? No reason can be imagined. He had been Rolph's familiar friend. If Rolph did only his duty, this was no reason to try to get him hanged. Wharton had educated Osborne, and procured him an honourable post. This he would not have done after a quarrel, and what opportunity had there been for a quarrel since?

There is always the possibility that Osborne's story was partly or wholly true. Wharton claimed in 1660 that before Osborne's letter there was 'never the least inkling of such a design'. Wharton must have known, even in June 1648, that this was untrue. Threats by members of the Army had made the King flee from Hampton Court in fear of assassination. As early as November 1647, a newspaper hinted that Parliament might order Hammond to do what 'should have been done at Hampton Court', and another later called the plot alleged by Osborne 'a *second* design for murdering the King'.[15] Wharton claimed the King was safer under Parliament's protection that with the Cavaliers. This he knew to be untrue,

14. Clarendon State Papers (Select) 91, No. 2979, 86v.
15. *Mercurius Melancholicus*, No 13; *Mercurius Elencticus*, 14-21 June 1648.

for Hammond's first loyalty was to the Army from which came threats to the King's life, and which had taken the King from Parliament's protection once before. Hammond had left the (field) Army in disagreement with its intentions towards the King, but he apparently regarded himself as an Army officer first and steward of Parliament second; and as the King's gaoler he appeared to be unnecessarily harsh. He was said to be much under the influence of Rolph, his principal adviser and himself a notable Army leader, 'prime confident' of Cromwell, and noted for speaking against the King.[16]

Wharton, it is claimed, sent Osborne to Carisbrooke to spy on the King. It is certain that Osborne was a latecomer to the royal household, and, unusually, appointed by Hammond, not by the Parliamentary commissioners. It is curious, and perhaps significant, that Wharton reproached Osborne for betraying the trust placed in him by not merely the Parliament, but also by the Lord General: this in fact meant Cromwell, who directed the Army and sent letters in the name of Fairfax. Parliamentary pamphlets emphasised the violence of Osborne's language against the King, and for the Army, at Carisbrooke.[17] This may have been to divert suspicion, but if it was genuine, at least originally, then his original role in Carisbrooke may have been even worse than that of spy—something more like *agent provocateur*.

However slight the chances of a genuine compromise between Charles and Presbyterianism, there was no chance at all of the continued existence of the Army or of toleration for Independency from a restored Charles or an established Presbyterianism or any combination of the two. Yet the obvious assassination or open execution of the King would certainly arouse opposition among neutrals and moderate Parliamentarians. The King would never abdicate, and while his sons were loyal to him, his deposition was pointless. In

16. Hillier, *Attempted Escapes*, 224; Clarendon, *Rebellion*, ed Macray, XI, 195.
17. Hillier, *Attempted Escapes*, 85; Firebrace, *Honest Harry*, 81; *The Moderate Intelligencer*, No 171, 22-29 June 1648; *Two Letters from the Isle of Wight*; Cromwell's letter to Hammond, 3 January 1647-8, referring to 'the letter the General sent thee, of which thou wast not mistaken when thou didst challenge me to be the penner'.

such circumstances, to prevent an agreement between King and Parliament the solution provided by the formula 'shot while escaping' might well seem best. Hillier wrote:

> It cannot be supposed that the . . . Lords would have pursued so firm a resolve [in prosecuting Rolph] or the . . . Commons so great a laxity . . . if there had not been strong reasons to believe . . . that the accusation rested on a truthful foundation.[18]

Osborne's basic claim (that the King's life was endangered) I have discussed separately, since the evidence is confusing as well as conflicting.[19] However, it is also considerable and there are strong grounds for believing at least that some extraordinary chicanery and violence occurred.

The end of the affair was decided, as was the fate of the three kingdoms, by the fortunes of war. The dates of Osborne's letters cover the critical period of the Royalist–'Presbyterian' revolt, when the trained bands of much of the Eastern Association, original recruiting ground of the Ironsides, seemed about to side *en masse* with the Cavaliers. This danger passed, but the Cavaliers' obstinate defence of Colchester held up much of the field Army for months. However, between 17 and 20 August, Cromwell destroyed the Scots-Cavalier army in Lancashire, by which time Colchester was starving. With apologies for his long silence, Hammond dared at last on 25 August to write again to Wharton, still cautious in his wording although God was now beginning to clear 'innocency'. The capitulation of Colchester, releasing the bulk of the Army, was signed on 27 August. The next day at Winchester Rolph underwent a harmless pretence at a trial. He showed clearly that he had, rightly, no fears of its result (which was in fact a foregone conclusion) by publishing on the day of his trial a pamphlet which was less a defence of himself than a demand for redress from the Commons for his long and allegedly unjust sufferings at the hands of the Lords.[20]

That Osborne told some lies is certain, but his charges could be untrue in detail yet true in the essential point of an attempt

18   *Attempted Escapes*, 211.
    See Appendix II, pp. 275-82.
    MS Carte 80, 603; Clarendon, *Rebellion*, ed Macray, XI, 198; Hillier, *Attempted Escapes*, 66-7, 197, 205-6.

on the King's life. Whether there was such an attempt or not, logically Wharton could not know that there was no danger to the King. On the other hand, he could have known that there was. Osborne could see no reason for Wharton's silence

> unless it were to give those time that are concerned in it better to think of some stratagem to evade discovery.

Wharton claimed he had no reason to conceal the matter, since this was beyond his power, and the attempt could be to his disadvantage, which his revealing it could not be.[21] There was indeed danger in concealment, but there might have been more in revelation, without first finding 'some stratagem'. Wharton's duty was plain: to take the letter to Derby House, or the House of Lords, at once. Only strong motives could make him act as he did. It is unlikely he was swayed wholly by personal friendships. Wharton was on terms of close friendship with Hammond (as was Cromwell) but Hammond was not accused. He must have known Rolph, who was active at Army headquarters when Wharton was Parliamentary commissioner there in July 1647, but there is no evidence of friendship. Cromwell was a friend, and still more a political ally, and as Army leader one whom it might be dangerous to abandon or seem to expose to attack. Still, however much Wharton's motives remain enigmatic, the turpitude of his behaviour is apparent.

21. *Two Letters . . . by . . . Osburn.*

XIII

WHARTON AND THE REGICIDES

*'you were with us in the form of things : why not
in the power ?'*

Of the events of 1648, Wharton wrote for von Spaen only this:

> Mars favouring the Parliamentarians before the year 1648, (after
> some unsuccessful negotiations with the King) the King, im-
> prisoned in the Isle of Wight, yielded such concessions as
> many members thought would bring about a firmly established
> peace; and after a debate lasting twenty hours, it was decided
> in the affirmative.
>
> Next morning before the members met, sixty of them were
> imprisoned by the leaders of the army. From that day,
> renouncing all public life I withdrew to the country...

For once the emptiness of his political testament is in keeping
with the negative role he played, at least after the Osborne
affair. Perhaps there was little or nothing that any in the
doomed House of Lords could do, but some lords kept trying.
In whatever was attempted, Wharton had no hand.

For some time the 'Presbyterian'-dominated Lords refused
to declare against the Scots or the Prince of Wales, but the
logic of events made them see that they would be involved in
the Army's defeat. Their only hope was a quick agreement
with the King, so on 15 August they revoked the Vote of No
Addresses. By 28 August the New Model was fully victorious,
but there was still time to complete the negotiations at Newport
in the Isle of Wight while Cromwell was making peace with
the restored extreme Covenanters in Scotland. However, for
too long Parliament failed to accept that the King would never
entirely abandon his church, his friends and the control of
the militia.

Cromwell wrote to Wharton on 2 September. He was disturbed by the news of the repeal of the Vote of No Addresses, and hoped to speak of it to Wharton face to face.[1] Cromwell may have suspected that Wharton was no longer wholehearted in the cause of the Army. No doubt much shaken by the Osborne affair, Wharton also must have been affected by the 'wind of change' blowing through the House. His early, close and consistent colleague, Say and Sele, was now the most urgent and vehement for an accommodation. In the House, where even peers long 'Independent' fought for milder terms, Wharton was scarcely ever present. It seems he could or would neither help nor hinder these last efforts. Like many others, he appeared only to ask leave for weeks at a time.[2]

At last the Army struck. Predictably, Rolph was its instrument, with the miserable Hammond his helpless accessory. With little ceremony, Rolph took the King on the first stage of his last journey, while the Army occupied London before the King's concessions at the 'Treaty' of Newport were debated. However, on 5 December 1648, the Commons voted that they were a ground for a settlement. The next day, 6 December, Colonel Pride's soldiers arrested forty-one of the Commons and prevented twice as many others from entering the House.[3]

Wharton was in the House on 5 December when the Lords also voted that the King's concessions were a ground for a peace settlement. His next appearance, and his last till 1660, was on 7 December. Within a month of the Restoration, Wharton wrote:

> When the Army first invaded the House of Commons, in order to his [the King's] death I declared against that Horrid act and never came into the House after . . .

part of which his secretary expanded in one place to:

> that very day the Lord Wharton declared himself against . . . and declared he would never come to the House till that force were off . . .

---

1. Abbott, *Cromwell*, I, 646.
2. *LJ* 10, 566, 568, 570, 573, 586; Clarendon, *Rebellion*, ed Macray, IV, 433.
3. *LJ* 10, 614-15; Gardiner, *Civil War*, III, 522, 525, 537-8, 541.

and in another place further expanded a part to:

declared himself fully in the House.[4]

Many peers of 1648 were alive in 1660 to verify this statement, but in fact Wharton could not have said anything on 6 December, for the House did not sit. On 7 December 1648, nothing was done in the Lords. It was then presumably that Wharton made his protest. It was a good time to make a dignified withdrawal. Say and Sele, perhaps the most intelligent of the 'Independent' lords (his nickname was 'Old Subtlety'), also disappeared from the House after November; and after Pride's Purge attendance was slight. Only one lord appeared in response to a general order to attend on 28 December, and only seven troubled to send excuses, Northumberland, Middlesex, North and Dacres pleading ill-health, Hunsdon a dead mother-in-law, Lincoln merely a desire to go to Lincolnshire, and Wharton 'urgent occasions'.[5] When the House of Lords would not agree to bringing the King to trial, the 'Rump' of the Commons voted that the sovereign power in England resided in them, as elected by the people, the source (under God) of all legitimate power. A few days after the King's execution, the Rump abolished both Kingship and the House of Lords as useless and dangerous.

There are three groups of peers to consider when attempting to understand the implications of Wharton's withdrawal: a group of consistent, non-courtier 'Independents' (Wharton, Say and Sele, Montagu and de la Warr) who withdrew permanently; four consistent 'Presbyterians', who, with Northumberland and the waverer Manchester, all reappeared when the Commons sent up the ordinance for the King's trial; and the seven or eight (all save one consistent 'Independents') who were accustomed to sit after Pride's Purge. Firth equated the last group with the few who were 'sanguine enough' to believe that the existence of the upper House 'might be prolonged by submission'. He believed with Gardiner, that four of them (including and especially Denbigh) were concerned in an 'obscure negotiation to save the King's life',

4. MS Carte 80, 574, 557v, 553.
5. *LJ* 10, 639, 641.

although their visit to Fairfax was to assure him 'if rumour may be trusted, that they would agree to anything judged conducive to the safety of the nation.'

It is most probable that they were merely clinging to the last remnants of privilege, and hoping to obtain some share of power whatever happened. Six of them were named in the Ordinance as judges of the King. Five of them including Denbigh (and all courtiers save one) actually sat on the regicides' Council of State. Two of these (who figured among Denbigh's associates), Salisbury and that prime favourite of King Charles and King James, Pembroke, earned contempt from fellow-peers by watching Charles proceed to execution when his friends were praying for him, and finally plumbed the depths of ignominy by having themselves elected to the lower House. It is ludicrous to imagine that such as these had any more intention than they had ability to save the King's life. Gardiner dismissed as imaginary the evidence against the reality of Denbigh's attempt, but accepted evidence for it which requires the assumption of several improbabilities. Firth actually recorded how the despicable Pembroke refused to speak against the Ordinance for the King's trial on the ground 'that he loved not to meddle with businesses of life and death.'[6]

The withdrawal of the other peers reflects the well-founded belief that Pride's Purge meant that the Army had irrevocably decided the fates of King and House of Lords. The 'Presbyterians' and Northumberland returned to their seats obviously to make a last protest against the now openly intended regicide. Probably shamed by them, none of those who had continued to sit either spoke for the Ordinance or sat in judgement on the King. The non-courtier 'Independents' occupied a middle position between the courtiers' complaisance and the "Presbyterians'" indignation, unwilling to denounce the intentions of those with whom they had so long (and until recently, so closely) collaborated, yet unable to support or condone the actions and intentions of the now republican extremists. Political principles or rationalised class interests may have been the motives of some. In Say and Sele, some strong motive

6. *House of Lords*, 207-8.

was needed to balance his desire for church Independency, which the revolution of 1648-9 would make secure from the dangers inherent in any other settlement. According to Clarendon, Say and Sele worked hard at Newport for a settlement because he feared for the privileges of the peers. Certainly he was particularly proud of his nobility and sensitive in his dignity, frequently bringing before the House aspersions on his honour. In 1657, in a letter to Wharton, he put on record his belief in the classic theory of a mixed government, combining monarchy, aristocracy and democracy. Clearly as early as 1641 he had no wish to see monarchy have a real share of power, and he spent the next seven years both labouring to reduce the King to a figurehead and supporting the policies of the House of Commons in all clashes between the Houses, thus helping to weaken the power and prestige of the peerage. In New England, when he had considered, he had wanted an aristocracy of 'gentlemen' to balance even the democracy of godly puritans; in old England, with its unselected population, he clearly limited the 'democracy' of his beloved mixed government to the oligarchy of gentry in the House of Commons, linked with the aristocracy of the hereditary nobility in the House of Lords. By the end of the Interregnum, Say and Sele was called a *Presbyterian*, and apparently was so as much in religion as in politics, a significant shift towards the more aristocratic, authoritarian and orthodox, and away from the more democratic, popular and congregational.

Wharton shared the Independency of Say and Sele, but showed no sign of the latter's touchy and almost morbid pride of caste. On the contrary, he seemed far more democratically inclined in both the strict political sense and in the loose social sense. He attended conventicles during the height of the Restoration attack on non-conformity, when all other nobles and almost all gentlemen, however puritan their pasts, conformed strictly. About the time of the 'Glorious' Revolution he elaborated a fairly radical scheme of political reorganisation which left neither Crown nor peerage with much independence of the Commons.[7] Neither Wharton nor any 'Independent' considered the use of force by the Army against Parliament to

7. MS Carte 81, 766. Discussed later.

be bad in itself, since they had often profited by it and even perhaps provoked it. Strictly speaking, indeed, even the members 'secluded' by Pride had no real moral right to complain, for that violence was only one of a long series, beginning before the death of Strafford, and lasting till the eve of the Restoration, and all the future Parliamentarians were guilty of allowing, possibly provoking, and certainly profiting by the earliest examples. Obviously Wharton, like other Parliamentarians, would view an act of force on Parliament with complacency or horror according to the aim or result of the force. In his account, itself a post-Restoration apologia, Wharton implied that the 'horrid Action' which stuck in his throat in December 1648 was the intention of killing the King, but all he actually declared was that he would not return until the 'force' of Pride's Purge were removed. In fact, that 'force' did not last so very long, for many of the secluded members, yet Wharton did not sit in the Protectorate Upper House of a reasonably representative Parliament. Wharton gave no evidence of loyalty to the person of any monarch, nor to the institution of monarchy, nor to the inviolability of Parliament, nor to the privileges of the peerage. The conclusion seems inescapable: whatever he meant on 7 December 1648, and however much he may have believed whatever he meant, his real reason for withdrawal lies elsewhere.

Oliver Cromwell wrote again and again to his friend Wharton during the first three years of the Commonwealth, 1649-51, urging him to return to public life. 'You were with us in the form of things: why not in the power?' demanded the now Lord General after his Irish victories.[8] The question shows how little he understood Wharton's nature. Wharton never sought power for its own sake, or for his personal advantage: he would accept the responsibility of the exercise of power, but only when he could somehow satisfy his conscience that it was for some good other than private.

Cromwell usually chose to write at some military crisis, for to him every victory was a fresh 'seal' of 'God's approbation'.[9]

8. Abbott, *Cromwell*, II, 189-90.
9. R. S. Paul, *The Lord Protector*, London 1955, 213.

No other peer received so much as a single letter with such a burden. In these earnest pleadings from one puritan statesman (Independent in some sense) to another puritan statesman (also Independent in some sense) are the clues which provide the explanation for Wharton's withdrawal. It seems that Wharton doubted the righteousness of the revolutionary activity of 1648-9; he doubted the righteousness of the actions, of the aims of the actors, and of many of the actors themselves.

The puritans of the English revolution found strange bedfellows in their struggle against the established alliance of Church and King. Wharton had had experience of the venomous methods of unprincipled extremists when Mildmay aspersed his character. Probably he remarked on the doubtful character of some of the 'Independents' when corresponding with Cromwell. The latter wrote to Wharton after the victory at Preston, marvelling at the mercy of God to 'the whole society of saints, despised, jeered saints!' He continued, however:

> Let them mock on. Would we were all saints. The best of us are (God knows) poor weak saints, yet saints.[10]

Sixteen months later, Cromwell wrote again from Cork after his Irish victories, clearly and specifically answering Wharton's objections:

> Its easy to object to the glorious actings of God, if we look too much upon instruments. I have heard computations made of the members in Parliament: good kept out, most bad remaining.[11]

Later, Cromwell was to testify himself (with typical force and possibly exaggeration) to the villainy of God's instruments when he drove out the Rump to such pejoratives as 'whore-master'.

However, Wharton objected also to the way in which these men of dubious character acted. In the letter from Cork, Cromwell tried to excuse it:

> Be not offended at the manner . . . perhaps no other way was left. What if God accepted the zeal, as He did that of Phineas, whose reason might have called for a jury!

10. Abbott, *Cromwell*, I, 646.
11. Ibid, II, 189-90.

The citing of a noted Biblical precedent for lynch law, and the disclaiming the need for both reason and jury, strongly suggest that Wharton could not stomach the operations of a High Court of Justice based on no law, and punishing actions which were no crime when done. Yet the deaths of Strafford and Laud had been as unjust.

Wharton's doubts went further yet. In 1643 he had recorded his belief that the aims of some Parliamentarians were other than his own. Now he apparently questioned whether the lawless means of sinful men could be wholly good in their ends. Cromwell in Ireland had written his confidence that his actions were 'God's actings'. Although his letters to Wharton generally came on the eve or the morrow of a great victory, nevertheless the puritan general disclaimed (at least to Wharton) the notion that the success of the revolutionaries should be sufficient proof of the rightness of their cause. From Dunbar (4 September 1650) Cromwell wrote:

> The Lord persuade you . . . The results of your thoughts concerning late transactions I know are your mistakes by a better argument than success. Let not your engaging too far upon your own judgements be your temptation or snare: much less [let] success—lest you should be thought to return upon less noble arguments.[12]

It seems that at some time either shortly before, at, or after his withdrawal, Wharton began to feel that the old cause for which he had taken his stand in 1640 and (especially) 1642 had been dissolved by the split in the puritan ranks. A few days before the battle of Worcester, Cromwell wrote:

> Do not say, you are now satisfied because it is the old Quarrel; as if it had not been so, all this while.[13]

In fact, it seems probable Wharton did not wholly accept that the old cause had been revived, for he still failed to rally to the defence of the Commonwealth.

In this failure he was an exception. Cromwell's letters named five other men with Wharton in a group whose members

12. Ibid, 328.
13. Ibid, 453.

'helped one another to stumble at the dispensations of God, and to reason [themselves] out of this service'. They were the ex-colonels Robert Hammond, Richard Norton and Edward Montagu (later Pepys's patron and Earl of Sandwich), Henry Lawrence and the 'recruited' M.P. for Hythe, Thomas Westrowe, secluded from Parliament after Pride's Purge. The last was readmitted to the House in October—a month after Worcester—and the other four all rallied to the republic, Lawrence and Montagu later rising high under the Protectorate. The group had been in close contact, for Cromwell could urge Wharton to read to others the lines written to him. It could be that Wharton's persistence in remaining withdrawn from politics was due to his continued objections to persons and actions, even in a good cause. On the other hand, he might have begun to see the whole cause in a worse light. He was, after all, the only peer in the group, and the abolition of kingship and the House of Lords affected the status of peers enormously and adversely while hardly harming (possibly improving) the status of the gentry.

When Cromwell acknowledged that they had excluded good men from Parliament while most of those remaining were bad, he added, 'It has been so these nine years, yet what has God wrought.' This seems to admit that from its first meeting the Long Parliament had expelled good men and retained bad; that Royalist M.P.s were not necessarily worse men than the largely puritan mass of Parliamentarian M.P.s. Certainly Cromwell acted as if this could be true; men who at some stage had fought for the King such as Monk, Ashley Cooper and Broghill rose high in the Protector's service. On the other hand, Christopher Love, a fiery puritan preacher for the opposition to the government before the war, became a Presbyterian martyr for the cause of monarchy in 1653.

Wharton's continued resistance and Cromwell's increasing greatness and sureness of God's favour gradually cooled the friendship between the two men. His letter from Cork, Cromwell began:

My dear Friend, my Lord,
    If I know my heart, I love you in truth: and therefore if, from the jealousy of unfeigned love, I play the fool a little, and say a word or two at guess, I know you will pardon it.

Further on, Cromwell denied condemning Wharton's reasonings, he merely doubted them. Eight months later from Dunbar, Cromwell wrote:

> My dear Lord,
> I, poor I, love you!

but he went on to adjure Wharton to love the Lord and take heed of disputing, for he (Cromwell) now knew Wharton was mistaken. Moreover, although Cromwell acknowledged he had been 'untoward' when he last spoke to Wharton in St James's Park, speaking 'cross' indeed of his judgement of Wharton, yet he did not actually apologise. A year later, from Stratford-on-Avon before the 'crowning mercy' of Worcester, Cromwell began his letter:

> My Lord,
> I know I write to my friend, therefore give [me] leave to [say] one bold word.

No longer was Wharton desired to share in the power won by the 'Independents'; now he and the other stumblers were merely informed:

> Now . . . you have an opportunity to associate with [God's] people, in this work . . . against His and His people's enemies . . . Let it appear you offer yourselves willingly to His work . . . I am persuaded it needs you not, save as our Lord and Master needed the Beast [ass colt], to show His humility, meekness and condescension: but you need it, to declare your submission to, and owning yourself the Lord's and His peoples.

There is no evidence that Wharton was ever offended by condescension, or that he ever objected to submission *per se.* On the matter of Wharton's attitude to associating with God's people (as understood by Cromwell) and owning himself theirs, the evidence is conflicting.

XIV

WHARTON AVOIDS TEMPTATION

'nor, except during a few months, did I have house
or lodging in London till the year 1659'

THE above lines were presumably all that Wharton felt he
needed to say about the Interregnum in his autobiographical
letter. The 'few months' were presumably in 1650: perhaps the
cross speech from Cromwell in St James's that year helped to
decide Wharton against further residence in Clerkenwell. His
county seat was now (since the devastation of Healaugh during
the wars) Wooburn on the Buckinghamshire estates inherited
from Arthur Goodwin. He did not act under any of the commissions in which he was named for assessments or for ejecting
scandalous ministers.[1] Apparently the only official paper to
which he paid any attention was one asking him in November
1650 for a report on the number, size and wealth of the
parishes in his district. This request was presumably made by
the Buckinghamshire commissioners for the church survey
which was to prepare for the rationalisation of the parish
system by uniting or dividing parishes where necessary.
However, in the event Parliament did nothing until 1655-8,
when ordinances dealt with some particular parishes.[2]

Wharton's withdrawal in 1648 was not extraordinary in
spite of Cromwell's seeming obtuseness. His persistence in
remaining for twelve years cut off from any form of public life,
let alone any share of power, is perhaps harder to explain, for
he was at one time seriously tempted to return. This was when
the breach with the past seemed both irrevocable and

---

1. MS Carte 80, 553; *Acts and Ordinances of the Interregnum*, ed C. H. Firth
   and R. S. Rait, London 1911, II, 32, 295, 463, 481, 659, 678, 968-9,
   1084.
2. MS Carte 80, 66-7; Shaw, *English Church*, II, 251-2.

(paradoxically) to some extent healed: when few even of the Cavaliers could have had any lively hopes of a Stuart restoration. At the same time, the protectorate which had replaced the republic seemed itself to be changing into a monarchy, a monarchy similar in many ways to the ideal form of mixed government believed by many to have been the true constitution of England. Wharton's abstinence on this occasion seems not to have been due to principles of good or ill causes or persons, but more to a rallying to class solidarity, though this rallying may have been somewhat reluctant.

After the expulsion of the 'Rump' of the Long Parliament came the dismissal of its successor, the nominated Parliament of 'Saints'. The 'Grandees' or more ambitious generals of the Army had prepared a new constitution and, on 12 December 1653, Cromwell became Lord Protector. Seven days later Charles Wing wrote to Wharton (who was his employer in 1648), in great excitement. He had spoken with the leading Independent minister, Philip Nye, and learned that thirteen or fourteen of the Protector's Council had been chosen and the rest were soon to be added. Nye was eager that Wharton, whose name had been mentioned at the meeting, should come to London speedily. Henry Lawrence wished Wharton were in town, and sent a message from Whitehall.[3] There is no evidence of any further urging from Cromwell after August 1651, but there may well have been in 1653 a last implicit or even explicit appeal. No doubt Wharton's old friends and more recent fellow-doubters alike felt that he might now relent, but if so he disappointed their hopes and expectations. As he put it:

> Though he had many and large overtures to have been employed in places of greatest Trust and profit, he refused all.[4]

In fact, it was clear that the expulsion of the Rump and its successor extended rather than cancelled the outrage of Pride's Purge, which if not the cause was at least the occasion and excuse for Wharton's withdrawal.

In an abortive proposal in 1652 for a marriage alliance between the families of Wharton and Cromwell there is clear

3. MS Carte 103, 198.
4. Ibid 80, 553.

evidence of Cromwell's continued respect for Wharton and his eagerness to strengthen the bonds between them, possibly with a view to enlisting again Wharton's political support. No doubt it was Cromwell's daughter Mary who first proposed a match between her brother Henry and her good friend Elizabeth, Wharton's daughter by his first wife. However, Cromwell was so pleased with the idea that he wrote to Wharton that he intended to settle on his son in the event of this marriage the lands of Burleigh, Oakham and 'two other little things', together with Dalby and Broughton, in all £3,500 *per annum*:

> near twice as much as I intended for my Son; yet all is unworthy of the honourable person.[5]

When Henry married a Russell of Chippenham he received only Dalby and Broughton, less than half the settlement destined for the husband of Wharton's daughter.[6]

Firth wrote that but for the lady's unwillingness the match would probably have been made,[7] but Cromwell's words in the same letter do not allow this conclusion.

> My Lord, give me leave to doubt that the lady hath so many just scruples . . . although I know your Lordship so really, yet I believe you may have your share of difficulties to conflict with; which may make the business uneasy: wherefore, good my Lord, I beg it, If there be not freedom and cheerfulness in the noble person, let this affair slide easily off, and not a word more be spoken about it, as your Lordship's thoughts are.

Clearly Cromwell, unlike Firth, doubted the reality or the importance of Elizabeth's scruples, and acknowledged the existence of Wharton's own. The alleged scruples of Elizabeth may well have been magnified or even invented by Wharton. On at least one similar occasion, Wharton later ascribed to a young lady of his house objections which were in fact his own.[8]

If in fact it was basically Wharton's objections which prevented the match, there is yet no clear indication of the grounds of those objections. Wharton and his family, like most

5. Ibid 103, 189.
6. T. Carlyle, *Letters and Speeches of Oliver Cromwell*, London 1904, III, 285.
7. *House of Lords*, 231.
8. T. C. Nicholson and A. S. Turberville, *Charles Talbot, Duke of Shrewsbury*, Cambridge 1930, 62.

of the peerage, intermarried freely with the more prominent and substantial of the gentry. Did Wharton extend his objections to the revolution and the revolutionary associates of Cromwell so far as to reject a family connection with Cromwell? Or was Wharton's habitual caution at work, arguing against an alliance which might, after some future counter-revolution, be a disaster to his daughter and an embarrassment to himself? He later showed himself stubborn in protecting the interests of his eldest daughter.

On the other hand, after Cromwell had replaced the rule of Parliament with that of a 'single person' (as contemporaries put it), Wharton, according to his son's biographer, often spoke

> with some bitterness against Cromwell's Treachery and Usurpation, and that, too, in company of Colonel Sydney and Dr. Owen, who spent a whole Evening with him in Reflections on the Falsehood and Tyranny of the Protector.

Yet the same authority, although admitting that Wharton appeared no more among the revolutionaries until some years after the King's death, claimed that Wharton was a courtier under the Protectorate.[9] These statements at first appear contradictory, and even improbable in themselves, but both must be examined carefully. In the first place, Wharton could not in 1660 have claimed that he had no house in London during the Interregnum unless that was substantially true. In that case, it seems impossible that he could be called a courtier. It may be thought that retaining friendly relations with the Protector, and interceding with him for Royalist relatives, constituted the behaviour of a courtier. Wharton effectively protected the husband of a cousin of his, the Irish Viscount Claneboy. Using a Royalist title (Clanbrassil) not recognised at Westminster, Lady Claneboy, a daughter of that second Earl of Monmouth whose sister married Wharton's father, wrote to Wharton for a word to Cromwell, who in turn wrote to Fleetwood of the trusty information he had of Claneboy's relations, especially his lady, and asked that he should not be transplanted.[10] Wharton also protected his cousin, the 'excepted' (from pardon) Sir Philip Musgrave, from 1651 to

9. *Memoirs . . . of the Marquess of Wharton*, 6.
10. MS Carte 228, 2, 5, 7, 8, 10; MS Carte 80, 674.

1655, often writing to Cromwell or to his friends on the Council or to local commanders for a pass, or release from arrest.[11] But this is a small total of activity at 'Court' to compare with the more startling feats of Robartes, who took part in the pageantry of the Protector's second installation, and whose son helped carry Cromwell's train, while Warwick himself carried the Sword of State. Robartes consistently, and Warwick much of the time, had been 'Presbyterian'. Warwick became closely allied to the Protector by the marriage (admittedly not of his own choice), between his heir and a daughter of Cromwell, although Warwick's brother Holland had been executed at the desire of the Army's leaders. It was rumoured that even Say and Sele was to become Chamberlain. Another peer, Fauconberg, the son and nephew of Royalists, advanced his fortunes by marrying a daughter of Cromwell.[12] Yet of all the peers who took the side of Parliament, Wharton was apparently the only one to receive frequent pressing invitations from Cromwell to return to power. Cromwell had affection for Wharton, but affection did not blind him to the weaknesses of his friends, for when Hammond wished at last to return to public employment, Cromwell was bluntly discouraging.[13] Clearly he had great respect for either Wharton's integrity or his ability, or both.

What exactly were the political opinions which could make Wharton, Owen and Sydney unite in detesting the usurpation of Cromwell? Owen was an Independent divine who was also politically active as an 'Independent' during the Interregnum. Although willing to attempt a reconciliation in church affairs with the Presbyterians, he was so hostile to monarchy as to prefer the rule of Army or Rump, or any form of government, however illiberal, so long as it was by the minority of 'Saints'.[14] Algernon Sydney was a confused republican, who allowed a theoretical sovereignty to the people, but a near-absolute power to Parliament. However, he was (at least, after the

---

11. G. Burton, *Life of Sir Philip Musgrave*, Carlisle 1840, 24-31; MS Carte 80, 593-4; MS Carte 103, 191.
12. Abbott, *Cromwell*, II, 27; III, 152, 629n; IV, 178, 420, 561-2.
13. Carlyle, *Cromwell*, III, 431-2.
14. G. Davies, *The Restoration of Charles II, 1658-1660*, Oxford 1955, 26, 88, 175-6.

Restoration) in favour of a monarchical element in the government, but presumably this would be no more than in the
Venetian constitution which he so admired.[15] Professor
Trevor-Roper has pointed out that as the Protectorate
developed its own Court and central government,
'Independents' 'against the "perfidious usurper" . . . sharpened
all the bitter vocabulary of the 1630's'.[16] Thus all the
indications are that Wharton and his friends agreed in their
dislike of an effective monarchy or rule by a single person, and
from an 'Independent' viewpoint. Another near-contemporary
witness states plainly that Wharton was against government by
a single magistrate, but that if such a magistrate had to be,
Cromwell was the fittest person.[17] This at least fits both the
known friendship with Cromwell and the alleged hatred of
Cromwell's usurpation.

However, as the Protectorate moved away from the arbitrary
militarism of the regime of the Major-Generals towards its more
civilian and 'constitutional' form, Wharton began first to show
interest again in politics, and later seriously to consider
reentering public life. In the period December-April 1656-7,
during which Cromwell was offered the throne, a member of
Parliament who signed himself only T.B. wrote several
newsletters to Wharton. This was probably Thomas Burton,
the diarist, who represented Westmorland (the original,
pre-Reformation Wharton county) and who was on visiting
terms with Sir Thomas Wharton. The head of the house of
Wharton also kept himself informed of the activities of the
next Parliament to which Cromwell summoned him, in
December 1657.[18] Firth wrote that Wharton 'was favourably
disposed, and thought of accepting the writ sent him', and that
Say and Sele not only dissuaded, but also rebuked Wharton.[19]
I do not agree that Wharton was rebuked. All that is certain
is that Wharton wrote to ask his old associate's opinion of, and
intentions towards, the new upper House. His letter may have

15. G. P. Gooch and H. J. Laski, *English Democratic Ideas in the Seventeenth
    Century*, Cambridge 1927, 282-6.
16. 'The Gentry', 48.
17. *Memoirs of Ambrose Barnes*, London (Surtees Society), 1866, 114.
18. MS Carte 228, 81-9; Ibid 80, 751, 755; Ibid 103, 205.
19. *The Last Years of the Protectorate*, London 1909, II, 13.

been either cautiously and hence obscurely worded, for Say
and Sele replied to 'this which I take to be the cause of your
writing', or, possibly, slightly incoherent from anxiety or
urgency, for Say and Sele concluded 'your man is in hast
therefore I must end.'[20] Urgency could be understandable if
Wharton had just received a summons, such as Say and Sele
had not yet received, to a Parliament which would begin in
three weeks' time.[21]

Say and Sele began his reply with a full rehearsal of the
claim that the English constitution was an example of mixed
government, having the quintessence of the three lawful kinds
of government each holding the others in check so that
monarchy, aristocracy and democracy did not 'slip into' their
respective extremes of tyranny, oligarchy and anarchy. To Say
and Sele the most important and effective element of the three
was, naturally, the peerage with its powers and privileges in
the House of Lords:

> Long experience hath made it manifest that they have preserved
> the just rights and liberties of the people against the tyrannical
> usurpation of Kings, and have also . . . upheld the Crown from
> falling . . . by the insolency of the multitude from the throne
> of government.

Thus it would be as unjust as dishonourable for a peer to
become a *felo de se* to the nobility and the constitution of the
kingdom by helping to overthrow the House of Lords and to
set up a house 'chosen at the pleasure of him that hath taken
power into his hands'. Say and Sele pointed out that the
half-dozen real peers among the new lords would be there
merely to give some countenance to the design, which, he
declared:

> I am resolved never to do, nor be guilty of seeming to allow . . .
> a bare-bones Parliament is not worse . . . If a writ be sent me,
> I shall lay it by me and sit still. If I be sent for by force I cannot
> withstand it, but when I come up I will speak that I hope by
> God's assistance which shall be just in his sight and just to this
> government being now about unjustly to be subverted.

20. MS Carte 80, 749, ed Firth, *EHR*, X (1895) 106-7.

21. Say and Sele's letter was dated 29 December 1657; the new Upper
     House was to meet on 20 January 1657-8.

In his indignation he apparently overlooked both the far-reaching subversion of the government which he had promoted and led since 1640 in Parliament's usurpation of the Crown's executive powers, and also the revolution which had formally abolished two-thirds of his beloved classical mixed government. Possibly his protest was inspired by principle, by his abhorrence of a mixed government in which the most essential aristocratic element would be too weak to perform its mediating function; but it seems more likely that it was his stiff-necked pride of birth and selfish clinging to the privileges of his caste (which, as one of the poorest of the peers, he prized the more as they were almost all he had) that made him abhor a mixed government in which the *parvenu* monarchic element would be in effect hereditary while the hereditary nobility had not their ancient place.

Say and Sele concluded his letter by disposing of legal arguments mentioned by Wharton as supporting the *de facto* government:

My Lord for your lawyers I look upon them as weathercockes which will turn about with the wind for their advantages.

Their doctrine that, 'where there is might there is right, it is dominion if it succeed, but rebellion if it miscarry', he thought a good argument for pirates, thieves and atheists, but not for Christians.

There is no obvious rebuke for Wharton in the matter or tone of Say and Sele's letter, unless a rebuke could be inferred from the need to dissuade Wharton from what was to Say and Sele so clearly an unrighteous, dishonourable, disloyal and subversive act. Wharton may have been dissuaded by the Viscount's forthrightness, and made loth to show himself no better than an atheist. The important thing is that he seems to have needed to be dissuaded. No doubt he paid at least lipservice to the ideal of mixed government. However, there were two ways of looking at the constitutional role of the new upper House: Say and Sele saw it as a stalking-horse or Trojan horse, but his son Nathaniel, sitting in it as Commissioner of the Great Seal, attributed to it all the mediating value and virtues of the necessary middle element of his father's beloved mixed government.[22] Significantly, Nathaniel Fiennes was a younger

22. Firth, *House of Lords*, 253.

son of the Viscount. Perhaps Wharton in his inclination to sit was merely anticipating the event which many expected, the full restoration of the monarchic element of the constitution by the settlement of the Crown on the house of Cromwell; even the haughty Earl of Northumberland was willing to serve a crowned Cromwell in a restored House of Lords.[23] On the other hand, Wharton may well have been less attached to the privileges of his order than even Northumberland (let alone the obsessively aristocratic Say and Sele) and therefore willing to accept a permanent bar to the restoration of the old peerage as a necessary bar to a Stuart restoration. Cromwell appeared to be opposed to arbitrary government whether by a republican clique, an assembly of 'Saints', the Army's Major-Generals, or a single person, and could perhaps be trusted to reserve to himself the minimum of power as a crowned monarch.

The old 'Independents' were divided on the question of whether a new House of Lords was desirable or not, but most (if not all) would agree that its creation tended to restore the *status quo ante bellum*. It was apparently the 'Presbyterian' element in the Protector's House of Commons who most resented the new Lords as a further instalment of the revolution and as a permanent bar to the restoration of the old Lords.[24] Wharton had before objected to the character of some of the revolutionaries, but now, despite Say and Sele's insinuations, it was obvious that many of those supporting the new-style Protectorate, and entering the new upper House, were neither rogues nor atheists, but soundly puritan conservative gentlemen. Cromwell had written to Wharton in January 1649-50:

> I am persuaded your heart hankers after the hearts of your poor friends, and will, until you can find others to close with: which, I trust (though we in ourselves be contemptible), God will not let you do.

Wharton's hankering heart was not able to impel him to rejoin even under the second version of the Protectorate, conservative and respectable though it appeared. On the other hand, it does not seem that Wharton had 'closed' with any other group, in opposition to the government.

23. Ibid, 270.
24. Trevor-Roper, 'The Gentry', 48.

Probably a most important bar to Wharton's participation was the boycott of the new House by all the other summoned survivors of the original Parliamentarian lords. To his 'other House' the Protector called (with a score of colonels and generals, and a hundred other gentlemen), seven English peers. The two who attended were Eure and Fauconberg, both sons of Royalists, and the latter now Cromwell's son-in-law. The five who had sat in the old House neither attended nor made any excuse.[25] Mulgrave was to die in 1658, and perhaps only ill-health kept him away; at least a political satire represented him as saying to the Army's leaders:

> I was something scruple whether play were lawful . . . so sate out the last game, which had like to have undone me; for the future I shall play at whatsoever game your honours please especially since you pay so wel.[26]

Warwick was also soon to die, else he too might have obliged his new friend Cromwell, whose rule he praised, and who grieved so at his death.[27] Manchester, unlike most peers whether Parliamentarian or Royalist, had refused to take the Engagement (to be faithful to the republic) and had lost his Chancellorship of Cambridge University.[28] He was hardly likely to unbend. It is improbable that Wharton hesitated to refuse the writ of summons through fear, despite Say and Sele's statement on what he would do if forced to attend, and the sentiments attributed to Mulgrave. He could always plead sickness. Had he attended, Wharton would have acted out of character, and contrary to the pattern which can be seen in the careers of those of the Parliamentarian peers who lived through the Interregnum.

This can be seen by an analysis of the behaviour of the different categories of Parliamentarian peers. Of the Independents, five (Howard, Pembroke, Salisbury, Denbigh and Mulgrave—all courtiers save the last, and all save the two last of proved moral worthlessness) served the regicide republic from the first; another group of five (Northumberland,

25. *HMC House of Lords*, IV, 522.
26. *A Game of Piquet*, quoted *HMC Bath*, II, 114.
27. Firth, *House of Lords*, 250; Paul, *Lord Protector*, 379.
28. Abbott, *Cromwell*, II, 386, n 19.

Nottingham, Say and Sele, Wharton and Grey) withdrew
from politics and served neither the Rump nor the Protector;
and two (de la Warr and Montagu) became Royalists. Of the
'Presbyterians', one (Robartes) became a Protectorate courtier;
two (Dacres and Stamford) entered the House of Commons;
Hunsdon and Suffolk withdrew altogether; while Maynard,
Bruce, Rutland, Berkeley, Lincoln and even the Earl of
Stamford, M.P., became in varying degrees Royalist. Of the
waverers, predictably enough, one—Warwick—became a
courtier, while North and Manchester withdrew, the last to
dabble in Royalist intrigues. Obviously, and naturally enough,
the 'Independents' supplied the regicide Rump with its noble
servants, while the 'Presbyterians' and waverers provided the
bulk of the neo-Royalists and all the Protectorians. Whether
from principle or pride, the non-courtier 'Independents' (save
for Mulgrave) neither served the Rump nor later rallied to the
Protector—and of these Wharton was thus typical.

In 1660 Wharton wrote, 'What I did for twelve years since
is well known,'[29] and the statement was as true as the activities
were innocuous. For want of any more serious occupation, he
turned his energies to building (Wooburn and Winchendon,
also in Buckinghamshire, absorbed many thousands of pounds
in the 1650s and 1660s) to landscape gardening or making a
park (four hundred trees were bought in 1650) Van Dyke
paintings (bought from the younger Vane) and the establishing
of a school.[30] He also pursued with moderate diligence attempts
to increase his estates.

Among the forfeited estates of the Duke of Buckingham were
some manors forfeited still earlier by his wife's ancestor, Arthur
Lord Grey of Wilton, executed in 1604 as implicated in the
Cobham plot. Even before Arthur Goodwin's death Wharton
secured evidence from Grey of Wilton's niece. After the Act of
Confiscation (July 1651) Wharton added further evidence and
made his petition, but had to submit to the decision of a
Parliamentary committee which determined that the lands
should go to Skippon.[31] In September 1653, an act was passed
to clarify the claims of Adventurers and soldiers to Irish lands.

29. MS Carte 80, 574.
30. Ibid 228, 70-1; MS Rawlinson Letters 104, 78-9; Ibid 52, 69.
31. MS Carte 80, 604-29; Ibid 117, 228-31; MS Rawlinson Letters 53, 6.

Wharton apparently had little inclination to attend the land lottery at Grocers' Hall, although his presence would have helped his agent, for there were only 40,000 acres to satisfy claims for 70,000. As a result, perhaps, Wharton in 1656 obtained for Arthur Goodwin's 'adventure' only £1,460 worth of good land in Westmeath, and had to be content for the rest with 1,200 acres of bog.[32]

Wharton took a greater interest in family alliances. Two years after the Cromwell proposal, Wharton offered Elizabeth to the young Lord Brooke. However, from the first he saw that the dowager Lady Brooke was cool towards the match. Not until three years had passed did a formal 'treaty' take place, and this Lady Brooke stultified, breaking each day agreements made the day before. She was determined to ensure that the Wandesford lands should go to the house of Greville, whether or not Elizabeth had children by her son, but Wharton was impervious to bribes and unwilling to sacrifice the interests of his daughter and her possible future children by a second husband.[33]

Wharton again met with reluctance from the other side when he proposed to marry Elizabeth to Lord Willoughby of Eresby, and almost ruined his daughter's chances by trying to insist on agreements protecting the beauty of Grimsthorpe park. However, he gave way in time, and the marriage took place in 1659. It seems very probable that there was a political significance in some of Wharton's match-making. While he had apparently discouraged an alliance with the Commonwealth's Lord General, although the latter was his personal friend and eager for the match, yet he swallowed rebuffs and accepted unpalatable conditions to marry his daughter to the reluctant heir of a staunchly Royalist house. At one time Lord Willoughby of Eresby wrote that he had absolutely refused to treat further with Wharton, and hoped he would not be any more 'courted into it'. His grandfather and father, the first and second Earls of Lindsey, had been respectively mortally wounded and captured by the Parliamentary army in which Wharton served at Edgehill.[34] One factor in Wharton's first decision may well have been the instability and

32. MS Carte 80, 662, 664, 672; Ibid 117, 244.
33. Ibid 103, 248-9.
34. *HMC Ancaster*, 430, 434.

unpopularity of the regicide republic, and a factor in his later persistence could have been the collapse of the Protectorate after Oliver Cromwell's death. If the more clear-sighted Royalists could see a chance of a restoration in the chaos of parties that resulted, so presumably could some of the Parliamentarians.

XV

THE 'JUNTO' AND THE
RESTORATION

'with full resolution to endeavour a happy settlement'

BEFORE the collapse of Richard Cromwell's Protectorate a considerable number of Parliamentarian peers had begun cautious negotiations with the exiled Court of Charles II. All, regardless of their factions and associations of the 1640s, were now described by the Cavalier Royalists as *Presbyterians*. Exactly when Wharton became one of these pseudo-Presbyterian intriguers is not certain, but it was probably much later. At first Manchester and Denbigh had been named as their more moderate leaders, asking no more than guarantees for their lives and estates, whereas Say and Sele and Robartes led those who demanded the Newport concessions made by Charles I just before his trial.[1]

When Wharton had been tempted in late 1657 to support the Cromwellian Protectorate as the best attainable constitution, he was untypical of the Parliamentarian peers. He (and the commoners with whom he agreed) apparently objected from an 'Independent' standpoint to this virtually hereditary monarchy, too little limited by the elected House of Commons, while Say and Sele, Northumberland and others, now 'Presbyterian' in outlook, would not accept a form of government which did not conform superficially to the old constitution, with an hereditary royal figurehead (Cromwell or Stuart) severely limited by a Parliament in which the Lords had powers equal to those of the Commons. In early 1658 they regarded

1. Much of the information about pseudo-Presbyterian lords and their intrigues was published by Firth, *House of Lords*, Chapter IX, especially 269-83.

with despondency the elevation of one who at any crisis thought and acted as Lord General of the Army rather than Protector of the State. However, the next two years saw the separation of these offices, the abolition of the second in favour of the Rump, the latter's second collapse before the Army, and finally the overthrow of the Army's ambitious 'Grandees' and the firm management of the again restored Rump by Monk, the only New Model general who refused to attempt, himself, to assume the reins of government.

In his military promenade from Scotland, Monk was greeted with many petitions for a full and free Parliament, and all Parliamentarians seemed to agree that such a body would almost certainly restore Charles II. In Wharton's original province of Yorkshire Sir Thomas Fairfax, in arms to aid Monk against the majority of that Army which he himself had originally led, tore up a declaration against government by a single person and, with many of the Parliamentarian gentry of Yorkshire, drew up a declaration which demanded either the re-admission to the Commons of those 'secluded' by Pride's Purge, or a freely elected new Parliament. They declined to pay taxes until one or the other of these demands should be granted. In the event, Monk granted both, consecutively, and there followed, as foreseen, the restoration of the Stuart dynasty.

Wharton returned to the hub of politics, London, only in February 1659-60, the month of Monk's arrival there. Some months later he was to write that he made this move 'with full resolution to endeavour a happy settlement under the King' for it was the first time he had seen 'anything towards it',[2] but as this was written after the Restoration, to excuse himself in the Osborne affair, it could not be dispassionately objective, and we cannot accept it unreservedly. Even if it were true without qualification, the questions remain: what did Wharton in February think were possible settlements, and what settlements did he then think 'happy'?

In his autobiographical letter Wharton claimed that he returned 'when it was easy to see the coming Restoration of the King'. However, Monk did not force the re-admission of the Secluded Members till near the end of February, well after

2. MS Carte 80, 553.

Wharton's decision to return, and probably after his arrival in London.[3] This re-admission filled the pseudo-Presbyterian lords with a confidence that *their own restoration* was imminent, and this in turn led them to a hardening of their terms for a *royal* restoration. It was now that Manchester and his group combined pressure on Monk for the re-opening of their House with the bribe to Monk of a promise to promote an act to confirm the soldiers in their estates, that is to confirm the dispersal by sale of the lands of the Church and the Crown, many now in the hands of Army officers. Simultaneously, Manchester's group insisted that the King must confirm those sales, showing what the Cavalier agents thought 'so insolent a spirit' that it seemed as if an aristocracy, rather than a monarchy, was their aim. Moreover, in his offers to Monk Manchester had used words to this effect:

> *if* it should be thought convenient for the good of the kingdom to receive the King, he could not upon any conditions with so much safety be restored as should be made by Act of Parliament . . .[4]

that is, the King's restoration was neither certain nor necessary, let alone imperative or urgent, unlike the restoration of the House of Lords.

The confidence of the pesudo-Presbyterian lords was somewhat dashed by Monk's refusal to re-establish their House, and they expressed great indignation at the Secluded Members' failure to honour a promise to promote that re-establishment. Nevertheless, soon a considerable number of peers were meeting with a number of Commoners who were mostly both Secluded Members and members of the newest Council of State set up by the restored Commons to act as a caretaker government till the election of a new Parliament. All these men were now called Presbyterians, and many of the Commoners—Annesley, Holles, Waller, Gerrard—had been leading 'Presbyterians' in the 1640s, but Wharton's old associate St John had been an

3. However, it was perhaps a sign to Wharton that one of the most outspoken of the petitions to Monk for a free (as presumably pro-Restoration) Parliament came from Buckinghamshire, where Wharton had lived throughout the Interregnum, and which had been so strong a centre of opposition in 1640-42.
   Firth, *House of Lords*, 273-4. My italics.

'Independent', and Pierrepoint had been once somewhat Independent in religion. This 'junto', as it was called by Royalist agents who corresponded with Hyde, planned to impose on the King the 1648 Newport concessions of his father before Monk or the new parliament could bring the King back 'upon his own terms'. It was 'not affection' but 'pure necessity' made them think of the King. Apparently some who had made the greatest promises to the King (such as Manchester himself) were now 'violent in this design', expressing 'great bitterness' against the old party of the King, whom himself they wished to have 'so fettered as he should not write a letter but they must know the contents of it'. Northumberland insisted that 'all the places of trust, and those of judicature, should be disposed of as both Houses should agree', as they could not be safe with less. Clearly their thinking had not changed substantially since 1642.[5]

One letter of 23 March from 'Sambourne' or Slingsby reported that this 'junto' met sometimes at Manchester's house and sometimes at Wharton's; Northumberland's was a later rendez-vous. From this it would be natural to assume that Wharton shared the group's strongest opinions, and also that he had some influence and prominence among them. Yet there is evidence that he was by this time hedging, or following an equivocal course. His own brother Sir Thomas not only signed but presented to Monk the Yorkshire gentry's declaration, and, soon after the King was invited to return, wrote to his former general, the arch-Cavalier Ormond, to recommend some Presbyterian ministers who preached 'honestly and boldly' for the King, in a way liked by episcopalian divines.[6] The brothers had puritanism in common,[7] but there is nothing to suggest that Sir Thomas had any interest in Independency, or much in politics. Both Whartons were put into the militia committees of several counties by an act of the restored Commons by which it is claimed

---

5. Ibid, 277-9, quoting letters from Sambourne and Mordaunt already printed in *Clarendon State Papers*, III, 705, 730.
6. T. Carte, *Original Papers*, London 1739, II, 347; *CSP Dom 1659-60*, 356.
7. They republished jointly the book in which Samuel Wales praised their father's puritanism. Dale, *Good Lord Wharton*, 31.

not a few were omitted who . . . had . . . shown their hostility
to the readmission [of the Secluded Members] or were suspected as likely to oppose the restoration of kingship.[8]

However, the exceptions to this partial purge included
Wharton's old associate Haselrig, a strong opponent of
monarchy. Wharton probably neither displayed nor felt any
desire for a restoration of kingship. On the other hand, it is
possible that secretly he may have favoured a Cromwellian
restoration.[9]

When Manchester and the others said they could not be
safe if so much as a kitchen boy of the old Cavalier-Royalists
were allowed about the restored King, we can be sure that
Wharton shared their fears and perhaps was foremost in
expressing them. His position might be awkward if Osborne
and Dowcett became the trusted servants of an unfettered
King. Yet the same just fears could lead so cautious a nobleman
as Wharton to act a double role, playing for safety. As early
as 16 March, a week before the Sambourne-Slingsby letter
above-mentioned, Lady Mordaunt included in a letter to Hyde
a list of visitors to that leading Royalist agent, her husband:
the English lords included (or comprised) Northampton,
St John, Strafford, Willoughby, Oxford and—apparently—
Wharton, the only original and consistent Parliamentarian in
a group consisting of Royalists and of 'young lords' who had
come of age since 1642.[10]

8. Davies, *Restoration*, 298.
9. It seems that Thurloe, the Protectorate's Secretary to the Council of
   State and intelligence chief and now a close friend of Wharton, was
   intriguing for Richard Cromwell's restoration with, among others,
   that Edward Montagu who had once shared Wharton's doubts and
   Cromwell's affection. Davies, *Restoration*, 309.
10. Clarendon State Papers 70, folios 184-5. All the persons listed in this
    letter and many other persons mentioned in other letters from Hyde's
    correspondents were not actually *named* by the writers; the names have
    been written in, presumably by the recipient, each above a number of
    groups of figures, presumably with the aid of a key to the cipher.
    I would be happier and more confident of the correctness of the
    deciphering if each name had been represented always by the same
    set of groups of figures, but it seems that Lady Mordaunt alone used
    at least four distinct cipher-forms for Wharton's name, only two of
    which even resembled one another. It seems quite impossible that the
    general code used by Hyde and a single correspondent could have

Wharton's colleagues in the 'junto' according to Sambourne-Slingsby, tried to combine profit with precaution when they (prematurely) 'shared the bear-skin' and assigned the offices of Admiral and Treasurer to Northumberland and Manchester and other posts to Holles, Gerrard, Pierrepoint and Lewis. Hyde would be fully prepared to believe that Wharton was seeking more than the pardon for which he had asked at or soon after his visit to Mordaunt, and as the King's minister, Hyde wrote to say that his master intended to give 'the party' other rewards. Wharton seems to have ignored this suggestion, which does not recur, and instead to have thrown himself into the task of working his passage to safety by aiding the unconditional recall of the King in return for a pardon rather than demanding favours and office as the price of even a severely limited restoration. On 23 March when Sambourne-Slingsby wrote of the arrogant plans of those who met at Wharton's house, Lady Mordaunt wrote that Wharton himself, who would look on his pardon as a particular favour (although of course all would be pardoned except the King's murderers) was at present by Lord Mordaunt's direction 'taking off St Johns'.[11] On 19 April when Lord Mordaunt sadly reported a new plot of Northumberland and Manchester with Holles, Lewis, St John, Pierrepoint, Gerrard and Ashley Cooper (to exclude from sitting in a restored House of Lords all save seventeen surviving Parliamentarians, to impose the Newport terms on the King and to divide amongst themselves the great offices of state) he had no ill to say of Wharton. Probably he even meant that Wharton, 'that lord who I dare say will almost believe himself in heaven when he receives his pardon',

---

been changed four times in as many weeks. Yet the identification of Wharton seems in every instance to be indisputable, from references in clear in other letters to Hyde and in copies of Hyde's letters. Hence the only possible conclusion seems to be that Hyde and the Mordaunts had in their original code several distinct alternative ciphers for Wharton, although this seems almost incredible when Wharton was so little known to the exiled Royalists that neither Hyde nor any one else at Court knew his 'denomination, Christian name and barony' for making out a pardon.

11. Clarendon State Papers 71, folios 32-3. Presumably 'St Johns' was Lord St John, the heir of Bolingbroke, listed among the visitors of the week before.

was the one whom he never heard ask any question concerning concessions from the King, but the sentence is obscure.[12]

Apparently Wharton now regarded himself as an active supporter of the King. The next day Lady Mordaunt reported him as saying (after he had denied naming Mordaunt to the Earl of Northampton as a source of information) that he was disheartened by such things (as, presumably, that accusation) 'for if the King's party show such malice towards one that serves him, what can those expect who have been against him?'[13] Apparently Wharton was as concerned to have his pardon in perfect and unexceptionable order as he was to keep it dark, for Hyde several times referred to the difficulties of having the document drawn up, engrossed and docketed by those qualified to do so while still preserving secrecy.

The new Parliament or Convention met on 25 April 1660. The 'junto' had planned to exclude from the Lords not only Cavaliers and their heirs but all 'young lords' who had come of age or succeeded since 1648, and who would be inclined to Royalism. With more justice, the 'junto' planned to exclude also any peers who had sat in any House of Commons. Wharton listed various groups of lords in the order of their claims to the right to sit.[14] First were seventeen 'lords who sat' (after the Civil War began), next sixteen whose ancestors had sat, then four who 'withdrew a little' (from the Parliamentarian cause), then six who 'sat in both houses'. The three remaining lists, of lords who were Royalists or Catholics or whose fathers had been Royalists, together totalled sixty-two adults; the first four groups totalled only forty-three.

The 'junto' had claimed that of the seventeen whom they would allow to sit, ten would 'follow Northumberland'.[15] But of the ten who first took their seats, four—Suffolk, Hunsdon, Lincoln and Maynard—were staunch 'Presbyterians' of 1647 or earlier, the last two by now Royalists. These would 'follow' Northumberland, the consistent 'Independent' of the mid-

12. Ibid, 305-6. Mordaunt could be referring to 'the President'.
13. Ibid, 332-3. However, the 'one that serves him' could possibly refer to Mordaunt, in which case 'those who *have been* against him' would include Wharton.
14. MS Carte 81, 63. Hitherto unpublished, so far as I know.
15. Clarendon State Papers 71, folios 305-6. Mordaunt's letter of 19 April.

1640s, only where they wished to go. However, Northumberland was appointed, with Wharton, Say and Sele and (significant concession) Hunsdon, to a committee to advise which other lords should be summoned. Wharton reported, and it was approved, that Nottingham, North, Montagu, de la Warr, Bruce and Rutland should be called, although the last four of these had become more or less Royalist.[16]

Even restricting the privilege of sitting in the Lords to the seventeen could not guarantee control to the 'junto', or to any group seeking to press for the "Presbyterians" 1648 objectives. Yet even this restriction could not be maintained for as long as a single day. Monk had agreed with the 'junto' to support their exclusion of all but the seventeen. According to the French ambassador, Monk excluded the 'young lords' or dissuaded them from attending, until the third day of Parliament. This report ignores the facts—of which its author may have been ignorant—that three 'young lords' took their seats unopposed on the afternoon of the first day of Parliament and that two more were among the three who joined, on the second day, the total of thirteen peers who had sat on the first. Accepting the ambassador's version also entails ignoring the evidence of Joseph Butts whose letter to Hyde of 27 April reported that Denbigh inveighed bitterly against the 'young lords' (to whom he would have preferred to see the Oxford lords seated as more likely to be moderate) and would not have admitted any of them if the General had not used powerful argument.[17] Northampton wrote that Dorset, Middlesex, Rivers and Petre went into the House 'with a gallant resolution' and found that the General did not 'desire their seclusion'.[18]

16. *LJ* 11, 3-4. Curiously, Robartes—earlier associated with Say and Sele —was not mentioned by this committee.
17. Clarendon State Papers 72, folios 59-60. Firth accepted the French ambassador's account: *House of Lords*, 282, n 4. He recorded without explaining the unopposed (and by the ambassador unmentioned) sitting on the first day of three 'young lords', but did not mention that two of the three additions of the second day were also 'young lords'. Of Denbigh, Firth recorded that even during the Commonwealth 1649-53, he was 'slowly and cautiously veering round to Royalism': *House of Lords*, 229. Evidently the change was so slow as to be not very marked by 1660.
18. *Clarendon State Papers*, IV, 679.

The five 'young lords' already seated by the time Monk allegedly decided to admit them, and by that time amounting to almost a third of the attendance of the House, comprised representatives of most of those classes of peers whom the 'junto' had determined in agreement with Monk to exclude from the House—the Royalist plotter Middlesex; Pembroke, who had sat in the Commons; Dorset, heir of a noted Cavalier; the Catholic Petre; and Rivers, Catholic heir of a Catholic Cavalier! These were clearly and fully accepted by the House, for Dorset was put on a committee the day after he first sat.

Whatever the reasons which allowed five 'young lords' to enter the House on 25 and 26 April, no decision by Monk or the 'junto' on 26 or 27 April could have reversed the trend, for none of those demanding admission on 27 April could have been refused on any grounds which did not apply to some or all of the five by then seated and accepted. Resistance to the mass entry would logically entail the expulsion of the five, but these five, with four neo-Royalists (Lincoln, Maynard, de la Warr and Rutland) and two staunch former 'Presbyterian' moderates (Suffolk and Hunsdon) were now an overwhelming majority of the House.

It seems clear that, in the face of what must have been a deliberately organised challenge to the 'junto's' policy of exclusion (a challenge such as Mordaunt earlier had planned to make through the Earls of Oxford and Strafford[19]), Monk had not only failed to support the 'junto' but had actually, from the first to some extent supported the 'young lords'. It is clear that no peer could have entered the House against the wishes of any who commanded such support as the 'Independents' had received from Colonel Pride in 1648. Very probably neither the 'junto' nor Monk would wish to incur the odium of a practice which had overthrown both Houses and against which Monk had declared, especially after the popular clamour for a full and *free* Parliament, and after Monk's great and successful efforts to break the Army of its habit of meddling in politics and coercing members of Parliament. The whole Restoration was in a sense the result of the failure in nerve or will of the Army and republicans, weakened by their quarrels and faced by general

19. His letter to Hyde of 19 April, referred to above, printed in *Clarendon State Papers*, III, 730 and quoted by Firth, *House of Lords*, 278-9.

hostility. This particular failure (to bar the entry of 'young lords' and thus, later, of Cavalier-Royalists) has been called the 'crucial point' and 'decisive factor' in the whole process of the Restoration, in that it made it impossible to expel the many Cavaliers and sons of Cavaliers elected to the Convention Commons in defiance of the election ordinance passed by the last session of the Long Parliament.[20]

The elections for the Commons must have shaken the confidence of the 'junto'. The counties—best index of public opinion—chose only Cavaliers or their sons, or failing those, Royalist 'Presbyterians' and a few army officers who had opposed the 'Grandees'. Cromwellians of old family were defeated by unknown men. Even in boroughs, men active during the Interregnum found it hard to obtain seats, and if by chance they were returned, as like as not the Commons arbitrarily excluded them. Two of those ejected were the regicides Francis Lascelles and Thomas Scot, who had been returned for Northallerton and Wycombe, both within Wharton's sphere of influence. In general, the Parliamentarian nobility did badly.

The 'junto' lords may have simply failed to control the first meeting of the House. To have a majority on 25 April Northumberland, Manchester and Say and Sele needed the full support of Grey of Wark, Wharton and Denbigh. The last was obviously of their mind, but there is nothing to suggest that Grey, who in the 1640s had been in turn War Party, Peace Party and Independent but never notoriously extremist, would now near his 70th year prove intransigent, and Wharton had been to some extent 'nobbled' by the exiled Court. Yet the words of Butts suggest that the admission of the original three 'young lords' hung on whether Denbigh would be swayed by Monk.

The likelihood or actuality of failing to command a majority among the ten peers first sitting must have caused the 'junto' leaders to abandon finally all thought of imposing conditions on the King's return, and may have made them eager to close with the Court before it was too late to make terms. The rewards given to their three principal peers—Northumberland

20. J. R. Jones, 'Political Groups and Tactics in the Convention of 1660', *The Historical Journal*, VI (1963) 169.

became Lord High Constable; Manchester, Lord Chamberlain; and Say and Sele (appropriately) Lord Privy Seal—point to a debt of gratitude inexplicable by their feeble and grudging intrigues with the exiled Court. In those intrigues, they demanded still greater rewards for even a conditional restoration, but some Royalist agents suspected at the time that many of the 'junto' were merely raising the price of their complaisance. However, as another of Hyde's correspondents pointed out, by promising the 'junto' that only the 1648 Lords should sit, Monk had discredited them and got them the name of Rumpers, while the failure of General Lambert's rising caused the 'malice of the Presbyterians' to decline, presumably because the end of the threat of Army resistance to a Stuart restoration trumped their last ace. Say and Sele and Northumberland were now reported to be great zealots for the King.[21]

Whatever Wharton's part in this ignominious collapse of a sordid plot, there is evidence that bitterness and perhaps fear and anger such as may have moved Denbigh were at work in Wharton too by the third day of Parliament. Butt's letter reported how Wharton said 'looking on the bench where the Archbishops did sit, that his blood did rise to see where that cursed man did sit'. Clearly he was stirred by memories of what Laud and his bishops had effected before they were banished from the government, the House and finally the church. But what stirred those memories just then, and so impelled him to voice his feelings with unwonted vehemence? In the attempted explanation of this outburst and of the statement which Wharton repeatedly denied making to Northampton may lie the key to what Wharton meant by 'a happy settlement'. Briefly, it appears to me that his behaviour just before, during, and for the months following the Restoration is explicable only on the thesis that Wharton was much concerned to get a religious settlement favourable to puritans and little concerned to get a political settlement favourable to the war aims of the Long Parliament, whereas almost the opposite could be said of most of the 'junto' peers.

Northumberland and Manchester followed the same religious exercises as did Wharton, for on the very eve of the meeting of the Convention Parliament, Alderman Bunce found

21. Barwick to Hyde, 27 April, printed *Clarendon State Papers*, IV, 679-80.

Northumberland's coach on the way to Wharton's house for prayers, and extracted from the two earls a promise to make easy conditions for the King's return. However, just as it is clear that the two earls acted very dissimilarly to Wharton in their secret politics,[22] so it is probable that in their attitudes to the church the three were not united. The *real* Presbyterians— the ministers—were applying to the Parliamentarian lords as their last refuge,[23] but it was not to prove a safe resort. Manchester had been already promising the Royalists to 'dispose' the Presbyterians towards admitting episcopacy, but while some of them would accept the *name* of bishops all wished to limit their *powers* to little or nothing.[24]

Wharton had been accused of telling Northampton that the King would pass in England what he had passed in Scotland, and of giving Mordaunt as his source of information. In Scotland Charles II had signed the Covenant—an engagement to extirpate prelacy—as the price of his acceptance as King of Scots and of his receiving military assistance from the Presbyterian Covenanters against the Independents of the New Model Army and its regicide republic. This bargain was the most controversial of Charles II's many dubious acts, and it was never more controversial and fraught with significance than in 1660. It was notorious that he had been no sincere convert to Presbyterianism, and it should have been well enough known that since the collapse of Scots support he had continued to maintain the full episcopal Anglican ritual at his Court in exile. Nevertheless, the English Presbyterians and to a less extent other puritans clung to this precedent for what might be made a part of the return of the Covenanted King. The Declaration of Breda did not exclude Presbyterianism, as it promised royal support for a settlement to be achieved by Parliament and a synod.

Mordaunt may well have given Wharton hints or even unwarranted assertions: he blithely reported that he was

22. As recently as 20 April Northumberland had been reported as saying that Hyde himself would be excepted (from pardon) for advising the King not to treat with Parliament, that is, for working for an unconditional restoration. Coventry to Hyde, *Clarendon State Papers*, IV, 670.
23. Barwick to Hyde, 16 April. *Clarendon State Papers*, IV, 666.
24. Morley to Hyde, 13 April. *Clarendon State Papers*, IV, 654.

accounted a Jesuit at one end of the town and a lay-elder at the other.[25] However, to members of the old Royalist party such as Northampton the episcopal Church of England was an integral part of their cause, linked with the throne and the Cavalier aristocracy and gentry by mutual loyalties, shared sufferings and common enemies. It seems indisputable that they supported episcopacy far more wholeheartedly in 1660 than they had in 1642, while the Book of Common Prayer, equally abolished by the puritan revolution and equally incompatible with a Presbyterian settlement, had always had their fullest support. Hence the gravity of the charge against Wharton, virtually, that by his lack of reticence he risked provoking a quarrel between the different religious factions whose temporary alliance (effected by such as the Jesuit lay-elder) was essential for the success of the Restoration.

Wharton's explosion of bitterness on 26 April may have been provoked by a realisation of deception or impending defeat. Possibly he now suspected that his fears for his own safety had made him gullible in believing in a favourable religious settlement and weak in not supporting political safeguards, or he may have perceived that the other 'junto' lords were abandoning or likely to abandon the cause of the puritan revolution in the way they had abandoned that of the Parliamentary revolution.[26] If it is as true as it seems probable that some 'junto' peers sacrificed principles to personal gain, then it is equally true that some of the 'junto' did not move with the times, or did not move fast enough. Wharton alone of those intriguers named earlier by Royalist agents was not among the eight peers chosen on the first day of Parliament to go to thank Monk for his prudent management. Bedford had been high in the 'junto's' counsels. He was presumably no more bitter against

25. Clarendon State Papers 71, folios 305-6. It is just possible but not at all probable that the Jesuit-lay-elder remark refers not to Mordaunt but to Wharton.
26. Allegedly, at the very time when Monk was (half-heartedly?) urging Oxford to persuade other 'young lords' to refrain from sitting for some days, Northumberland was urging Oxford himself to sit, which Oxford refused to do until he had again consulted Monk! If this be true, it seems that some 'junto' lords betrayed their agreement with Monk even before Monk himself did. Mordaunt's letter, *Clarendon State Papers*, IV, 674.

the Cavaliers than Manchester and Northumberland[27] (he had been in the Peace Party when Manchester was in the War Party, and had joined Charles I at Oxford when Northumberland merely dabbled in desertion); yet at the Restoration only he and Wharton of the 'junto' peers received no reward.

It was the House of Commons which heard the only open attempt to impose conditions on the return of the King, and that after the joyful acceptance by both Houses of the King's letters and declaration (the Declaration of Breda). Matthew Hale moved for a committee to ascertain which of the Newport concessions of Charles I should be demanded of Charles II, but Monk's opposition 'was echoed with such a shout' that there was no further attempt.[28]

On 1 May, immediately after the King's letter had been received and ordered to be printed, Wharton obtained leave to be absent from the House as often as his indisposition and 'lameness' made necessary.[29] The willingness to give way to the ills of the flesh may have been caused by political discouragement, such as certainly accompanied the trouble in his arm in 1647. In fact, for the whole of May and the first half of June Wharton attended regularly, serving on committees and at conferences, and reporting to the House. If he had lost heart on realising that the King was about to be recalled unconditionally, he soon recovered it. However, on 4 May the House of Lords annulled the vote by which, on 20 July 1642, it had suspended a number of Royalist peers, and shortly after invited and obtained the attendance of leading Cavaliers. These were followed by the mass of the old Royalists, and before May was out, even the peers created since early 1642 were admitted. For some time opposition to Cavalier policies ceased to be practical politics in the House of Lords.

There had been perhaps some rallying of the old Parliamentarian lords in the face of common danger, for the day after

27. Bedford and Manchester were among those showing great bitterness against the King's party, as Lady Bristol informed Sambourne (letter of 23 March above). Bedford and Clare were encouraged by the 'junto' lords to come and sit. Legge to Ormond, 13 April. *Clarendon State Papers*, III, 731.
28. Davies, *Restoration*, 346.
29. *LJ* 11, 8.

Wharton's lameness made his excuses, he was appointed to a committee to settle the militia. Of its twelve members none was a Cavalier or son of a Cavalier, if one excepts Buckingham, now son-in-law to Fairfax. Possibly the old Parliamentarians were felt to have the administrative experience necessary for this business, but more probably they were anxious to control it. But if so, this was a last flicker, of no real significance. Wharton's collaboration in the next few months was not with any of his fellow-peers, but with new, non-noble colleagues in a bid for a satisfactory religious settlement, and his only other pre-occupation in the first few weeks was to save himself from the ill consequences of his activity.

XVI

DANGER AND DELIVERANCE

'I had nothing to do in the king's Death.'

IN his autobiographical letter, referring to the return of the King, Wharton recalled:

> and the same day on which he returned to London, and even until the coronation, I was careful to be among those surrounding the King with an equipment for which I paid no small amount.

Indeed, while still wearing mourning for his second wife, Jane (although she had died nearly two years before) Wharton added diamond buttons to his apparel as a sign of rejoicing, while his horse's trappings were valued—almost incredibly— at £8,000. He also pointedly took in his coach to Greenwich, to meet and escort the King to London, his Cavalier cousins, Sir Philip and Sir Edward Musgrave.[1] This display of loyalty may have been no more than normal caution, but possibly Wharton had already heard rumblings of the approaching storm. As his account to von Spaen continues:

> A few days after the King's return certain persons unjustly sought to have me excluded from amnesty.

A first blow came on 4 June 1660, when a proviso was proposed for the Act of Indemnity to leave Wharton liable for the £4,000 he had accepted from the estate of Sir George Savile, the future Marquess of Halifax, for the fruitless embassy to Scotland in 1645. Wharton successfully fought off this attack, claiming that all his acts had been authorised by Parliament. He further alleged that he had helped to keep the person of the child-

---

1. *HMC Le Fleming*, 26; *Life of Thomas . . . Marquess of Wharton*, 8.

baronet, from the hands of someone in power during the Interregnum, although others claimed that the orphaned Savile children had been left destitute of maintenance.[2] In any case, this skirmish hazarded only a portion of Wharton's wealth, unlike the main onslaught.

On 14 June, Osborne and Dowcett repeated their evidence before the Lords who committed Major Rolph to Newgate, and referred to the Judges his possible exception from pardon.[3] No doubt it was Wharton's life, rather than Rolph's, which was aimed at. It seems probable, however, that Wharton was not taken by surprise: that his daughter Elizabeth overheard a casual mention of the plot against her father's life is alleged by the biographer of Wharton's son, the Marquess.[4] Certainly Wharton at once, before he could himself be attacked, made to the House a clear statement of his case. Later he wrote, or rather probably dictated, an account giving the gist of what he said,[5] as follows: that he had obtained for Osborne his appointment, and that he supposed this was why Osborne chose him to write to; that in return for his kindness, Osborne had complained of Wharton's not revealing the information in the letter, which, however, Wharton had sent 'within not many hours' of receiving it, to the Governor; and that this was done before the letters to the Speakers were delivered.

Some lords made several attempts to have a committee appointed to examine the matter. It is tantalising and frustrating in the extreme to have no evidence as to the identity of these lords, any more than of those 'persons' mentioned by Wharton as trying to exclude him from pardon. However, some of those who rallied to Wharton's defence are known. The Earl of Stamford had been a 'Presbyterian' in 1648 and a 'Presbyterian'–Royalist rebel in 1659. His evidence therefore would be valuable. It is true he was possibly not altogether disinterested. He had a skeleton in his family cupboard, that of his dead but not forgotten regicide son and heir, Grey of Groby, who had distinguished himself by pointing out

2. MS Carte 103, 252-3; Ibid 81, 18; Ibid 80, 745, 738.
3. *LJ* 11, 61-3.
4. *Life of Thomas . . . Marquess of Wharton*, 6-7.
5. MS Carte 80, 574.

'Presbyterians' to Pride for arrest or seclusion.[6] Stamford was busy having this hushed up, and wanted no precedent for nosing out scandals. What he told the young Duke of York, the King's brother and heir-apparent, was that in 1648 the matter had been 'sifted to the bran' in the House, and that by persons 'tender of the King's safety'.[7] The sequel was recalled later by Wharton for the benefit of von Spaen:

> but the Duke of York, unsolicited by me, spoke a few friendly words on my behalf, and the plot failed.

The next day a pardon was promised for Wharton.[8]

The Duke of York had no closer connection with Stamford than he had with Wharton, but he may have been convinced by the earl's account. In any case, York moved that the House lay aside the matter of Wharton's conduct and go on to the 'main business' concerning Rolph,[9] and it was largely, or even entirely, as a result of this that Wharton was spared further investigation. York's action may have been inspired by pure benevolence—a wish to see justice done, or a spirit of forgiveness and conciliation. This was how Wharton professed to regard it in his autobiographical letter:

> Although it was expressed in few words, and he has probably forgotten it, yet I shall always remember it, and attribute it to God's providence and the duke's friendship.

Yet in fact Wharton showed little practical or observable gratitude, and it may well be that he regarded the assistance of the already Roman Catholic heir to the throne as a piece of political calculation. If he thought this he may well have been correct.

In spite of the promise of a pardon (which he had obtained three months before, and which was fulfilled if not before at least soon after the Restoration), Wharton felt no real security for some time after the Osborne affair had been revived. He busied himself intensively collecting evidence from the Lords' Journals and the Clerk of the House, preparing lines of defence

---

6. B. Whitelocke, *Memorials of the English Affairs*, Oxford 1853, 359,361; *The Memoirs of Edmund Ludlow*, ed C. H. Firth, Oxford 1894, I, 210.
7. MS Carte 80, 577.
8. *CSP Dom 1660-61*, 53.
9. MS Carte 80, 577.

and influencing or endeavouring to influence people in his favour. How many copies Wharton circulated of his account of the affair can be guessed at only, but they were clearly numerous, for many remained in his own possession.[10] He listed or prepared to list peers who would speak to others. He would have to know from each to whom they would speak, and what account they had of the affair. He would ask each 'What became of such a business, and it if be at an end?' and 'according to the answer' he would be able to lay more or less weight on it. Obviously some lords felt the matter was not closed. Wharton wished to give the impression (certainly misleading) that he was concerned only to prevent scandals:

> In respect of the buzz of it, and not the crime which is not apprehended, desire if it be moved, that they will speak to lay it aside and if they be not speakers, that on the speaking of any Lord who shall speak that way they will say well moved and to any who shall move otherwise, no, no.[11]

Among those named in various capacities were York, Mr [Secretary] Nicholas, the Earls of Bedord, Suffolk, and Lindsey, Lords de la Warr and Hunsdon (Rochford in Wharton's papers), Sir Thomas Wharton, Sir Philip Musgrave and some Parliamentarian aldermen. Thus his nets were flung wide enough to encompass the social spectrum from burgess to prince, the political from Cavalier to 'Independent', and the religious from Roman Catholic to puritan. Some of those listed were to be consulted for their influence, some for their memories of the events of 1648. The name of Hunsdon (Rochford) was queried by Wharton, who presumably remembered how keenly the 'Presbyterian' leader had pursued the prosecution of Rolph. Lindsey was now father-in-law to Wharton's daughter, but his name was also queried. This would appear to negate the assertion of the Marquess of Wharton's biographer that Wharton's son-in-law, Lindsey's son, was the means of saving his wife's father.[12] Willoughby d'Eresby does not even appear in the lists.

Wharton's impeccably Cavalier cousin, Sir Philip Musgrave,

10. Ibid 80, passim.
11. Ibid 80, 555.
12. *Life of Thomas . . . Marquess of Wharton,* 6-7.

returning the good protection Wharton gave him during the Interregnum, was an impressive witness and staunch friend, as he was to prove again later. Sir Thomas Wharton, equally loyal, was in almost as good odour with the new government, having just been granted the office of Keeping the Money in the Tower.[13] These relatives with servants and ex-servants Wharton arranged to have present and ready to testify to the length of time which passed before Osborne wrote his first letter, and to the length of time (two or three days) during which Mr Wing had kept the letter before giving it to Wharton, who now admitted that he sent it on in a day or two. Wharton also listed questions to ask Osborne.[14]

A little after this, Wharton prepared a long paper covering what he should say and do if there were any move in the House to reopen the affair.[15] His first counter to such a move would be that the Duke of York had moved to lay it aside. Because of this and because of his clearance by the House in 1648, Wharton would answer no questions. Although he reserved the right to take every chance of saying what he thought fit of his own 'carriage' or behaviour, he resolved to say 'little or nothing to the merit of the business'. In these decisions Wharton was wise: it would no longer serve him so well to express indignation at Osborne's betrayal of his trust, or to claim that this betrayal made Osborne's evidence worthless, or to claim that the late King had been safer with Colonel Hammond than he would have been with the Cavaliers; while Wharton's own account of his 'carriage' might not stand up to close questioning. The paper included an appeal to the sympathies of the prospective hearers. He had been so far from profiting by the late 'troubles' that he had lost nearly £10,000 in the ruin of his chief seat and park, yet he was so magnanimously free of the spirit of revenge that he had purposely avoided learning who had injured him. His account (in the third person by a secretary's hand) continued:

> by the fitting himself with a habitation in lieu of that ruined seat, and by the troubles he is at present in a considerable debt, and hath Six young motherless children wholly unprovided for.

13. *CSP Dom 1660-61*, 50.
14. MS Carte 80, 555.
15. Ibid 80, 557, 572.

Wharton's final line of defence was to be the assertion that he had not read Osborne's letter before sending it to Hammond. This incredible and certainly mendacious statement throws some light on Wharton's character, while it raises the question of the honesty of his brother, for Sir Thomas, 'a person of as much truth and integrity as lives' (according to Wharton), was to depose:

> he heard me and my dear wife (who was a person of singular honour and truth) often say in private discourse that upon the opening of the letter (she being by) as soon as I saw at bottom who it was from, I read it not but said I would send it away to Coll: Hammond and accordingly I did seal it up and send it away to him.

Wharton deliberately reserved this implausible defence to the last. He wrote:

> Though this be truth I forbore to give account of it because it is the least credible part of the story.

Probably he was reluctant (whether from shame or conscience) to lie in a statement made on his honour before his fellow-peers. Yet he was willing, or at least (in the strict sense of the word), prepared so to lie, if necessary, to save himself. This may have been merely the instinct of self-preservation, but it is possible that Wharton felt all means were justified for the true ends of justice in the defence of those unjustly persecuted. Later we find him prepared to urge and organise wholesale perjury in the interests of law-breaking non-conformist puritans. As for Sir Thomas Wharton, we can only guess whether he was willing to perjure himself to save his brother, or whether Wharton (and the second Lady Wharton) persuaded him (and possibly even themselves) that what could scarcely have happened did in fact occur.

To von Spaen, Wharton did not mention even the ostensible grounds of the attempt to exclude him from amnesty. There is no hint in Wharton's papers of what provoked or impelled that attempt. It is possible but unlikely that he had powerful enemies whom he had offended on non-political grounds. The Savile interest is a possibility. The more obvious possibility that there was a genuine desire to have justice or vengeance on Rolph and Wharton and to rehabilitate Osborne must be discarded in the face of the evidence. Despite the fact that the political scene was vastly different from that of 1648, Rolph was soon released, while Osborne dropped back into the obscurity from which he had so dramatically reappeared. Unlike his fellow-servants and royal-escapists, Firebrace and Dowcett,[16] Osborne received no place and no obvious reward, despite Charles I's recommendation of him to his heir, when that heir was restored as King in 1660. Wharton concluded his planned defence by pointing out that he had 'not been wanting to himself for his preservation', but had 'laid hold of his Majesty's gracious pardon'. This was true, and almost singularly so. As he told von Spaen later:

> My pardon was made out, not only in common with other noblemen, but even before theirs.

Bedford, the other 'junto' member who failed to obtain preferment at the Restoration, also made sure of an early and separate pardon. It is possible that he felt the need to do this because of some notoriety in continuing to support to the last the scheme to impose conditions on the Restoration, but Hyde and the King knew well that Wharton was clear of any such reproach.

Apart from regicides, very few were excepted from amnesty at the Restoration; not many were even suggested for exception. Not all regicides were excepted: one even received a knight-hood. Wharton indignantly protested: 'I had nothing to do in the king's Death.' Nor had he had anything to do in any of the governments of the Interregnum. The attempt to exclude him from pardon was therefore extraordinary. Even more so was another, made a few days after that on Wharton, to exclude Sir Richard Onslow on grounds that seem utterly trivial. They were that, during the Civil War, Onslow compared the then King to a hedgehog.[17] The disparity of alleged offence and proposed retaliation, even greater than in the case of Wharton, suggests all the more strongly some ulterior motive. Onslow had failed to win a county seat in the Convention because he

16. Firebrace, *Honest Harry*, 207.
17. *DNB* (s.n.).

wanted to impose 'bad conditions' on the King.[18] However, Bedford faced no exclusion attempt. In fact, it appears certain that the link between Wharton and Onslow, and the reason for the malicious attacks on them, lie in their post-Restoration political activity, in which they were closely linked, and which it is now time to consider.

18. Davies, *Restoration*, 322.

XVII

THE HEAD OF THE
PRESBYTERIAN PARTY

'the only tug is betwixt Episcopacy and Presbytery...'

THERE is no word in his autobiographical letter of Wharton's
political activities during and immediately after the Restoration, nor is there, so far as I know, any account of them in his
or other contemporary papers, official or private. However,
there was printed, two and a half centuries ago, a brief account
of the attempt against Wharton which also claims to explain
it. The biographer of Wharton's son wrote that the attempt
was made by 'the Court, looking on Philip Wharton as the
Head of the Presbyterian Party'.[1] This is so extraordinary a
statement that perhaps it was ignored because it seemed so
obviously and wildly inaccurate. In the first place, if the
'Presbyterian Party' is interpreted as the mass of 'Presbyterians'
secluded by Pride and re-admitted to the Long Parliament by
Monk, they could and did claim (with some truth) to have
made the Restoration. Certainly their leading members were
either favoured or at least treated with circumspection, until
the election of the Cavalier Parliament of 1661 showed the
Court that it was independent of puritan support. In the
second place, the Presbyterian clergy of 1660 fall into two
categories: the 'Reconcilers' aiming at a compromise Church
of England which should be more presbyterial than episcopal,
and the majority, who held out for the full Scots–Presbyterian
discipline.[2]

It is hard to believe that Wharton would even co-operate

1. *Memoirs ... Marquess of Wharton*, 6.
2. E. W. Kirby, 'The Reconcilers', *Essays in Modern English History in
   Honour of W. C. Abbott*, Cambridge Mass. 1941.

with the larger group, in opposition to whose aims he had first become Independent. It is quite incredible that the Court would molest any prominent lay supporter of the Reconcilers, a group which it was treating with every courtesy. Although Wharton might co-operate with the 'moderate' Reconcilers, he could hardly have been a leader of this group which also, in the final analysis, could not admit of toleration, not even (or possibly especially not) for independent congregations of Independents or Congregationalists (as they now preferred to be called). Finally, if the Court wanted to attack a Presbyterian or 'Presbyterian' leader, there were surely many more eminent than Wharton and more fit to be called 'Head' of such a party. Yet—for want of others—Wharton was the head of a 'Presbyterian' party, and the evidence for this is still among his papers.

The main issue in the Convention was that of church government: as a letter-writer put it, 'The only tug is betwixt Episcopacy and Presbytery . . .'[3] The restored 'Presbyterian' majority of the Long Parliament, after Monk's reversal of Pride's Purge, spent a deal of time establishing, so far as legislation without the King could establish anything, a Presbyterian system of church government and worship. It is agreed that even in May 1660, and especially from early June to late November 1660, numerous attempts were made in the Commons of the Convention to establish some form of church government and worship which should be more presbyterial than episcopal, and to preserve from eviction the thousands of more-or-less puritan ministers then in livings of the Church of England. One authority (without naming the planners) mentions plans and preparations made, during a Parliamentary recess, for action at the next session;[4] another dealing with the next Parliament mentions (without naming them) the 'old leaders' of the opposition of 1660.[5] Indeed, the leadership and organisation behind the Presbyterian attempts in the Conven-

---

3. Letter of E. Gower, quoted L. F. Brown, 'The Religious Factors in the Convention Parliament', *EHR*, XXII (1907) 58.
4. R. S. Bosher, *The Making of the Restoration Settlement, 1649-1662*, London 1951, 194-5.
5. W. C. Abbott, 'The Long Parliament of Charles II', *EHR*, XXI (1906) 56.

tion Commons were, until recently,[6] so little identified that one account of the leadership and organisation of the Court party in the Convention claims that the Presbyterian interest was unorganised, and implies that it was leaderless.[7]

One source suggests that Bampfield was a leading spirit of the Presbyterians; others, that four members of the 'junto'— Holles, Pierrepoint, Annesley and Sir William Lewis—with Swinfen 'and others of that gang' (assisted by Monk himself) were portending 'high opposition' when they foiled the more Royalist members of the Convention by electing another arch-'Presbyterian' of the 1640s (Sir Harbottle Grimston) as Speaker.[8] There is no evidence to connect Holles, Annesley and Monk with the 1660 opposition to the restoration of episcopacy. All three soon received peerages and offices from the restored monarchy. So did another of the 'junto', Ashley Cooper, as well as two more leading politicians of the Interregnum, Crew and Booth. We have already considered the rewards received by three 'junto' peers. Another of the 'junto', Sir Gilbert Gerrard (like several others, one of the eleven leading 'Presbyterians' driven out by the Army in 1647), was by November 1660 petitioning the Crown for the right to search for concealed lands and money and for two-thirds of the profits from them. Another of the eleven, Serjeant-at-law John Glynn, had become notorious for his pliability: for Cromwell, he prosecuted Royalist conspirators, and for the restored monarchy he prosecuted Sir Henry Vane. Major-General Browne, Lord Mayor of London, was at first a defender of puritan divines, but within a year lost his zeal. Edward Harley remained a confidant of the Presbyterians till late in 1660, but he was then made Governor of Dunkirk.[9] Indubitably, the Court had a deliberate and wholesale policy of buying the support of prominent lay puritans by giving them a share or an interest in the new Court and government. Prynne remained staunch to the cause of Presbyterian church government, but

6. Until the writer's note, *EHR*, LXXIX (1964) 307-54.
7. Jones, 'Political Groups', 162-3.
8. Letters to Hyde, quoted Brown, 'Religious Factors', 56.
9. For statements on the careers of these M.P.s, the sources, unless otherwise stated, are generally *DNB*, the *Calendars of State Papers*, and other obvious sources.

he was no leader, while his frequent speeches in the Convention often hampered rather than aided his cause.[10] A correspondent wrote to Hyde in April 1660:

> As for the grandees of that party, they [will] come in of themselves, when they see the tide begins to turn . . .[11]

which as Dr Bosher writes, was a true prophecy, for:

> From now on the support given to the puritan clergy by the 'grandees' was lukewarm. They felt a growing embarrassment at connection with a party soon labelled 'factious' and 'seditious' by the Court, and endeavoured to keep their new-found loyalty above suspicion.[12]

Just as it is certain that Wharton received no favours from the restored Court, so it is clear that he was among the few who continued to defend and protect puritan clergy and the puritan cause both publicly in the House of Lords and privately, by manoeuvres. Before the Convention met, he obtained a list of the names—526—which appeared on any returns as elected to the House of Commons. To more than half of them he put either (before) symbols, or (after), the names or initials of twenty-three persons.[13] Wharton apparently marked with a diagonal bar twenty-seven names of those whose elections were disputed, or who were otherwise unlikely to sit, or who were returned for two seats. Fourteen bars he converted to St Andrew's crosses, recording elimination by non-confirmation of election, expulsion, elevation to the peerage, emigration or death. In fact, however, between forty and fifty of those listed either never, or not for long, sat in the Commons. Wharton, it seems, went through each county list for those likely to support the puritan cause, either assigning them to 'managers' —local men wherever possible, and preferably magnates—or marking them (if at first no local manager was available) with a series of signs. These ranged from one dash for very hopeful

---

10. Jones, 'Political Groups', especially 166-7.
11. Quoted Bosher, *Restoration Settlement*, 148.
12. Ibid.
13. MS Carte 81, 74-7. Endorsed 'Names of the members of the Commons howse 1660'. Edited by the writer, and published *EHR*, LXXIX (1964) 307-54.

to many dots for very doubtful. The two systems were originally distinct, several counties having only or mainly one or the other, but many came to have both signs and 'managers' as the manager-system was extended to cover as many as possible of those at first simply marked. Some at first merely marked became themselves 'managers': these included Sir Thomas Wharton and Sir Wilfred Lawson, both called by some authorities Royalists (as opposed to Presbyterians).[14]

The basic territorial assignment of M.P.s to local 'managers' appears plainly: Onslow had a string of Surrey and Sussex representatives, James Darcy had thirteen other Yorkshiremen, and Edmund Petty's charges mostly (like himself) held seats in Buckinghamshire. Petty had some non-territorial assignees also, apparently some of the difficult cases, and so did Sir Wilfred Lawson. However, the main exceptions to territorialism were the two Whartons. Sir Thomas's charges came from a wide range of counties, but half of his dozen were actively Royalist 'Presbyterians', mostly with considerable military records—Booth, Browne, Waller and Harley. Presumably, he had a good deal in common with them. To 'M' (for 'Myself') Wharton assigned, apart from a territorial group of Buckinghamshire M.P.s, several notable 'Presbyterians'— Massey, Sir Richard Temple, Bampfield, James Fiennes (another son of Say and Sele) Prynne and Hale; the knighted regicide, Ingoldsby; and several prominent public servants of the Interregnum—Rushworth, Downing and Sir Charles Wolseley. There were also ten (out of the twelve assigned) of the members of the latest (largely 'Presbyterian') Council of State—Lewis and Pierrepoint of the 'junto', Speaker Grimston, Swinfen, Colonel Birch, Sir John Holland, Knightley, Serjeant John Maynard, Sir John Potts and Sir Thomas Widdrington. The last two were also 'managers', as were seven other men assigned to Wharton. These nine included no fewer than five out of the six most important (in the number of their charges) after Wharton himself—Sir Thomas Wharton, Sir Wilfred Lawson, Darcy, Petty and the industrialist Thomas Foley. The only leading 'manager' not in turn managed by Wharton

14. Bosher, *Restoration Settlement*, 135; H. N. Mukerjee, 'Elections for the Convention and Cavalier Parliaments', *Notes and Queries*, CLXVI (1934) 398-403.

was Sir Richard Onslow. The implications are plain: Wharton was the head of a hierarchy and the chief of the party, and Sir Richard was the most trusty of his lieutenants. The future was to make this still more evident.

To a total of only seven 'managers'—himself, Onslow and the other five named above—Wharton assigned no fewer than ninety M.P.s, while the remaining sixteen 'managers' accounted for no more than thirty-one. Of the ninety, Wharton alone managed nearly half. This again emphasises his personal share, and adds a final conclusive proof of his leading role, in the work of organisation. The quantitative difference between the activity of the seven and that of the sixteen suggests a qualitative difference. Possibly some of the sixteen were more 'contact-men' than 'managers'. Probably the sixteen were less staunchly puritan than the seven (this description might fit Glynn, Gerrard, Widdrington and Manchester) or more Royalist (Edward Harley, Potts and Viscount Wenman) or not very influential (Ellis, Thomas Bacon, Bennet, Raynsford and Thomas Hatcher) or too notorious (Goodwin, Thurloe and Sir John Trevor). Those assigned to them sometimes suited the characters suggested above for them: two of Harley's charges (Hinson and Meers) and one of Wenman's (Lord Falkland) were already (or proved to be) Royalist–Anglicans; Hatcher and Raynsford had only relatives assigned to them.

Surprisingly but significantly, only two of the seven chief 'managers' had reached any eminence in national (as apart from local) politics: Wharton himself, and Onslow, who had been a member of the last Council of State. The sixteen, on the other hand, included four of that Council (Gerrard, Potts, Harley and Widdrington—the last a former Speaker and Commissioner of the Great Seal), as well as Glynn, Trevor and Thurloe, Secretary to Cromwell's Council of State. The most notable statesman of the whole twenty-three, the Earl of Manchester, barely figured as a 'manager', since the only name assigned to him was done so with a query. Pierrepoint, Swinfen, Bampfield, Grimston and Prynne were not among the twenty-three; nor, of course, were any other English peers or any of those soon to receive peerages. This confirms the Royalist prophecy of the 'coming in' or falling off of the Presbyterian grandees.

It is impossible to be certain of the meanings of many, or even most, of the symbols used by Wharton to differentiate groups of M.P.s. Patient examination of all that is readily accessible of the careers and characters of the 526 (or rather of the five-sixths of the 526 about whom anything at all is on record, in print) has made possible useful comparisons between the general characteristics of separate groups. One useful yardstick is the difference in complexion of the militia committees of July 1659 and March 1659-60. Unfortunately, a person appointed under both ordinances could be anything from Anglican–Royalist to Rumper–Independent, since (despite Davies's statement[15]) it seems likely that in at least some counties only enough obvious opponents of the secluded 'Presbyterians' were dropped (in Buckinghamshire, a dozen[16]) to ensure that the attitudes of the new appointees (in Buckinghamshire, thirty-seven) would prevail over that of the majority of the survivors of the July 1659 appointees (in Buckinghamshire, survivors also numbered thirty-seven, several already clearly neo-Royalist). However, a group of M.P.s of whom many served on only the later committees, and of whom few served at all (let alone only) on the earlier committees, is clearly more Royalist and less puritan than a group in which the proportions are, or tend to be, reversed. Yet a note of caution is necessary: the position is confused by the fact that in the 'puritan revolution' one man could be extreme in religion and moderate in politics, while another might be extreme in politics and either more conservative in or less concerned with religion. In particular, Presbyterians who were politically staunch monarchists could be more opposed to an episcopal Church than some Independents who, possibly republican in theory, could nevertheless accept both King and Bishops so long as the King by toleration exempted them from the authority of the Bishops in the same degree as the Commonwealth had exempted them from the authority of Presbyterian synods. However, whatever the antecedents of particular M.P.s, it is not too cynical to assume that, generally speaking, where a golden handshake was accepted, it was effective— that honours, promotions, gifts, offices and preferments either

15. 'A clean sweep was made. . . .' *Restoration*, 298.
16. *Acts and Ordinances of the Interregnum*, ed Firth and Rait, passim.

rewarded, or ensured for the future, abstinence from opposition.

It is possible that Wharton failed to calculate the scale of the success of this policy. Either that, or he was misinformed about a great many of his prospects, as he certainly was about some; or else he was very optimistic, or careful to throw his net as wide as possible, and would rather attempt to influence moderate Royalists than fail to contact and confirm some possible supporters. The most common symbol—a dash—marked over a hundred M.P.s who seem to have been considered as (at first sight) the most likely to support a largely Presbyterian church settlement. A quarter of the group had been secluded by Pride's Purge; well over half had sat either in the Long Parliament during the Civil War or in Protectorate Parliaments. However, sixteen proved to be opponents of the puritan interest. Some, such as the 'manager' Widdrington, presumably turned their coats during the Convention; others probably concealed their real attitude during the Interregnum, as did Charlton—Royalist plotter, yet militia-committeeman in July 1659. The smaller groups marked with symbols include Rumpers and Cavaliers. Some groups have few or none with Royalist pasts or futures, others have many. One small group consisted mainly of Royalists having no obvious connection with puritanism. The only explanation possible seems to be that Wharton regarded them as moderates who might be influenced to be neutral in the struggle. He was later to attach some importance to moderates.

Nearly half the names on the list—250—were neither marked nor assigned. These M.P.s undoubtedly furnished the bulk of the Anglican–Royalist strength in the Convention Commons. One hundred and sixty-two of them had sat in no previous Parliament—a high concentration of those two hundred-odd young men who were (as contemporaries and later historians agree), by and large, Anglican Royalists.[17] Another thirty-one sat for the first time in Richard Cromwell's Parliament. Between forty and sixty of the unmarked are identifiable as known Cavaliers or Anglicans. The whole 250 contained a far smaller proportion of secluded Presbyterians than did the marked groups, no more than between an eighth and a seventh.

17. E.g. Clarendon; and Brown, who claimed that 208 out of 473 in the Convention Commons were new to Parliament ('Religious Factors', 55).

Some of these were very Royalist in 1660, such as the rising, soon-to-be ennobled Crew; others were clearly of Wharton's faction, though unmarked, such as Onslow himself. To this extent at least, Wharton's party was 'Presbyterian'.

The issue of the Church was raised early in the Convention and never forgotten. On 9 May, a bill was reported 'for establishing ministers settled in ecclesiastical livings'. On 28 May (the day before the King's return to Westminster) the Commons drew up a declaration which, on 1 June, the King issued as a proclamation against forcible evictions from estates or livings acquired since 1642. Some Presbyterian ministers now attempted to submit to Parliament a petition to put the King in mind of the Covenant and declaring against Bishops. This was thwarted about 10 June. Meanwhile some more moderate Presbyterians, disassociated from that attempt, were conferring with the King at Manchester's lodgings on the terms of a comprehensive and compromise Church settlement.[18] Within four days of the attempted anti-episcopal petition, Wharton faced the revival of Osborne's charges. Obviously the Court had good reason to attack the head of a party opposing Hyde's aims in the Church. The question remains why the heir to the throne should thwart such an attack. It is however known that as early as 1659 York was trying to form a party in his own interests, which were 'frequently inimical to Hyde's'.[19] Nearly thirty years later James Stuart was still trying to use puritan support for a basically Roman Catholic policy.

If the attacks on Wharton and Onslow were meant to disable or intimidate them from opposition, they failed of their purpose. In late June and early July Wharton studied and annotated a copy of 'The Larger Proposals of the Presbyterian ministers to his Majesty'. Although these men were the 'moderates', they not only demanded a stricter discipline, but also inveighed against the Prayer Book, with the veiled threat that its re-imposition would lead to widening breaches. However, they were willing to accept episcopacy, in a moderated form.[20] To this the Bishops' reply was (not surprisingly) unyielding, if

18. Bosher, *Restoration Settlement*, is the authority for this period.
19. D. Underdown, *Royalist Conspiracy in England, 1649-1660*, New Haven 1960, 291.
20. MS Carte 81, 144.

polite.[21] Wharton was still more concerned with the 'Proposals and Considerations' of the Congregationalists (or Independents). He helped to draft these, adding or deleting phrases where this seemed necessary for clarity. In this paper the threat was less veiled, for the Congregationalists, after claiming that episcopal oppression brought the nation into 'war and blood', hinted that the same would recur if they were not granted the toleration they exactly defined. They wished to depend immediately on the King's supremacy in ecclesiastical affairs, which they fully admitted, and they stressed the gratitude and loyalty which the King would gain by toleration.[22]

On 27 June a bill was introduced for the maintenance of the 'true Reformed Protestant Religion'. The Commons debated this on 6, 9 and 16 July, but on 20 July (despite the Presbyterians' efforts) they laid it aside. However, the next day the House voted to read a petition against the ejection of puritan ministers, reviving the earlier bill on this subject, left in committee since early May. From early August to late September the Court lost control of the Commons' actions on religion. By 7 August, Anglicans were gloomily reporting that the Commons were being very severe on the Bishops.[23] By the end of August, Wharton, Thurloe, Bulstrode, Sir William Roberts, Philip Nye, Gervase Bennet, Colonel Clarke, Captain John Stone, Mr Hillesly, 'etc' had been noticed meeting regularly, two or three at a time.[24] Largely because the 'Presbyterian counter-offensive' had become a 'grave threat to the government's whole policy',[25] Parliament was adjourned from 13 September to 5 November. Between 28 August and 22 September five Bishops (new and promoted) were nominated and elected. A month later, presumably to still the consequent puritan alarm and resentment, the King and Chancellor had the Bishops join with the moderate Presbyterians to frame a royal declaration foreshadowing an interim church government almost more presbyterial than episcopal. When Parliament reassembled on 6 November,

21. Bosher, *Restoration Settlement*.
22. MS Carte 81, 140.
23. Bosher, *Restoration Settlement*.
24. *CSP Dom 1660-61*, 207.
25. Bosher, *Restoration Settlement*, 176.

the 'Presbyterian party' in the Commons made their carefully-prepared move.[26] They introduced a bill to convert into statute law that most favourable royal declaration.

Wharton in his usual manner listed those whom he had prepared or tried to influence for this crucial attempt. He headed his paper 'List of Persons To whom papers are delivered in and to be delivered 6th Nov: 1660'.[27] Actually there were eight short lists in two sets of four. The first four were headed: 'The Cases', 'The Case with Objections and Answeres', 'The Case with some Circumstances', and 'The Case as Stated with Considerations'. The whole second set (of four short lists) was headed: 'These following are Supposed already to have papers delivered them and not returned in.' Presumably, those in the first set of four lists were still being circularised on 6 November, with four different papers, each putting the Presbyterian case in a different way, while those in the second four had received, but not yet answered, communications of the same four kinds. Unfortunately, there is no way of knowing, or even of guessing, the differences in the ways of handling 'the case', nor whether these differences were of any great importance. Forty-five names in all appear. They include eight of Wharton's managers or contact-men (among them Onslow, Lawson and Petty), with many other leading 'Presbyterians' such as Prynne, Lewis, Bunckley, Bampfield, Swinfen, Birch, Sir Richard Temple, Knightley, Sir John Northcoat and Sir Anthony Irby. Yet not all could have been seriously expected to speak for the Presbyterian bill. Two of the three in the fourth list of the first set—Thurland and Edward Stephens—had in July spoken against the Presbyterians, as had another—Barton—erased in the fourth list and added to the third. Charlton in the sixth (or second of the second set) had shown himself a strong Court–Anglican. True, he was not of the old Cavalier party, and had seemed loyal to the Rump in 1659, while Stephens had been a secluded 'Presbyterian' in 1648. Possibly they were regarded as deserters who could yet be recalled to support a compromise settlement.

Wharton and his fellow-organisers may well have thought that the strongest supporters of the Court and of episcopacy

26. Ibid, 194-5; Jones, 'Political Groups', 175.
27. MS Carte 80, 559. Published *EHR*, LXXIX (1964) 307-54.

could scarcely attack a bill identical with a royal declaration approved by the Bishops. They may even have believed that the declaration embodied the true aims of the Court, although this would perhaps suppose them to be rather naifs. Certainly the 'Presbyterian' speakers made a great deal of play with the claim that the bill represented the King's expressed attitude, and certainly this fact was a great embarrassment to their opponents, who were compelled to repeat the illogical or betraying statement that while the declaration was a very good declaration, the bill was a bad bill.[28] Their claim that the bill was premature, since the declaration envisaged a national synod to settle the Church, was quite disingenuous: negotiations between Bishops and even the minority of Presbyterian divines willing to make any compromise with episcopacy had shown both parties to be basically intransigent—a fact which in itself rendered suspect the Bishops' acquiescence in the very Presbyterian declaration. Nobody thought a synod would be called. Shrewd observers were sure that the negotiations, and the request to the 'moderate' Presbyterians to submit their proposals (eventually embodied in the declaration) were simply to gain time and smooth matters over until the episcopalian party should be stronger.[29] It seems clear that the Earl of Clarendon (as the Chancellor, Hyde, now was) conveyed his real aims implicitly or explicitly to the Court's supporters.[30]

Its opponents succeeded in having the bill laid aside at the second reading on 28 November. This defeat ended the Presbyterian successes in the Convention, which was shortly after dissolved. One view of this defeat is that it was caused by the defection to the Court–Anglicans of the anti-Presbyterian puritans, the 'Independents' (or 'Commonwealth' men as they were sometimes called) resenting the Presbyterians' abandoning them, and hoping for a toleration from a fully episcopal church which no Presbyterian or semi-Presbyterian would give. According to this view, the earlier successes of the 'Presbyterians' had been due to their co-operation with the 'Indepen-

28. E.g. Masham. The debates are printed in the *Parliamentary History* and summarised by Bosher, *Restoration Settlement*.
29. Bosher, *Restoration Settlement*, 162.
30. Jones, 'Political Groups', 165, 169-70, 175-6.

dents'.[31] This view has been challenged recently on the grounds that no swing of 'Independents' was needed to give the Court its majority in November.[32] Unfortunately, Wharton's papers make no obvious contribution to deciding this argument. Like many puritan 'Grandees', whose peers' rights to private chaplains safeguarded them from personal danger of religious persecution, Wharton may not have felt sufficiently the tension between the two wings of puritanism. He was on corresponding terms with several prominent (and moderate) Presbyterian divines. During the Interregnum, he (like Manchester) presented both Independent and Presbyterian ministers to his livings. Wharton left no evidence that he fully appreciated the incompatibility of the positions of the Congregationalists and the Presbyterians in 1660. The former fully admitted the King's supremacy in ecclesiastical affairs, so as to depend on the King, rather than on a national Church or a uniformity-conscious Parliament, and so gain toleration. The Presbyterians denied the King's authority in Church affairs and even Parliament's, apart from a grudging acceptance that statutory confirmation of a Church settlement was necessary for its enforcement. If Wharton's eight short lists of 6 November could be seen to show differentiation between Presbyterian 'Presbyterians', strongly Royalist 'Presbyterians', Royalists with some sympathies for the puritan attitude, and 'Commonwealth' men or 'Independents', some light could be thrown on this problem. However, no obvious system can be made out from a paper which put Charlton, Sir Richard Temple, Sir George Downing and Colonel Birch in the same list as Messrs Petty and Bacon and which lists pliant Glynn and turncoat Widdrington with Prynne. Some significance probably lies in the concentration of eminent or staunch 'Presbyterians' in the very first list, and in the fact that Sir Richard Onslow had one list (the last) to himself.

31. Brown, 'Religious Factors'; Bosher, *Restoration Settlement*, especially 167, 174-8.
32. Jones, 'Political Groups'.

XVIII

SWIMMING AGAINST THE TIDE

'refusing to bow their heads to prelacy and ceremonies'

THE narrow failure in the Convention was followed by an utter collapse in the Commons of the next Parliament. *Faute de mieux*, Wharton's efforts were now concentrated in the House where he himself sat, and largely in his own person. Yet barely two years later he was a leading engineer of an extraordinary combination of dissident lords which threatened to overthrow the Cavalier Chancellor.

All puritan factions in London combined to elect anti-episcopalian members for the next Parliament, and their organisers and sympathisers attempted to have this example followed throughout the country.[1] The Court was alarmed by this, but for a number of reasons, including the senseless rising of Venner's Fifth Monarchy group in London, the elections greatly reduced the number of puritans in what was to be called the 'Cavalier Parliament'. However, when this met in May 1661, Wharton listed as 'Friends', 135 Members of the Commons. It could hardly have been a coincidence that the minority later voting vainly against the Corporation Act numbered 136.[2] Wharton's 'Friends' included only sixty-three survivors of the Convention, and of these only forty-seven had been marked or assigned on Wharton's master list. Some of the new M.P.s were puritans—there were three anti-episcopal London aldermen among the 'Friends'—but for the most part Wharton had to rely on moderates. These included strong Royalists and Cavaliers such as Bramston and Lord Mansfield,

1. Bosher, *Restoration Settlement*, 162, 195-8.
2. MS Carte 81, 79-80; Abbott, 'Long Parliament of Charles II', 28-9.

who might oppose punitive measures from mildness, but who did not approve the cause of those against whom the measures were aimed. When the House of Commons voted to burn the Covenant, only 103 voted in the negative.[3] Wharton in fact made a list of twenty 'Names'—his Musgrave cousins and other northern gentry, some unmarked, unassigned Convention men and some 'Cavalier' M.P.s not among the 'Friends'—ending with the note 'several other Moderate men whose names I do not remember at present.'[4]

The greatest difference between the Presbyterian party of the Convention and Wharton's 'Friends' in the Cavalier Parliament was the shrinking of the group of 'managers'. Many of the twenty-three had not been re-elected, but others simply fell by the wayside. Only three continued their previous roles. They were reinforced by three obscure recruits, Messrs Lever, Stevens and Browne, responsible respectively for seven, eight and nine M.P.s. One of the three survivors was Petty, who had a smaller group than before, still mainly of Buckinghamshire members. Only one of these—Sir William Bowyer—had been in Petty's group in 1660, and he since then had acquired a baronetcy. Wharton and Sir Richard Onslow were responsible for forty-two and forty respectively. In addition, they were responsible *adhuc* for twenty-nine and twelve more respectively. Nothing could show more clearly the shortage of managers (greater even than the shortage of potential supporters) and the near-collapse and demoralisation of Wharton's party.

Nevertheless, Wharton continued to combat the vengeful episcopalians of the Cavalier Parliament, but his efforts were now mainly personal, and in the House of Lords. He had been put at once on all the standing committees, and he also served on many other committees during his regular attendance in the first session. However, one of the first acts of the new Parliament restored to their seats in the Lords the Bishops, driven out by mob pressure confirmed by the King's unavailing concession early in 1642. Not until January 1661-2, during the second session, did the Uniformity Bill, introduced into

3. Ibid.
4. MS Carte 81, 83.

the Commons in July 1661, come before the Lords. No doubt the Court deliberately delayed the measure which would enforce the use of the Prayer Book, which a Royal Commission was actually engaged on revising.[5] Although the Lords committed the Bill to a large committee of forty-four, Wharton was not among them. Only half-a-dozen former Parliamentarians were, but on the other hand there were eleven Bishops. However, Wharton contrived later to have himself added to the committee. He made notes on the content of the Bill, and had several copies made of that part of the Declaration of Breda which concerned the accommodation of tender consciences.[6] One of the many provisos with which he was concerned stipulated that the Act should not invalidate the King's concessions in pursuance of the Declaration.[7] Presumably this was an attempt surreptitiously to give to the King's Presbyterian–episcopal declaration of October 1660 the statutory recognition refused it by the Convention in November 1660.

The dramatic fall of puritanism from its peak of prosperity to its nadir of persecution obviously made a strong and lasting impression on Wharton. From this point, his letter to von Spaen becomes much more detailed, if not more accurate:

> Shortly before his return in 1660 (while Parliament was yet sitting) the King, to the great joy of all good men, published a declaration from Breda granting freedom of conscience to all but Papists.

There was in fact no exception made in the King's declaration. There was, however, a qualifying clause common enough in seventeenth-century toleration proposals: no man was to be called in question for differences in religion *which did not disturb the peace of the kingdom*. The Cavalier Parliament was to show that it held all differences which entailed nonconformity would disturb that peace—a view for which recent history gave considerable corroboration—but the embittered Wharton a generation later seemed to blame the King:

5. Bosher, *Restoration Settlement*, 224.
6. *LJ* 11, 400; MS Carte 81, 100, 102, 107, 108.
7. Ibid 81, 121, 133.

In 1661 he summoned a new Parliament and there followed in the next year a great change of policy, for by a single act of Parliament two thousand Dissenting Pastors of the most deserving virtues, refusing to bow their heads to prelacy and ceremonies or submit to Episcopal ordination (after being ordained by a Presbytery) were ejected from office and benefice.

This exaggerated estimate of the number of the victims of 1662 has persisted. Seven to eight hundred ministers had lost their livings in 1660, mostly by the return of the Anglicans whom they had supplanted, but those ejected in 1662 may have been fewer than a thousand, and certainly were not more than 1,129 including undergraduates, and of all these, nearly two hundred later conformed. Many were displaced because they petitioned for the King's trial in 1648.[8] Many of the ejected of 1662 had not only enjoyed for fifteen to twenty years the benefices of the men they had supplanted but had also denied their predecessors' families their legal dole, and had acted as judges in the tribunals of 'Triers' who ejected Royalist Anglicans. The victims of the puritans numbered between 3,000 and 3,600.[9] Of these Gardiner wrote that whether more or fewer than two thousand suffered was of no historical importance.[10] The same could be said of the victims of the so-called 'Bartholomew Day massacre'.

Wharton had to do with at least nine more provisos, some drafted entirely in his hand, and others altered by him. They qualified the Act in every possible way, from delaying ministers' deprivations of benefices for six months after its publication to allowing liberty of conscience for all who accepted the Testaments and the Apostle's Creed and the right of public meeting to all who accepted the thirty-nine articles of faith.[11] He served on a committee to draw up a proviso leaving it to the King to provide for deprived clergy,[12] though whence the King was to obtain the wherewithal was not specified and cannot be imagined.

8. A. G. Matthews, *Calamy Revised*, Oxford 1934, xiii-xiv.
9. P. H. Hardacre, *The Royalists during the Puritan Revolution*, The Hague 1956, 42, quoting Tatham, *Puritans in Power*, Cambridge 1913, 90-1.
10. *Civil War*, III, 10.
11. MS Carte 81, 106, 112, 114, 120, 131, 113, 108, 110.
12. *LJ* 11, 424.

Although puritan and Catholic lords acted together against the bill, Wharton in particular complained that it gave easier terms to Catholics than to Calvinists. His own account for von Spaen was as follows:

> While this was being debated, I complained seriously and openly in the House of Lords judging it unjust that pastors ordained by a Presbytery, or from foreign parts, should be prevented from performing the ministerial office or obtaining church preferment unless re-ordained while it would be possible for those who had been Romish priests, without re-ordination, by a single profession of our faith, to enjoy that liberty. To this a great prelate (at that time of London and not long after Archbishop of Canterbury) replied that those pastors might have the same liberty if that lord or anyone else could show that it belonged to them as to the Roman priests by an equal law. After saying this he sat down without offering any argument for his proposition, at which various peers in private expressed their displeasure.

The significant point is that those other peers who disapproved of Bishop Sheldon's contemptuous attitude, did so privately. Manchester had urged the 'Reconcilers' to remove offensive passages from a petition to the King, but in this he did no more than the Anglican Clarendon,[13] and thereafter he seems to have done little enough for those whose religion gave the name of 'Presbyterian' to the party he had been supposed to lead.

Wharton was reluctant to accept the unpalatable fact that the revived Anglican Church would be not only fully episcopalian in government but even Laudian in form and doctrine. When the puritan divines already could be called 'nonconformist', he kept their long paper of 'reasons against the Liturgy' and a tract by Baxter on 'universal accord' in the communion of the Church.[14] However, he was probably more concerned with practical suggestions for compromises which would allow the maximum number of puritans to remain in the Church. In his own hand he drafted two pages of proposals for comprehension, including a modified episcopal laying-on-of-hands for the presbyterially-ordained, a simple declaration by

13. Kirby, 'The Reconcilers', 75.
14. MS Carte 81, 84-95, 66-71.

clergy of agreement with the doctrine and acceptance of the worship and government of the Church, the making optional certain ceremonies and the surplice, and the revision of the liturgy and canons before they were made obligatory. For a three years' indulgence of those who would still be outside the Church, he proposed that members of a congregation who were listed by name might meet for the public exercise of religion (presumably this listing was to overcome Cavalier fears of conspiracy); that they should be disabled from public office and not exempt from parish duties and tithes; and that conventicles (secret, unlicensed meetings) should be punishable by the confiscation of estates. Later he expanded and modified his scheme.[15]

The puritan divines were encouraged by some of the peers who favoured them not to submit to the terms of the Act of Uniformity. Wharton, on the other hand, tried to induce individual ministers to accept it. Apparently Wharton's arguments did not prevail with Benjamin Agas, but four clergy in his livings—William Cole, Francis Higginson, Thomas Dodson and John Dalton—conformed at once or later.[16] No doubt the reason for this difference was that Wharton did not share the illusions of most Presbyterians, who believed that the Act would have to be suspended for their benefit.[17] Wharton claimed that the chief obstacles to puritans' conforming were ceremonies and episcopal re-ordination. Some puritans conformed in spite of these, and so might others have done but for an obstacle that Wharton omitted to mention. Some Bishops were even anxious to make it possible for the presbyterially-ordained to receive episcopal ordination (without any humiliating admission that they had not been ordained before) by the use of the sentence 'If thou hast not been ordained, I ordain thee.'[18] As for ceremonies, it was generally agreed that they were neither enjoined nor forbidden by scripture, and so could be decided legitimately by any Church.

Neither Wharton nor others suggested that there was any doctrinal test imposed on Calvinists. Instead, according to the

15. Ibid 81, 346, 350.
16. Nightingale, *Ejected of 1662*, s.n.
17. J. Ralph, *The History of England*, London 1744, I, 74.
18. Kirby, 'The Reconcilers', 66.

Bishop of Winchester in 1665, many nonconformist divines admitted that they could subscribe to the Prayer Book and use the ceremonies, but could not forswear the Solemn League and Covenant.[19] Wharton's own version made pride, and refusal to accept the majority opinion of a Protestant Church and Parliament, the great stumbling blocks to comprehension. In fact, it seems that another obstacle, more dangerous to Church and State, was the puritans' obstinacy in adhering to a declaration which was a manifesto of their unchanged intention to make the great changes in the Church which were attempted during the Civil Wars. To the great majority of the nation the Covenant was a manifesto of rebellion.

Wharton himself apparently saw that the real issue was the matter of apportioning blame, saying to one minister that the Anglicans were resolved either to 'reproach' the puritans or to 'undo' them.[20] Yet Wharton himself was asked by one minister, at first ejected but later conforming, to approve letters thanking a Bishop for his favour, goodwill and kindness.[21] Even Sheldon, Bishop of London, supplied Wharton with a copy of the proposed alterations in the Prayer Book, which contained many concessions to puritan feeling. Subsequently, Wharton drew up long papers of the 'amendations' in the Book of Common Prayer sent by Convocation to Parliament, and a long extract of the alterations in the Book of Ordination.[22]

It has been claimed that for the most part the Lords merely aggravated the harshness of the Act of Uniformity.[23] Yet the Chancellor Clarendon brought in a proviso for the King's power to dispense with the act for any 'peacable and pious' minister, which was later rejected by the Commons. Even one Bishop attempted to qualify the clause obliging ministers to declare against the Covenant, and other bishops helped to add a proviso to give ministers ejected under the act one-fifth of the profits of their lost livings. The Commons rejected this on the very good ground that the similar ordinance of the Long Parliament had been largely ignored.

19. MS Carte 80, 757-9.
20. Ralph, *History of England*, I, 74.
21. Nightingale, *Ejected of 1662*, II, 1085-6.
22. MS Carte 81, 117-9, 134-5, 128-9; Bosher, *Restoration Settlement*, 247.
23. Ibid, 249-53, 241.

In December 1662 another royal declaration announced an intention to extend toleration to nonconformists. Unlike that of October 1660 this owed nothing to Clarendon, being the work of the King, of another pro-Catholic, Henry Bennet, and of the self-appointed champion of the puritans, Lord Ashley. Consequently it explicitly and really looked for Parliament's aid to ratify the promised toleration. Nevertheless, the King expressly maintained his claim to an inherent power of dispensing with laws, presumably with or without Parliament's goodwill.[24] Oddly enough, Wharton in his autobiographical letter made no mention of this attempt to reverse the tide of persecution which he was himself so vigorously combating. It is true that this declaration explicitly extended the proposed toleration to Roman Catholics. Twice in the letter to von Spaen (once untruly as we have seen) Wharton emphasised that the toleration schemes which he approved expressly excluded Papists. He had been unimpressed by their appeal of June 1661 for the removal of the 'sanguinary' penal laws, and actually added menaces, including the penalty of *praemunire*, to a draft bill against recusants.[25] Yet in fact there is reason to believe that he was at this time not entirely above co-operating with Catholics. Apparently he often received at his house a Jesuit who 'tampered' with the nonconformists to obtain a political alliance for the common goal of toleration.[26] However, although Wharton's papers are full of evidence of his efforts against the imposition of penal laws against Protestant dissenters, there is no evidence that Wharton supported the toleration attempt of December 1662. The bill, introduced into the Lords in February 1662-3 by Robartes, now Lord Privy Seal, and strongly supported by Ashley, was to give the King power to dispense with the Act of Uniformity and other similar laws. On 5 March 1662-3, the Lords voted to limit its scope to the Act of Uniformity, but later the bill was dropped. Of all this there is no hint in Wharton's papers. Since he kept so much from this period, including some

---

24. *English Historical Documents*, ed D. C. Douglas, London 1953, VIII, 373; D. T. Witcombe, 'The Cavalier House of Commons 1663', *BIHR*, XXXII (1959) 181-3.
25. MS Carte 81, 143, 522-3.
26. *HMC Ormonde NS*, IV, 349.

possibly potentially dangerous, this omission seems significant. We must admit the strong probability that Wharton took no active part in, and presumably distrusted, a scheme largely concocted by two of the five future Ministers of the Cabal for a toleration which would include Roman Catholics.

In the event, despite the efforts of Court speakers such as Bennet and his clients, the House of Commons denied that the King had any prerogative power to dispense with laws. They then not only pointed out that the reasons for uniformity remained the same as when the Act for it had been so recently passed, but also emphasised their total disagreement with the King and his new advisers by bills against Roman Catholics, nonconformists' conventicles and even against the public employment of any nonconformist who had been in any office before the Restoration. This last was eventually dropped by the Commons. The bills against recusants and conventicles passed the Commons but could not pass the Lords before the end of the session of 1663. It is possible that Wharton had a hand in preventing their passage, for it was the affair of the Earl of Bristol, in which Wharton was deeply concerned, which took up the time of the House.

The Roman Catholic Earl of Bristol was another who was at this time seeking puritan support for toleration. This was the George Lord Digby who had attracted so much hostility from the opposition in the House of Commons of the Long Parliament before becoming one of the most influential and most disastrous of the King's advisers during the Civil War. By 1662 he was allied against Clarendon with several ex-Parliamentarians including Robartes, the 1659-60 'junto' members Annesley and Cooper (now Earl of Anglesey and Lord Ashley respectively) and two of Wharton's old friends, Thurloe and Edward Montagu, now Earl of Sandwich. He was also allied with the Duke of Buckingham, whose father had tried to make a scapegoat of Bristol's father and who as a crony of the King, a Cavalier of the second Civil War and a son-in-law of Fairfax, had an ambivalent political position, generally posing as a patron of nonconformists.[27] Early in July 1663, when Bristol began to attack the Chancellor, some at

27. D. Townshend, *George Digby, Second Earl of Bristol*, London 1924, 220-9.

least of the nonconformists thought their chance had come.[28] However, when he accused Clarendon to the King, the latter's angry response was enough to deter Bristol's associates.[29]

Nevertheless the Earl proceeded on Friday 10 July to make what is generally called a 'fantastic'[30] attempt to impeach the Chancellor. In his own name and (by all accounts) on his own, he exhibited articles of alleged treason committed by Clarendon. The charges were even more improbable than was usual in seventeenth-century impeachments.[31] They included, incredibly enough, the allegations, first, that Clarendon had encouraged the King to solicit from the Pope, for one of his relatives, a cardinal's hat, and secondly, that he habitually defamed the King by alleging he favoured Roman Catholics.[32] True, the matter in the charges of a seventeenth-century impeachment seems sometimes to be of almost secondary importance. Anything could be alleged, for given the right treatment, something could be made to stick. The important thing was to have the victim imprisoned and denied legal counsel or other help while Parliamentary committees collected evidence and invited delations. To do all this it was necessary to have a majority of opinion favourable to the attacker or at least not active for the defence. This Bristol had failed to obtain, for in spite of his urging the House declined to commit Clarendon. The latter at once declared his innocence, and the Lords ordered the Judges to report on Monday whether the articles had been brought in legally, whether the House could proceed in the matter, and whether the charges were of treason.

Clearly the Chancellor was in no great or immediate danger of ruin, and this had as a corollary, just as obvious, that his assailant was in grave peril. Bristol confirmed his reputation for 'impetuosity and indiscretion'[33] by attempting privately to influence, or possibly intimidate, the Judges.[34] He was now

28. F. Bate, *Declaration of Indulgence, 1672*, London 1908, 40.
29. Townshend, *Bristol*, 220-9.
30. Witcombe, 'Cavalier House of Commons', 189.
31. Hume likened them to 'incoherent altercations of a passionate enemy'. Quoted in Cobbett's *Parliamentary History*, IV, 283.
32. The charges are printed in *Parliamentary History*, IV, 276-9 and *History of the House of Lords*, printed for E. Timberland, London 1742, I, 56-9.
33. Hume, quoted in *Parliamentary History*, IV, 283.
34. *Timberland*, I, 59.

claiming mendaciously that his articles were an information and not a charge. Unmoved, the Judges on Monday 13 July gave their opinion that no one peer could originally exhibit to the House of Lords a charge of high treason against any peer (so that Bristol's charges were 'not . . . regularly and legally brought in') and that if the matters were true yet they had no treason in them. The Lord Chamberlain then read a message from the King, who had had from the House a copy of Bristol's charges. Charles from his own knowledge testified to the untruth of several of them, and ominously promised to deal with Bristol for many 'scandalous Reflections' on himself and his relatives in what he looked on as a libel on himself and his government.[35] Nevertheless, Bristol challenged the Judges to give their reasons for their opinion. It was unprecedented for the Lords to make such a request when the Judges' opinion was unanimous, as it was in this case. Yet Bristol and his supporters seemed to have the backing of the House, and as a result the astonished and indignant Judges agreed to give their reasons the next day. They felt it was necessary to make it very clear that their opinion that what Bristol had done was not legally done did not necessarily imply that Bristol had committed any criminal act.[36]

It appears, contrary to all accounts from Clarendon's to those of the biographers of Clarendon, Bristol, Buckingham and Shaftesbury, that Bristol not only expected considerable support in his attack, but also had good reason to expect it. Certainly Bristol had considerable support to cover his retreat in two days of heated debate. In preparation for this there was an attempt to organise an alliance between all who were either hostile to the Chancellor or friendly to toleration or both. The evidence for this is in Wharton's papers. Indubitably Wharton was deeply involved in this attempt. This strongly suggests that there was also some attempt to organise support for Bristol's attack on 10 July, but any such preparation would be limited to a few peers both from the need for secrecy and from the greater danger of such activity.

On one paper Wharton listed in his own hand nearly ninety

35. *Parliamentary History*, IV, 283; *LJ* 11, 559.
36. *Timberland*, I, 60.

lords expected to be present on 13 July.[37] In this, one group of forty-four (miscounted apparently as forty-three) together with another group of fifteen, whose proxies were held by ten or eleven of the forty-four, were made to total fifty-eight lords[38] obviously expected to support Bristol. Another total of fifty-one was made up from a group of twenty-six[39] firm supporters of the Chancellor, eight proxies held mostly by that statesman, and, undoubtedly, the seventeen Bishops shown in the Lords' Journals to have been present that day, though unnamed on Wharton's paper. There, however, a list of fifteen[40] others had symbols before or after reminiscent of those used by Wharton to mark Convention M.P.s. The twelve (out of these fifteen) who were in fact present apparently divided evenly. Other absences reduced the votes of those listed as Bristolians to forty-nine, and of the anticipated Clarendonians to forty-two. Seven lay peers were present whose names were not listed by Wharton.

Wharton kept fairly extensive but only partially legible notes of the two days' debate.[41] From these it appears that on 13 July Ashley spoke once, expressing pleasure that the Judges found no treason; that Lucas attacked Bristol for 'evil imputations'; and that Southampton wanted a vote according to the Judges' opinion. Wharton alone made a protest against the way in which so important a matter was carried on, saying he had observed 'great silence, and in any motion such an unwillingness to speak that what was moved was always ordered'. He desired to vote honestly and equally, and he required time before voting. He was not satisfied by the questioning of a lord for what he did in Parliament.

On Tuesday 14 July, when the debate was resumed, the Duke of York urged the House not to delay the business of the

37. MS Carte 81, 224. Being prepared for publication.
38. Including at least seventeen Roman Catholics and twenty-four of Parliamentarian or Cromwellian antecedents.
39. Including only two Catholics and two Parliamentarians, but with nineteen Cavaliers, nine of them (including Clarendon) ennobled during or since the war.
40. Two princes (York and Rupert), two Parliamentarians, several Cavaliers (including Lindsey) and some who had been minors during the troubles.
41. MS Carte 81, 226-7. Being prepared for publication.

Judges' opinion. The Bishop of Winchester insisted that Bristol had said he was making an accusation—that is, not as now pretended, laying an information. Buckingham suggested that they might vindicate the Chancellor. Wharton roused Clarendon's ire by propounding that Bristol merely moved a matter to be debated. Southampton pointed out that no lord could move anything in the name of all the peers, to which Wharton replied that one could on behalf of all. Southampton gave his opinion that Bristol's action 'had been done in heat'; Buckingham opposed this. After further debate, they returned to Wharton's suggestion, which Lucas attacked and Ashley defended. One peer said Wharton had moved it unnecessarily and that the fundamental laws had been ill-quoted. To this Buckingham and Winchester replied, as well as Wharton, who said that two or three others desired it, and that he had not mentioned laws but privileges, of which he thought some were fundamental, and this (that a lord should not be questioned for actions in Parliament) he thought was one.

In the end the House voted *nemine contradicente* to agree with the Judges' opinions. Wharton copied out this vote in his own hand, together with their order giving Bristol ample time to make good his charges as misdemeanours.[42] The attack had failed, and so had Bristol's attempt to extricate himself, in spite of the prolonged defence, chiefly by Wharton and those whom Wharton prompted. The King gave orders for the arrest of Bristol, who lost for ever all credit in Parliament and Court, and who remained in hiding or obscurity till Clarendon's downfall. It is notable that on Monday 13 July only one of Bristol's known associates spoke. This was Ashley, and all he could express was an hypocritical pleasure that the Judges found no treason in the charges. On the second day both Ashley and Buckingham defended the opinions expressed by Wharton, but this was one stage further removed from a direct attack on Clarendon than was Wharton's energetic defence of the accusing Bristol. Buckingham's fawning proposal was taken up, and he himself was appointed to the committee to vindicate Clarendon. Manchester's only part was to convey to the House the King's message, full of menace to Bristol.

42. Ibid 81, 233.

Two Cavalier lords outspoken in this debate, Southampton and Lucas, were later on the same side as Wharton in opposition to the Five Mile Act. Their unhesitating support of the Chancellor in 1663 was perhaps due to the strong line taken by the King. This may have influenced a sufficient number of lords to be decisive. However, party lines were becoming fluid. Several ex-Cavaliers were listed as Bristolians, and a number of ex-Parliamentarians as Clarendonians. Bristol's attack on the Chancellor was obviously prompted less by the refusal of some grants, recorded by Hume, than by Clarendon's constant opposition to the King's favour for Catholics, also recorded by that historian.[43] In particular, Clarendon had not approved the declaration of December 1662, and it was this split in the Court interest which doomed to failure that attempt at toleration.[44] Although his attempt ruined Bristol, it had not been for the Chancellor the easy triumph he would have us believe in his account of the affair. In this he described Bristol, on 13 July, lamenting in utter confusion, and omitted any mention of the debate on that day and the next.[45] It has been claimed that the 'delays caused by the Bristol "impeachment"' which had prevented the passage of the Acts against Papists and conventicles were not deliberate obstruction.[46] There is no proof that this result was not the one aimed at. Certainly the aftermath of this affair for Wharton suggests that he had incurred great resentment.

---

43. Quoted in *Parliamentary History*, IV, 283-4.
44. Witcombe, 'Cavalier House of Commons', 182-3.
45. *Life*, Oxford 1857, II, 23-7. *Parliamentary History* is similarly uninformed, and actually ascribes the vote of 14 July to 18 July. Only *Timberland* gives an inkling of the truth.
46. Witcombe, 'Cavalier House of Commons', 189, n 7.

XIX

THE GREAT ADVERSARY

'Lord Wharton . . . might lose much . . .'

PLOTS and rumours of plots, with their roots in the restless
politics of the past two decades, continued to trouble the
monarchy for several years after the Restoration. Although
most plotters were ex-New Model soldiers and either republicans or Fifth Monarchy men, the government did not much
distinguish between these and the mass of nonconformists
whom they even attempted to involve. After crushing the most
dangerous of the plots the government allegedly determined to
make an example of severity upon some men of high standing.[1]
Nevertheless, no great men were successfully implicated and
apparently only one was seriously threatened. This exception was—not surprisingly—Wharton. Also not surprisingly,
Wharton said nothing of this threat to von Spaen: he would
not wish to suggest that he was always thought of whenever
a plot was exposed.

It was in October 1663 that the government finally crushed
the widespread Northern or Derwentdale Plot which in its
long course was constantly betrayed and which collapsed
finally when the insurrection which was its aim amounted to
barely two hundred men, mostly republican ex-soldiers,
meeting in pouring rain in Farnley Wood near Leeds.[2] On 26
November a rebel prisoner, Captain Robert Atkinson, gave
information that Wharton, Fairfax and Manchester had been
acquainted with the plot.[3] The two latter disowned it and

1. A. Browning, *Thomas Osborne, Earl of Danby and Duke of Leeds*, Glasgow
   1944, I, 28.
2. H. Gee, 'The Derwentdale Plot', *TRHS*, XI (1917) 125-42.
3. *CSP Dom 1663-64*, 352.

no one gave them another suspicious thought: the Chamberlain Manchester was so far from his puritan past as to attend his royal master to plays which mocked puritanism, while Fairfax had rebelled against the 'Grandees' and the republicans of the Army he once commanded in order to aid Monk and the Restoration. The government sent 'stringent orders' for the prosecution of prominent men—Sir John Hotham was one suggested victim[4]—but nothing came of it save danger to Wharton.

The prolonged and serious attempts to implicate Wharton, and Wharton alone, can be explained most easily by his prominence in opposition during and since 1660. It was only a few months before that Wharton had aided Bristol and publicly denounced the overbearing and arbitrary conduct of the Chancellor's Cavalier–Anglican majority in the Lords. Moreover, Wharton had drawn and continued to draw attention to his old associations by supporting nonconformist ministers and employing men who had served eminent Protectorians. Sir Thomas Gower wondered, when the rebel prisoners first began to name 'great men', if Wharton might be one, although he saw that by such subversive attempts Wharton 'could get little and might lose much considering his wealth'.[5] Gower, the most vigilant of the Yorkshire Deputy-Lieutenants and the one who caught the most active rebels, was one whom Wharton in 1661 had hoped to influence through Sir Richard Onslow, but now Wharton was to Gower only a person whose carriage was much suspected. Wharton had recently made a journey into the north, a proceeding which was unusual and which in the circumstances aroused suspicion.

However, the evidence of this attack on Wharton is not only scanty but most confusing, with startling hints of a 'great adversary' attempting for some unknowable reason Wharton's ruin. It would simplify the problem if this adversary could be a Minister of the Crown made hostile by Wharton's political activities or cold-bloodedly choosing him as a victim more suitable than Hotham. Unfortunately his adversary is more likely to have been one of a group of Yorkshire magnates (the Duke of Buckingham, Sir George Savile and Sir Thomas

4. Browning, *Danby*, I, 28.
5. *CSP Dom 1663-64*, 313.

Osborne) in which case Wharton's real enemy was very probably an ostensible friend.

Wharton already knew himself to be endangered by rumours connecting him with the plot when Sir Henry Bennet, Secretary of State, wrote to enquire about a steward or secretary of Wharton (apparently Walter Jones formerly servant to Cromwell's Comptroller, Colonel Philip Jones) who had been committed a year ago and released on Wharton's entreaty. Bennet did not summon Wharton to his presence (as even Strafford in his pride would not) but his letter was probably intended to bring about an interview. Wharton was sufficiently impressed or—most probably—alarmed to visit Bennet the same day although so late that he had to excuse the lateness on the grounds that he was newly come to town. Unfortunately, Bennet had heard that Wharton had been in town a good while. He said the King had ordered the enquiry a fortnight before, but his delay in questioning Wharton, his inability to remember the suspect's name, his change of mind over the 'very letter of his letter'—that Wharton should send the suspect to him—and the earnest way in which he looked at Wharton all suggest that Bennet intended the interview as a polite form form of examination. If so, he got little change from Wharton, who while profuse in expressions of loyalty and obligation to the King, somehow neglected to tell Bennet either the name or the whereabouts of his former servant (an omission, however, which he repaired the following day).[6]

Wharton in turn got little comfort from Bennet, for although the Secretary assured him of the King's 'fair opinion', Wharton had to ask twice before he would promise to keep the affair in his own hands. This repeated request to a semi-Catholic ex-Cavalier whom apparently Wharton had never met before[7] suggests that Wharton already feared lest his affairs fall into the hands of someone more hostile than neutral. He already suspected that the rumours about him had been started deliberately; apparently the person he suspected of this was one who could see that charges against Wharton were followed up. Wharton passed on his suspicions when he wrote to his

6. MS Carte 81, 189, 195; *CSP Dom 1661-62*, 607.
7. When Wharton noted that Bennet looked earnestly at him, he added 'perhaps in his method', which implied unfamiliarity.

brother a few days later. A week later still Wharton was
certain ('by several circumstances and information from
strangers who knew not he suspected it before') whose hand
was behind the business.[8]

He may have been certain, but for a future biographer he
left neither certainty nor even a clear probability. Wharton
wrote a whole series of letters to his brother; and the drafts
of some with some answers and other papers, including accounts
of the trials and executions of more than twenty plotters, fill a
considerable portion of his surviving papers.[9] Unfortunately,
if understandably, his extreme caution made him name as few
names as possible: even Sir Thomas he addressed as his
'friend', and he referred to himself as 'your friend'. Still, some
things emerge even from such a morass of circumlocution:
someone of considerable power and influence must have
pursued Wharton, for although the King was allegedly
satisfied of his innocence, yet Wharton's servants were examined
and his visitors enquired into so that the highest and best-
informed, outside the Privy Council, discussed whether the plot
could be fastened on Wharton.[10]

How great was Wharton's danger in his own opinion—and
presumably in fact, since he was not without experience—can
be seen from his requests to Sir Thomas in a stream of urgent
letters. He wanted his brother to inform their cousin Sir Philip
Musgrave and to enlist the services of James Darcy, a 'party
manager' in Wharton's 1660 list, and some other of several
past or present Yorkshire M.P.s. These were to stand by in
turn at York while the plotters were tried and to act as need
arose; for example, they could prevent witnesses from giving
false information (in response to leading questions) by asking
pertinent but awkward questions about times and places.
Wharton saw no danger save in false oaths, but he claimed
that it might need a judicious friend to save his life and fortune.
Yet for all this his brother must keep these efforts private, for
Wharton must not seem concerned.[11]

He had explained his northern journey to Bennet as con-

8. MS Carte 81, 194.
9. Ibid 81, 191-4, 196-203, 211-22.
10. Ibid 81, 194.
11. Ibid 81, 193, 196, 194.

cerned purely with business (presumably that of his estates and mines): to Sir Thomas he described the unwarlike retinue he took of fifteen or sixteen women and children and only three men, apart from butler, cook and coachman. Such a train would be highly inappropriate for a peer allegedly considered for the post of rebel general. In view of Wharton's military record, it seems incredible that any plotters, however pushed for a leader, should have so considered him, but this claim by the King's-evidence prisoner, Walters, was one of the most disturbing items of news from Sir Thomas. Fortunately, another prisoner, alleged by Walters to have been the plotters' messenger to Wharton, denied everything. Later (in January 1663-4) Captain Atchison—a more prominent plotter—named Wharton, but this again was unconfirmed. By this time Sir Thomas Wharton had cause for anger in the slurs and slanders against his brother, whom however he could now assure that he had 'back friends' or defenders.[12]

It was in the second half of January that Sir Thomas referred to possible assistance from a person who had great influence (which he would certainly 'improve' for Wharton's service) with a merry gentleman who in turn was both as able as any to do Wharton 'good offices' and as versed as any in the examinations and business of the plot. Wharton's response was to refer again to the same fomenter of all 'the late discourse' about himself, adding 'the circumstances you hinted to me of the Imployment of his friend is [sic] considerable'; later he was not sure whether his brother meant that it was a real friend or his 'great adversary' who had such influence with the important and merry gentleman.[13]

It seems impossible clearly to identify the persons referred to in such tantalising hints. The Deputy-Lieutenant most active against the plotters in Westmorland was Sir Philip Musgrave, openly named in Wharton's letters. Wharton had for years protected his Cavalier cousin, who now in his turn was the puritan peer's good and unfeigned friend. From his activities and those of plotters and others we are led from the relative simplicity of political plots into a maze of possible or probable business or family connections, confusions or duplications of

12. Ibid 81, 216, 221, 250-2, 201.
13. Ibid 81, 203, 192, 196.

names, and local jealousies or even feuds. It may have been the prisoner Captain Robert Atkinson of Westmorland (first to mention Wharton's name to the authorities) who was in 1657 with Wharton on the Commission for Assessments for Cumberland—on which Wharton never acted—and it could well have been the same Robert Atkinson who in that year wrote to Wharton, whom he was soon to see.[14] This Atkinson's companion in 1657, when they apparently did some business for Wharton, was an Edward *Braithwaite*, brother-in-law to one of Wharton's puritan ministers, Francis Higginson. In 1663-4 it was through two Westmorland gentlemen named *Braithwait* that Captain John *Atchison* of Wensleydale—who gave the second information against Wharton—offered to surrender and make disclosures if assured of pardon: he should have applied to Musgrave who because of this improper proceeding (and perhaps his concern for Wharton) became increasingly angry with the Braithwaits.[15] An ex-Leveller named *Braythwaite* was made estate-steward by the Duke of Buckingham, whom he later betrayed.[16] A 'Captain *Atkinson*' returned safely to Westmorland boasting that only the King, Buckingham and the two real friends who went with him to London were privy to his release.[17]

This brings us to consider whether Buckingham could have been Wharton's 'great adversary'. Much depends, of course, on exactly what Wharton meant by the phrase: that is, whether he meant a great or powerful person who was opposed to Wharton, or a person not necessarily of *great* power, who had, whether on public or private grounds, a great aversion to Wharton. Some light might be thrown on this could we but identify the two members of 'the council above' (presumably the Privy Council) who particularly ordered Gower to make Wharton's agent and messenger John Gunter give security for

14. Nightingale, *Ejected of 1662*, I, 408; *Acts and Ordinances*, ed Firth and Rait, II, 1084.
15. *CSP Dom 1663-64*, 449, 451, 465. Presumably Atchison, if originally from Wensleydale (in the Wharton country) now lived and plotted in Westmorland (also Wharton country).
16. H. C. Chapman, *Great Villiers*, London 1949, 135.
17. *CSP Dom 1663-64*, 492. *CSP Dom* seems to confuse Atkinson and Atchison, not mentioning the latter. Gee ('Derwentdale Plot', 132-4) distinguishes John *Atkinson* and Robert Atkinson.

his appearance *in case Wharton should be questioned.*[18] Buckingham was not yet a great Minister of the Crown, but he was a great magnate especially in Yorkshire and the King's friend. As Lord Lieutenant of the West Riding he was the one most concerned in dealing with the plot, but though he showed energy in suppressing the rising, he showed relative leniency thereafter. In contrast to the Deputy-Lieutenants who were Cavaliers or sons of Cavaliers, Buckingham was son-in-law to Fairfax, and closely connected with the pseudo-Presbyterians whom Wharton led and defended and for whom he himself set up as patron: he even maintained friendly relations with republicans.

Buckingham could be called great, but if he was Wharton's adversary, it must have been on private grounds, and for such a postulate there is only the slightest evidence. Wharton felt he had a claim to some forfeited Wilton estates granted to Buckingham's father, but he had not obtained them, and Buckingham had been willing to regain his lands by marrying Fairfax's heiress. Wharton, in his interview with Bennet, mentioned his enemies and said Bennet would know on whose account he had them, implying a bond of sympathy or common interest which could refer to the various efforts for toleration in which the two were (separately) concerned. On the other hand it could refer to Wharton's defence of Bristol, the original patron of Bennet, whom he had advanced for the disadvantage of Clarendon. Bennet seems generally to have honoured obligations of gratitude. Wharton's requests that Bennet keep control of his affairs could have been inspired by fear of Clarendon, but there is no evidence of Clarendon's personal concern in prosecuting plotters. Bennet was by now a rival of Buckingham, against whom he intrigued, and although the Duke had been leagued (against Clarendon) with Bristol, he had so feebly supported the latter and so abjectly truckled to the Chancellor on the occasion when Wharton so stoutly defended the one and opposed the other, that a coolness might well have grown up between the two peers. Wharton might conceivably have needed and expected Bennet to sympathise with and protect him against Buckingham.

Sir Thomas Wharton had written that he knew of none more

18. MS Carte 81, 197.

versed in the plot than the gentleman who had been so merry in Wharton's house in the 'wooing time' of Wharton's daughter. In 1659 Buckingham (whose wit and gaiety need no emphasis) was a leading spirit among the younger Yorkshire magnates, which could bring about his presence at the marriage of a Yorkshire heiress even had his new connections, the Fairfaxes, not been old friends and neighbours of Wharton. Buckingham could well have been the 'merry gentleman'; in fact, it is hard to imagine who else could have been. If so, he must still have been *either* the 'great adversary' *or* that mysterious personage's friend—when Wharton responded to his brother's news, he mentioned the fomenter of all the trouble, and added 'you hinted to me of the Imployment of his friend'. Sir Thomas hoped to employ for Wharton both a close friend of the 'merry gentleman' and (through him) the 'merry gentleman' himself. Wharton later doubted whether his brother meant that a real friend, or Wharton's great adversary, had such influence with the 'merry gentleman'. This would seem to preclude the identification of 'merry gentleman' and 'great adversary' in the one person, but it is not conclusive. From Wharton's first reaction it could be taken that he imagined that someone who was a friend to both Wharton and his enemy could avert from Wharton the ill-will of a merry adversary. However, one circumstance militates strongly against supposing Buckingham to be the 'great adversary': Wharton was later for several years a close political ally of the Duke.

　Sir George Savile was in 1663 a young Yorkshire magnate, a Deputy-Lieutenant and on intimate terms with Buckingham. He may well have frequented the house of one who had been, by Parliamentary ordinance, his own guardian. Since his wit was even more remarkable than the Duke's, it would be tempting to cast him for the role of 'merry gentleman', but for the slightness of his involvement in the business of the plot. Could Savile have been the 'great adversary' of Wharton whom Sir Thomas (in his innocence) thought could be used to influence a more important 'merry gentleman'—Buckingham? If so, this could perhaps explain Wharton's doubts and the apparent cross-purposes of the brothers. The Savile family regarded Sir George's wardship to Wharton as a period of plunder and oppression, as Wharton well knew—he would remember the attempted proviso to the Act of Indemnity to retrieve the £4,000 spent on Wharton's Scottish embassy. Sir Thomas may not have been aware of this, and may have thought from Sir George's manner that he was neutral or even friendly, especially as Wharton claimed to have protected Savile's interests during his minority. Nothing in Savile's career or character suggests that he bore Wharton any grudge or that he ever pursued a vendetta; hence if Sir Thomas thought him friendly he was probably right and if Wharton thought him a great adversary he was very likely wrong. Yet Wharton was tolerably shrewd, and in such a matter—literally vital—could not afford a mistake. Like Buckingham, the Marquess of Halifax (as Savile was to become) was later politically allied with Wharton who, even when they took different sides, treated his former ward in debate with what seems almost exaggerated respect. This may have been respect for Savile's brilliance and oratory, but gratitude seems a more likely cause since the pious Wharton would not easily be brought to respect a man who by irreverent wit exposed himself to the charge of atheism.

Another Yorkshire magnate and Deputy-Lieutenant was Sir Thomas Osborne. In 1663 he was on intimate terms with both Savile and Buckingham, the latter being his patron. When Gower made Gunter give security for his appearance, Wharton's agent applied for help to Osborne, who said he would enquire into it when he reached London. This assistance, real or delusive, may have helped to create the misunderstanding between the Wharton brothers, which must surely have been connected with the close relationship between the three young Yorkshire magnates. At first Wharton may have thought that his brother meant that Savile would be used to influence Osborne—Osborne and Buckingham were the two most concerned with unravelling the plot, after its first stages. Later, after Gunter's application to Osborne for aid, Wharton may have feared his brother hoped to use Osborne to influence Buckingham.

Wharton's first reaction in this case is only understandable if Osborne as well as Buckingham had been 'merry' in Wharton's house, and this is by no means unlikely, for Osborne married into the same family (the Berties of Lindsey) as did Wharton's daughter in that year of 1659. This link by marriage could justify Sir Thomas Wharton in thinking—if he did think—that Osborne could be used as a friend. In fact, the two marriages make it rather difficult to accept that Osborne could have been the 'great adversary', especially as the future Earl of Danby always carefully nursed his family relationships to build up his political 'interest'. No evidence links him with Wharton's former bugbear, Richard Osborne. It is hard to believe that public grounds of politics or principles could make the client of Buckingham boggle at friendship with Wharton, but in his later career Osborne, in complete contrast to Buckingham, showed a thorough lack of sympathy for nonconformists. This feeling may have motivated him in 1663, and may have been apparent to Wharton but not to his less politically-involved brother. Any general dislike on Osborne's part may have been exacerbated, rather than mollified, by the marriage which Wharton successfully persisted in making between his daughter and the heir of the supremely Cavalier house with which Osborne was so proud to ally himself. One thing is certain, and perhaps significant: unlike Savile and Buckingham, Osborne never enjoyed Wharton's political aid, nor did Buckingham while he and Osborne were close together. Wharton's only contact with Osborne was to attack his government and to hound him in his darkest hour.

To repeat, it would be eminently satisfying if one could simply assume that the 'great adversary' was Clarendon, who had it in mind to crush his most outspoken critic. However, Wharton said he was confident of the justice of those in power *in London*,[19] and Clarendon cannot be made to fit the description of one closely concerned with the plot, and friendly with one who was a house-guest of Wharton in 1659, quite apart from the fact that neither Clarendon in his own memoirs, nor his biographers in their works, have a word that suggests any resentment, let alone action, against Wharton. For that matter, none of the biographies of the three Yorkshire magnates throws the faintest light on the question. In the absence of any better information, we can only assume—tentatively—that Osborne was, for some inscrutable reason, an enemy; Savile, in spite of the past, a friend; and Buckingham, in spite of similar interests and past allies in common, no more than a neutral.

19. Ibid 81, 221.

It is of course just possible that no malice was needed to connect Wharton with the plot, that is, he may have been less innocent than he claimed. He noted that:

> Robert A[tkinson?] of Westmorland knew little only was to command such a troop. John Atchison of Wensleydale knows much.[20]

This information he may have gathered from the reports of the trials. However the Deputy-Lieutenants, and Osborne in particular, excused their ill-success in implicating influential men by the latter's bribing or persuading the other plotters to remain silent.[21] Walters, the King's-evidence, alleged that when the plotters' messenger warned Wharton of two spies on him, he was answered that Wharton was 'too cunning to be catched'. But even Walters said they found Wharton was 'not to be dealt with', and Wharton pointed out that in twelve years he 'never did or would join with that gang' when they held their heads highest.[22]

It would not be surprising if both the plotters and the authorities thought Wharton disaffected, for his behaviour was far from circumspect. While Atkinson was denouncing him he continued to attend the conventicles so dreaded by Cavaliers.[23] The friends he entertained and the messengers and agents he used were such as to make his brother remonstrate with him because they might 'occasion . . . discourses' against him. Gunter was not only an ejected nonconformist, but also nephew to a Cromwellian Major-General, as well as being Wharton's estate-agent in the north. Wharton had a sense of loyalty to or sympathy for his servants, in spite of his own danger. Sir Philip Musgrave wanted another messenger, Richard Waller, kept in Yorkshire although he had good reason to go to Westmorland. Under pressure, Wharton said he would if necessary try to dispose of Waller to someone else, though he did not know how so helpless a man would fare when gone from him.[24] Perhaps it was as well for Wharton

---

20. Ibid 81, 213. In Wharton's own hand.
21. Browning, *Danby*, I, 28.
22. MS Carte 81, 221.
23. *CSP Dom 1663-64*, 484-6.
24. MS Carte 81, 203, 191; Nightingale, *Ejected of 1662*, I, 239.

that his brother, his cousin, and his former ally Darcy all stood by him effectively, and that the Duke of Ormond—a close friend and ally of Clarendon—chose this time to emphasise his friendship with Sir Thomas Wharton, insisting against the reluctance of Bennet and the King on the payment of Sir Thomas's arrears of pay for service in Ireland.[25]

Sir Thomas Wharton had told his brother that it was objected against him that he employed nonconformists, housed Mr Nye and Mr Dell and allowed a great number of dissenting ministers to frequent his house. This was no exaggeration by his enemies. Apart from the three already mentioned, Wharton employed, housed for a time, or assisted with money, at least a dozen—Matthew Hill, Theophilus Gale, Samuel Clark, William Taylor, John Howe, Cornelius Todd, Thomas Pickard, Anthony Proctor, Robert Bennet, William Cole, Samuel Birch, Thomas Gilbert, Humphrey Gunter and others. Some of these he managed to persuade to re-enter the established Church; others he established and protected as conventiclers. These and many others, who include some of the better-known names among the nonconformists—John Owen, Edmund Calamy, Increase Matther, Joseph Alleine, Rowland Stedman, Christopher Jackson, John Rogers, John Swynfen, John Dodds, John Rawlett, Samuel Hieron, Henry Lever, Thomas Rosewall, Lewis Stukeley, and Lazarus Seaman —were Wharton's correspondents for many years.[26]

It has been suggested that Wharton's patience must often have been tried by a 'somewhat mendicant tribe', and on the other hand, that their correspondence with Wharton, though mingled 'with a great deal of devotional matter', was 'good sound politics for all that'.[27] However, I have found no trace of impatience, and, regrettably, no trace of politics either. So far were Wharton's protégés from being mendicants, that they were often honourably and busily employed by him as tutors, chaplains, estate-agents, or even as marriage-brokers to inspect and enquire into possible candidates for the hand of his heir.

25. T. Brown, *Miscellanea Aulica*, London 1702, 312, 338, 340; MS Carte 81, 203.
26. Matthews, *Calamy Revised*, s.n.; Nightingale, *Ejected of 1662*, s.n.; MS Rawlinson Letters 49-53, passim.
27. Nightingale, *Ejected of 1662*, II, 1387; Carswell, *Old Cause*, 33.

One at least intervened freely and fearlessly to urge Wharton to give his consent to his daughter Anne's marriage with a penniless young man and to supply them with the fortune they needed.[28] He had some success, it seems, for Anne married the man, William Carr of Ferniehurst, a younger brother of her step-mother, the third Lady Wharton, but on the other hand it is claimed the indignant father in reprisal had the sacraments withheld from her on the ground that her disobedience involved a fall from grace.[29]

28. MS Rawlinson Letters 50, 10, 12 et cetera; 28, 29.
29. E. R. Wharton, *The Whartons*, 40. Quoted Stone, *Crisis of the Aristocracy*, 598.

XX

THE TIDE BEGINS TO TURN

*'they and their friends greatly increased
in influence.'*

In 1663 the punishment or persecution of the ejected puritans
had only begun. Wharton wrote in his autobiographical letter:

> However, as most of these pastors continued to preach in
> private conventicles, their reputation growing with their
> sufferings, in 1663 or 1664 heavy penalties were imposed by
> Parliament on the people who frequented their services.

He did not mention his own leading part in the unavailing
opposition to the Conventicle Act. For the debate in the Lords
he drew up a most detailed plan including every possible
argument or means of delay: first, to arouse hostility against
the pressure from the Commons, then to prevent the bill's
commitment by bringing up the Judges' opinion that the
statute 35 Eliz. c. 1, against sectaries, was obscure, and to ask
the Judges' opinion again. He and any possible helpers would
emphasise the dangers to the privileges of King and peers, to
gentlemen's family prayers and the Queens' chapels, to liberty,
security and Magna Carta.[1] As Wharton followed the progress
of the bill he must have noted with some bitterness the
Commons' rejection of all the mitigating provisos his tactics
had helped to win.[2] Even the Lords rejected a bill by which
the King could dispense with the Act of Uniformity.[3]

Wharton continued to von Spaen his account of the manner
in which the Cavalier Parliament enlarged the Clarendon Code
against puritan nonconformists who attended Conventicles:

1. MS Carte 81, 170. Much corrected in Wharton's hand.
2. Ibid 81, 157, 172, 182.
3. G. N. Clark, *The Later Stuarts*, Oxford 1947, 20.

However, as the people persevered (although many were punished, and not lightly) in 1665 Parliament prescribed an oath to be taken by the pastors with a penalty of six months imprisonment for those who refused it. All (except about twenty in the whole nation) obeying their consciences, refused it.

The real penalty for not taking the oath was a prohibition from living within five miles of any town. Wharton's notes of the debate show that he was the chief opponent of the bill.[4] This was natural enough. However, he was strongly supported by two former Cavaliers, Southampton and Lucas. Further support came from the ex-Protectorian Fauconberg and from a peer indicated by the initial 'C', but not identified. Another Cavalier, Northampton, and the ex-Parliamentarian Denbigh were at least sympathetic to them; and it has been claimed that Manchester and Ashley Cooper also opposed the bill.[5] The former probably did so. The letters 'Cam' certainly represent *camerarius* or Chamberlain, and although this means either Lindsey, Lord Great Chamberlain, or Manchester, Lord Chamberlain, the latter was elsewhere named by Wharton as an opposition speaker.[6] The alleged evidence for Ashley's opposition simply does not exist. The initial 'C' could be held to stand for Cooper only if it had not been Wharton's invariable custom to refer to his fellow-peers by their titles or offices, or contractions of those.

Wharton made the longest speeches for his party.[7] He said that the recommittal of the bill had been moved, seconded and thirded, with many reasons, which had been answered only by the Archbishop of Canterbury, himself answered by Southampton. The Primate charged that the nonconformists had emissaries in Holland, then at war with England. Wharton pointed out that there was no evidence for this, and asserted that the release of most arrested nonconformists 'tended to clear their innocence'. He also claimed they had in a body opposed the death of the late King, were loyal, peaceable and

4. MS Carte 80, 757-9.
5. Miss C. Robbins, who edited Wharton's notes. *BIHR*, XXI (1946-8) 221-4.
6. MS Rawlinson A 130, 56.
7. When his speeches were short, he so recorded them.

orthodox, and should not be 'made vagabonds and put into the case of Cain'. Wharton here confused in one body Independents who had petitioned for the King's trial and Presbyterians who had lost benefices by refusing the regicide Engagement. His chief opponent on this occasion, the Earl of Bridgwater, conceded that Wharton 'spoke as he thought'. If he did think as he spoke, Wharton had convinced himself of the truth of what was not true.

Though Wharton continued to agitate against the new penal code, he recognised that it was not as effective against the nonconformist clergy as had been hoped by the Cavaliers and feared by his own party. As he told von Spaen:

> However, it pleased the Lord (in spite of King and Parliament) to incline the hearts of many, and these not of the lowest rank, citizens and substantial merchants, to attend their ministry and hold them in honour. Seeing which the late King, moved by wisdom and clemency, thought fit so to arrange matters that very few suffered punishments according to the laws.

In his parenthesis, Wharton seemed to condemn equally as persecutors of puritans the Parliament and the King, ignoring the latter's early attempt to grant toleration. Perhaps this was due to resentment against the King's rapid withdrawal from that position followed by support for Clarendon, the stumbling-block, against Bristol, the zealot for toleration, and against the subsequent attempts made against Wharton by the King's Ministers, apparently unhindered by the King. However, it must be remembered that by 1686 Wharton's most recent and vivid memories would be of the renewed persecution of dissenters by the alliance of Crown and Tories since 1681.

Certainly Wharton was not content to leave it to the Lord's pleasure and the King's wisdom and clemency to protect the nonconformists. He either proposed or helped to draw up plans for a campaign to obstruct the administration of the Clarendon Code.[8] These showed how a friendly Justice of the Peace, especially in London, could avoid disturbing dissenters or nonconformists despite informations pressed on him, and yet avoid fines. He could waste time in questioning the credit of informers, have his servants deny them admission, or pretend

8. MS Carte 81, 161, 165.

sickness. If he had no witnesses to an interview, he could later perjure himself by denying the information and have an excellent chance of having a jury believe him rather than the informer. That Wharton even considered such unscrupulous devices is proof of his elastic morality in the service of religion. Clearly it permitted much in the way of means if they were justified by the ends.

Wharton's persistent and energetic opposition to penal laws against dissenters continued not only in spite of his apparent and perhaps very real peril from the Northern Plot, but also in spite of his real and possibly severe ill-health. This last is not only suggested by those absences from, and formal pleas of illness to, the House which so often in the past coincided with periods of political depression, but is also proved by the evidence of his private letters. Wharton missed the first fortnight of the session in March 1663-4, and was absent for much of April 1664. In the latter month he recovered from 'ague'. The strain imposed by the danger from denunciations may have contributed to that illness. He was absent again for much of December 1664 and January 1664-5; in the latter month he recovered from 'distemper'.[9] With the easing of the pressure on the nonconformists, Wharton seems to have allowed himself to give way more to his infirmities than he could in the heat of the conflict. His attendance was poor during 1666, and he was excused the House for all the session October-February 1667-8; but in March 1668 he began to attend again. His absences were not necessarily from lack of interest in politics, for an anonymous friend in the Commons informed him of the measures of the Lower House before they were officially notified to the Lords.[10]

Clarendon was at last gone, and most of the new Ministers of the Cabal—Ashley, Buckingham, Clifford, and Arlington—favoured toleration, from sympathy either to Catholic recusants or to Protestant dissenters. It would not be surprising if Wharton had attempted to share in some small degree in the triumph and power of these men. There are some indications of renewed or increased interest in public affairs, or improved health, or both. Sometime in 1668, Wharton unsuccessfully

9. MS Rawlinson Letters 104, 31; Ibid 53, 64.
10. MS Carte 81, 37.

attempted to take over from Albemarle, by an application from his wife to Albemarle's, some place or office.[11] He was again on all the Lords' standing committees in October 1669, and began to be appointed often to committees in that session and in the next from February 1669-70. This restoration of Wharton to the status he had formerly held almost 'of right' may have been connected with the changed position within the Lords: an attempt to pass a further penal law against the dissenters, although successful, met with opposition on a larger scale and in a more menacing form than had any of the earlier measures.

In March 1669-70 seventeen lords made the first considerable political protest of the reign. It was against the second Conventicle Act, and Wharton, who drew up a paper of objections against the bill,[12] was naturally among the protesters. Most of the others were also ex-Parliamentarians (or heirs of such)—Willoughby, Denbigh, Manchester, Delamere, Anglesey, Dover (formerly Hunsdon), Say and Sele, Clare, Holles, Montagu and Eure. However, some support for the dissenters now came from the breaking-up of the old Cavalier interest. Among the protesters, Essex[13] and Halifax were sons of Cavaliers. As such men became dissatisfied with the Court's policy, they showed their displeasure by favouring non-conformists. A clear example is another protester, Lucas, who had spoken against the Five Mile Act in 1665, and had made a violent speech for limiting the taxes voted by the Commons in February 1669-70.[14]

Notably absent from the protesters were Ashley and Buckingham, the self-proclaimed champions of dissent.[15]

---

11. Ibid 103, 243. The third Lady Wharton, widow of a Commonwealth Admiral, would have much in common with the wife of the former Commonwealth General, Monk.

12. MS Carte 81, 331.

13. No relation of the Parliament's Lord General, but heir to a Cavalier executed after the second Civil War.

14. MS Carte 81, 301; *HMC 9th Report*, II, 79; *Timberland*, 106-9.

15. 'However high Lord Ashley was to rise, he was never to break the bonds which united him to those leaders of Protestant dissent'. L. F. Brown, *The First Earl of Shaftesbury*, New York 1933, 93.

Clearly they sacrificed their principles (if they had any) to expediency, for they were still struggling courtier-fashion for the greatest shares of power. Wharton may have been disillusioned by this selfishness, or disheartened by the failure of even this increased opposition, but more likely he was reassured by the laxity of the enforcement of the laws against dissenters, concerning which he told von Spaen:

As a result, they and their friends greatly increased in influence.

Certainly, after the November 1670–June 1671 session and until after the session ending in October 1673 Wharton was not a regular attender of the House of Lords. However, he dined occasionally with the Earl of Arlington (his former interrogator Bennet, now one of the pro-Catholic members of the Cabal) and apparently helped Buckingham to draft a bill which aimed (vainly) at the 'ease and security' of Protestant dissenters.[16] By August 1673, he was even rumoured (incorrectly, of course) to have become a Privy Councillor.[17] In fact, that opposition of Wharton's which arose immediately from the Restoration had barely subsided before the beginnings of his second, and very different, phase of post-Restoration opposition.

It is just possible that Wharton may have had a hand in helping to launch the Declaration of Indulgence of 1672, but if so, it is strange that there is no evidence of it. Wharton would be glad to see a toleration, but was this the kind he would be willing to help launch? It was initiated by a Catholic Minister, Clifford,[18] and was (like that designed in 1662) to extend the right of private worship to Roman Catholics as it gave that of public worship to licensed Protestant dissenters; and it was promulgated at the same time as a war was begun, in alliance with the very Catholic King of France, to destroy the independence of the Calvinist Dutch in the interests, so far as England was concerned, of commerce. On the other hand, Wharton had an interest in neither foreign affairs in general nor in commerce, as is shown by their absence from his papers.

16. *Diary of John Evelyn*, ed E. S. de Beer, Oxford 1955, III, 564; MS Carte 81, 337.
17. MS Rawlinson Letters 51, 3.
18. Bate, *Declaration of Indulgence*, 143.

He disliked and distrusted Roman Catholics, but he had co-operated with Bristol.

On this point Wharton's 1686 testament is worse than useless: it confuses the issue. In it he wrote:

> From this in the year 1672, the King by a decree sealed under the great seal granted them the privilege of preaching, and of providing before a certain day places convenient for the purpose. In this it was declared that the Papists would have no privilege from it. My opinion then (in which I even now persist) was that such liberty would lead to the Glory of God and the building up of the church.

The claim that the Papists were explicitly excluded from any privilege was a perversion of the facts. Wharton either lied or deceived himself, and as no reason for lying can be imagined, we must assume that to him the benefit to Roman Catholics seemed so slight that his statement was no more than an exaggeration. In the same way Macaulay could claim that by this declaration 'the penal laws against Roman Catholics were set aside.'[19]

The reason why Wharton had no great part in pushing a design which he so approved may be a disinclination (such as he showed after 1648) to work with unworthy persons: half the Cabal Ministers were 'popish' and the others flagrantly immoral, and irreligious virtually to atheism. However, Wharton was to work closely with both Buckingham and Shaftesbury (Ashley) later. It is perhaps more probable that he was, as in the Interregnum, and in 1662-3, willing to accept benefits which he did not think lawfully bestowed, but not to have a hand in procuring them; 'but', he recollected fourteen years later for von Spaen:

> many in either House of Parliament, worthy champions of their country's liberty, feared that if the King were allowed to grant so much without consulting Parliament, he or his successor might be able to think of restoring Popery.

However, it is clear that he did not in 1672 fully share with those 'worthy champions' this fear of prerogative and the possibilities of a Catholic succession:

19. *History of England*, London 1880, I, 224.

by their importunity they got the King to revoke the declaration, nor did they labour less earnestly when they found the present King [that is, James II, in 1672 Duke of York] a supporter of that liberty. On these and all other occasions I took advantage of every opportunity to take up the cause of the Reformers (or dissenters as they were called) seeing which and believing me to be influential with them, the late King and the present very often honoured me with conversation on these matters. He who now bears the sceptre has indeed often said to me that he and I, moved by different reasons, had worked for the same ends.

Here at last Wharton's political testament justifies itself by explaining his actions and his fortunes: it becomes clear that Wharton's closeness to Cabal Ministers in 1673, and the royal favour which made it rumoured he would take office, were the result of his defence of the Declaration. Apparently until 1672 the King and his Ministers had forgotten Wharton's influence with, and prominent championship of the dissenters. Possibly Wharton's near retirement for much of the time after 1665 caused him to be overlooked, and this in itself may largely explain his lack of a prominent role in the launching of the Declaration. However, if the royal brothers now sought to repair an oversight, they were not successful. Wharton was to become increasingly suspicious that when the reasons for an activity differed widely, its ends probably were not the same.

XXI

WITH SHAFTESBURY
TO THE TOWER

'What Cooper designs Sawpit dares not oppose...'

IN the Lords, Wharton's almost lone stand against hopeless odds had come to an end by 1670 with the appearance in opposition of a numerous and vigorous group. In the Commons also the position had changed since 1661. There a group of about as many as Wharton hoped to influence in 1661 did indeed act together solidly and with constant resolution against the imposing of the Clarendon Code as late as 1664.[1] Its failure was due only to its being permanently and heavily out-numbered, but with the drift to opposition of some former supporters of the Court, and the steady infiltration through bye-elections of ex-members of the Convention and new M.P.'s of similar persuasion, the position of the opposition became more formidable. However, its aims were altered with its composition, and its leadership, probably never as solidly secured to Wharton as his paper hierarchy would make it appear, now passed largely to other hands. Wharton, in this new form of opposition, a 'Country' party rather than a 'Presbyterian', influenced a section, a puritan group, and apparently not even all the puritans who had been in his old 'Presbyterian' party. Some of the old 'Presbyterians' had even rallied to the defence of Clarendon in his final crisis, while the Cabal, in its attempt to introduce toleration, would have to count on the support of the dissenters' friends, the usual opposition, against the hostility to be expected from many or most of the usual supporters of the King's Ministers.

When Parliament met in January 1672-3 it was for the first

1. Abbott, 'Long Parliament of Charles II', 34-5.

time since the beginning of the third Dutch War. The govern-ment's lack of success in, and pressing need of finance for, its foreign policy gave the majority in the 'Cavalier Parliament', hostile to toleration, its power to wreck the government's domestic policy. By their insistence the Commons had the Declaration of Indulgence cancelled. The Houses then passed the Test Act, which barred from office all those who would not take the oath of supremacy, declare against transubstantiation, and receive the Anglican sacrament of communion: these provisions would affect all strict nonconformists and especially Roman Catholics. The Act drove Clifford from the Treasury and the Duke of York from the Admiralty. Shaftesbury, who had already admitted in the House of Lords that the Declaration of Indulgence was illegal, now suddenly attacked the foreign policy which he had so zealously prosecuted, and was dismissed from the office of Chancellor in November 1673. The secret diplomacy by which Charles II, assisted by Clifford and York, had secured French gold in return for promises to restore Catholicism, was now half guessed. No doubt this, as much as the failure to obtain toleration by use of the prerogative, caused Shaftesbury to change, but whether his pride or his principles (if any) were more offended, remains a mystery. Buckingham was dismissed in January 1673-4, and Arlington did not long survive his rival. Thus died the Cabal.

The 'Country' party in both Houses, whose 'Presbyterian' core had always opposed the policy of Anglican repression, now had in Shaftesbury a likely leader. The Catholics, still numerous in the upper House and smarting under the latest blow of the Test Act, were likely allies. Barely a year after his dismissal, Shaftesbury published a manifesto which made clear the great aim of all sections of the opposition: a new House of Commons to replace the Cavalier Parliament so immovable in its intolerance. He circulated copies of a letter, addressed to that Earl of Carlisle who had once sat in Cromwell's 'other House', in which were mentioned three other peers presumably linked with the letter's sender and recipient.[2] These were Holles, a leader of the 'Presbyterians' in 1648 and 1660, Fauconberg, son-in-law of Cromwell, and Salisbury, whose father, while a peer, had sat in the Commons, as had Fauconberg. The

2. Printed in Brown, *Shaftesbury*, 226-7.

antecedents of the five lords seem to epitomise the aims which were to be alleged against the party which was ultimately so well organised by Shaftesbury: revolutionary government as against Stuart monarchy, puritan oligarchy as against the alliance of Crown and episcopal Church, gentry democracy in Parliament as against hereditary aristocracy. Such aims could not of course be avowed, even if they were held, by members of the House of Lords.

Wharton received a copy of the letter early in February 1674-5.[3] Soon he was linked more closely with Shaftesbury than were any of the four indicated by that letter. Ranke wrote that in 1675 there was 'a society of confederate lords to which Buckingham, Wharton, Ogle and Shaftesbury belonged' who 'were the natural allies of the Presbyterians' led by Holles. The French ambassador frequently alluded to this group.[4] There is one obvious element of improbability in this statement, for Ogle was to prove as staunch a Tory as his father, the Duke of Newcastle;[5] but the old Cavalier's heir may have dabbled briefly in opposition. Certainly we should neither reject nor accept the statement out of hand; nor ignore it, as does every historian after Ranke.

After examination, it may stand, in a modified form. Wharton was not merely a potential ally of those called in Restoration politics 'Presbyterian': he was one of them, and one of their leaders, and possibly the most influential of their leaders. No doubt Holles and Wharton influenced different groups which had much in common. Co-operation between them would be possible, but the different and often opposing parts the two men had played since 1642, and especially the events of 1647 and 1660, would make a real union difficult, perhaps impossible. Shaftesbury may have turned first to Holles, as the Court may have ignored Wharton, because of Wharton's semi-withdrawal from politics for several years. That very withdrawal may have enabled, or even induced, the forming of a group around Holles, who, if a 'lost leader' in 1660, was certainly not a permanent loss to the puritans' cause. The close collaboration of Wharton with Shaftesbury and Buckingham and with a

3. MS Carte 81, 606. Dated 3 February 1674(5).
4. *History of England*, Oxford 1875, IV, 11.
5. G. E. C., *Complete Peerage*.

fourth peer—not Ogle of Ranke's statement, but Salisbury who figured in Shaftesbury's manifesto—was in two years' time obvious to the world. Wharton's renewed activity may have been in response to Shaftesbury's solicitation, but this would be merely the occasion, and the proffered means to do something in the face of a deteriorating situation. Sir Thomas Osborne, soon Earl of Danby, consolidated his power as first Minister by deliberately reviving the Cavalier and Anglican hostility towards dissent. Under the now strictly enforced penal laws, Wharton saw the conventicles he attended broken up, and he himself suffered the humiliation of arrest.[6]

When Parliament met on 13 April 1675, Wharton was at once put on the standing committees. That same day he and Shaftesbury, with eight others, defiantly protested when the Lords described as 'gracious' the King's speech which mentioned the necessity of enforcing the laws against dissenters. Of this little group, only one had been among the lords in Shaftesbury's letter of two months ago. This was Salisbury, related to Shaftesbury by marriage. Half of the ten, Winchester, Halifax, Clarendon, Mohun and Paget, were Cavaliers or their sons; the others were Stamford and Delamere.[7] Wharton that day made some almost wholly illegible notes, apparently of the actions of opposing lords such as Stanhope, Mordaunt, Darcy and the Duke of York.[8] The last was not long to remain a supporter of his brother's new Anglican government. Two days later the government introduced what has been called the Non-resisting Test Bill, to impose on all officials and members of Parliament an oath not to attempt to change the government of Church and State. Wharton made an extract from the Journal, of the long-drawn-out struggle from 15 April to 31 May, in which the House three times sat till 10 p.m. and once till midnight.[9] A partisan account, probably by Shaftesbury, was soon printed as *A Letter from a Person of Quality to a Friend in the Country*.[10] This summarises speeches against the Bill by Shaftesbury, Wharton, Halifax, Salisbury, Mohun,

6. *HMC Buccleuch-Whitehall*, I, 321.
7. *LJ* 12, 656.
8. MS Carte 79, 26v.
9. Ibid 79, 17.
10. Printed in *Timberland*, 129-60.

Holles, Grey of Rolleston, Bolingbroke and Winchester.[11] Only six of these were of Parliamentarian antecedents. Twenty other lords were honourably mentioned, of whom several were of Cavalier families and two were Catholics. Intentionally or by accident, the Duke of York and the Bishop of Rochester had seconded an opposition motion which Danby's followers defeated.

Wharton, described in the *Letter* as 'an old and expert Parliament man, of eminent Piety and Abilities, besides a great friend of the Protestant Religion and Interest of England', spoke at least three times. First he 'offered as a cure to the whole oath, and what might make it pass . . . without any farther Debate' the addition of the words 'as the same [the government of Church and State] is or shall be established by Act of Parliament'. As this alteration would have destroyed much of the point of the Bill, which was to prevent members of Parliament from attempting to alter the constitution, it is not surprising that the Court party at once rejected it. Next, on the Bishops' claim to a divine right, that is, to be of divine institution, Wharton asked them the embarrassing question 'whether they then did not claim, withal, a Power of excommunicating their Prince?' The Bishops were unwilling to answer, as well they might be, for this exposed the illogicality of their preaching non-resistance to the King. Other lords took up the cry, and received no better answer than that the Bishops never yet had done it. Finally, when Buckingham 'as Generall . . . coming last out of the Field', made a speech of 'eloquent and well-placed Nonsense'; Wharton, 'readily apprehending the Dialect', replied shortly and put an end to the debate. This is almost the only hint of a sense of humour in Wharton.[12]

The opposition made full use of the right of protest, and as a result brought that right under attack. The Court party voted that the reasons given for the protest of 26 April were a breach of privilege, and the twelve concerned seemed in danger of being sent to the Tower. However, no fewer than

---

11. Browning, *Danby*, III, 124-5, curiously lists Holles and Winchester as not named in the letter.
12. Thomas Gilbert, nonconforming minister, sent Wharton a 'piece of drollery' but apparently it was meant for one of Wharton's sons. MS Rawlinson Letters 53, 90.

twenty-one lords protested against this vote. Perhaps as a result of this incident, Wharton drew up a paper on the right of protestation, pointing out that the Court or Royalist party had made most use of it in 1642.[13] The staunchest of the opposition were obviously those who took part in all four of the protests during the struggle. There were ten such, half of 'Presbyterian' antecedents, the rest of Cavalier, including one Roman Catholic.[14] The chief supporters of the Bill were Danby, Chancellor Nottingham,[15] Lauderdale and some Bishops.

The opposition delayed the passage of the Bill until Parliament was prorogued. They never admitted a wish to alter anything in Church or State. Instead they claimed that to keep peers by an oath from sitting was an unprecedented invasion of their liberties, for that honour was so inherent it could only be removed with their lives.[16] The first part of this lofty argument was demonstrably untrue. Wharton and others could remember when Lincoln was kept out of the House for fourteen months for refusing to take the Covenant. The second part was in four years belied by those who argued it, when they used a test to exclude Catholic peers.

When the next session was three weeks old, the Court majority on 8 November 1675 ordered the *Letter* to be burned. Still the opposition grew in strength. They controlled completely a sub-committee on the bill regulating the trial of peers, and on 20 November very nearly carried an address to the King for the dissolution of Parliament. In this they had the assistance of almost all the Catholic peers.[17] These last were not very zealous allies, and were probably dragooned by the Duke of York. He was the only Catholic among the chief supporters of the motion, and only two were among the protesters.[18] Wharton carefully noted that forty-one lords, with seven proxies, favoured the dissolution and only thirty-four, with sixteen

13. MS Carte 80, 60. If not written in 1675, it must have been written when protests resumed after the Restoration. Published (so far as is legible) in *BIHR*, XXXI (1958) 211-15.
14. *LJ* 12, 665, 669, 671, 677.
15. This was no relation to the worthless Parliamentarian of the 1640s.
16. *LJ* 12, 665.
17. *HMC 9th Report*, II, 66, 79.
18. *Timberland*, 183; *LJ* 13, 33.

proxies, opposed it.[19] This rapid advance towards success was partly due to the organisation of the opposition by Shaftesbury. It was also partly the result of the continuing quarrel between the Houses, which had enabled the opposition to spin out the debates on the Non-resisting Test until the last prorogation, and which convinced some lords that an election was necessary to curb the insolence of the Commons. The same quarrel now caused another prorogation, this time for fifteen months. Wharton's summing up for von Spaen was:

> This Parliament (by which the King was supplied with more money than had been given to all his predecessors in the last fifty years) continued for fourteen years, but as it opposed his views not only as to the abovementioned concession of liberty but also as to other matters, (and its dissolution was eagerly awaited by the whole nation) he prorogued it for a year and three months, that is, from November 1675 to mid-February 1677.

At once Shaftesbury's eager mind seized on the unprecedented length of this prorogation. He pointed out that old but unrepealed statutes of Edward III and Richard II laid down that Parliaments should be held every year. Therefore, a prorogation of more than a year was illegal, and when a year was past, became a dissolution. A stream of papers reached Wharton and others, full of these arguments, objections to them and answers to the objections.[20] Some objections were unanswerable. It was pointed out that to say that a prorogation which sets a date for Parliament's meeting is a dissolution, is begging the question. In the end, Wharton was, according to his own account, convinced:

> Some jurists held that by this action of the King's, Parliament had been dissolved since by a standing law it was decreed that Parliament must be summoned every year, which would be impossible if it were not dissolved and another called. This view was maintained in some learned books published shortly before the time for the prorogation.

Wharton was by now a close companion of Shaftesbury. The two, with Lord Mohun, were noticed continually whispering

19. MS Carte 79, 19.
20. Ibid 79, 82, 84, 90, 92, 94, 96, 102, 104, 108, 110.

together during the trial of Cornwallis.[21] Apparently Wharton
on behalf of Shaftesbury's 'faction', attempted to persuade the
Duke of York to support the claim that a dissolution had
occurred. Shaftesbury apparently counted on the Prince's
Catholic group, although Wharton had obtained no definite
promise.[22] However, just before the next session, the Court had
a pamphlet published entitled *A Pacquet of Advices and
Animadversions to the Men of Shaftesbury*, which cooled the ardour
of sixteen of the twenty lords who, in the words of an anonymous
newsletter writer, 'were but 3 or 4 dayes before . . . in as firme
a league as could be', and caused even Shaftesbury to have
misgivings.[23]

Nevertheless, as soon as the House sat on Thursday 15
February 1676-7, Buckingham in a long speech argued that
they were not a Parliament.[24] At once Frescheville (on behalf of
his cousin Danby, who was amply warned of the opposition's
plans) moved to call the Duke to the bar. A debate followed in
which the Court speakers included Fauconberg, one of those in
Shaftesbury's manifesto of two years back, and two personal
enemies of Buckingham, the old Cavaliers Ormond and
Dorchester. Halifax, Winchester and the 'Presbyterians'
Aylesbury and Anglesey, though holding that Parliament was
not dissolved, yet thought that raising the question was either
commendable or merely indiscreet. No doubt Shaftesbury had
counted on the support of the Duke of York's Catholics. It has
been claimed that he received no support whatever from them,[25]
and although this is not strictly correct, it must have been a
severe disappointment that only two—Berkshire and Bristol—
spoke against punishment and none for dissolution. When a
parallel motion in the Commons, more cautious than
Buckingham's, had collapsed, Danby proposed afresh the
punishment of those who supported the dissolution theory.
Ormond moved that Buckingham should be questioned, while
the Treasurer himself proposed the same for Salisbury,

21. *Hatton Correspondence* (Camden Society), 1878, I, 136.
22. J. Macpherson, *Original Papers containing the Secret History of Great
   Britain*, London 1775, 79.
23. Browning, *Danby*, I, 218 n 2, 213 n 4.
24. MS Carte 79, 31-4, 37-44. Wharton's notes, and accounts made from
   them.
25. By Browning, *Danby*, I, 214-16.

Shaftesbury and Wharton. These three had been the only whole-hearted supporters of Buckingham in the five hours of debate, slightly aided by Holles and Bolingbroke.

Three of Wharton's speeches are recorded. First, he dealt with a point raised by Chancellor Nottingham and left unanswered by Shaftesbury, that the Triennial Act of 16 Car. c.1 (1641) implied that the King might prorogue for three years. Wharton said that this Act was repealed, so that nothing could be drawn from it, and that in any case its business had not been prorogations. He also asked whether it was for the good of the King's government to say that no laws bind the King. Next, Wharton answered the arguments of Halifax, with (in his own words) 'much respect to that Lord *as in reason he deserved*'. He said Halifax's precedents of the non-observance of old statutes for annual Parliaments did not touch the case, and asked if there were any precedent for a Parliament to be discontinued and to meet again. Finally, Wharton seconded Salisbury's motion to ask the opinion of the Judges. He argued that to admit they were not a Parliament did not mean they could not continue to act as a convention, citing the example of the Restoration Convention which made orders, addresses and committees. Fauconberg, formerly an ally of Shaftesbury but now a Privy Councillor, said he thought the Judges would desire to be excused giving their opinion in this matter, to which Shaftesbury replied with some justice that the Judges attended so that the Lords might have their opinion.

Perhaps it was that night that Wharton made marginal comments on his notes, answering some points with *esprit d'escalier* and against others putting an ironical 'Ha!' or even 'Ha! Ha!'. The next day the debate was resumed for two hours. The four lords who had been charged (with asserting and maintaining that Parliament was dissolved) urged in their defence that on three separate occasions it had been debated in Parliament whether the writs that summoned them were good, and no one had been questioned for debating it. Then Buckingham's original motion came to the vote, but was supported by only Stamford and Delamere[26] (in addition, presumably, to the four). The accused four were then ordered, by fifty-three votes to thirty, to withdraw, and then to ask

26. *HMC Rutland*, II, 38.

pardon of the King and the House for their assertions. They were called in singly. Salisbury, the first, was told that the House found that he had not asserted Parliament was dissolved, as he had disclaimed this upon his honour, but the House took great offence because he said the prorogation was illegal. His refusal to ask pardon of the King and the House was judged contempt, and as a delinquent he was committed to the Tower during the pleasure of the King and the House. Wharton was called in next, to his place at first (not the bar) and noted that he

> had the same words said by the Chancellor to him as to my Lord Salisbury and the same acknowledgement required which his Lordship refused to make saying their Lordships were witnesses, he had therefore before his withdrawing begged pardon of the King and the house (which [the] D[uke of] Buckingham had also done). The Chancellor required him to do it again, and his Lordship saying he had already done it, (after he was withdrawn again) the house judged this to be a Contempt, and that he should kneel at the Bar as a delinquent and be committed to the Tower during the pleasure of the King and the house.

Shaftesbury was brought direct to the bar, asked to acknowledge his endeavours to maintain that Parliament was dissolved was an ill-advised action for which he humbly begged pardon of the King and House, and on his refusal, similarly committed. When he returned to the House next day, Buckingham received the same treatment.

When Danby first proposed punishing those who claimed Parliament was dissolved, Buckingham had said 'this was hard, that men in that power should drive a thing so', and Halifax protested vigorously against sending them to the Tower.[27] However, it has been claimed that Danby was not merely vindictive in this action, but was emphasising the dangerously revolutionary nature of the collusion (or conspiracy) of the four.[28] There seems to be reason in this. In the second debate (on Friday, 16 February) the accused lords significantly pointed out 'that the Religion of the nation had at least three times been moved and debated in Parliament to be altered, and yet no questioning of them neither who moved or managed these

27. H. C. Foxcroft, *Life and Letters of* . . . *Halifax*, London 1898, I, 126 n 2.
28. Browning, *Danby*, I, 217.

Debates'. This was both a defiant reminder of Danby's failure
in the last session to pass his Non-resisting Test Bill, and also a
possible threat of counter-attack against the Anglican
supremacy. Collusion there had certainly been, and among
three of the four it continued in a way calculated to bring the
King's government into contempt. Inspired by Shaftesbury,
all save Wharton asked to have their cooks with them in the
Tower, and angered the King by this insinuation that they
feared poison.[29] Why one of the four did not do as his fellows
we can only guess. Impudence, which fitted Shaftesbury and
Buckingham like a glove, was hardly the wear for Wharton.
He may well have felt misgivings when made to kneel at the
bar, to which he had helped to send so many others, from
Strafford on. Often before in jeopardy, he had as often escaped
scatheless through luck, adroitness or powerful friends. Now,
in his old age, nearly forty years after he had first taken his
seat, he was caged.

Nevertheless, the collaboration which continued even in the
cage involved apparently all four of the prisoners. Hearing that
they talked together constantly in church, the House ordered
them to be held *incommunicado*, each guarded by two trusty
warders.[30] Meanwhile, some at least of the populace showed
pleasure at their imprisonment. Several bonfires were lit, but
gentlemen (of the Court, presumably) paid for at least one
of these.[31] A satirical poem lampooned them:

> What Cooper designs Sawpit dares not oppose,
> And George leads soft Cecil about by the nose,
> The first is a statesman, The second his tool,
> The third a d——— Atheist, The fourth is a fool.[32]

No one could quarrel either with the description of Shaftesbury
as the statesman who was the architect of the faction's designs,
or with the description of Buckingham as an atheist. However,
Salisbury though possibly foolish was not notably soft. In the
debate he had counter-attacked the Treasurer's supporters by
moving that those should be made known who had advised the

29. Ibid, 217 n 2.
30. *HMC Le Fleming*, 214; *CSP Dom 1676-77*, 564.
31. Ibid, 564; *HMC 7th Report*, 468.
32. *HMC Le Fleming*, 143.

long prorogation. If anyone led Salisbury, it would be his relative-in-law Shaftesbury, for Buckingham was by now a spent force, bankrupt in reputation, fortune and health. As for 'Sawpit', the future would show which designs of Shaftesbury he would further, and which he would not. If he was a tool for the breaking of Danby and the Cavalier Parliament, he was being 'used' to do the very things he would most wish to do and to have others do.

However little public sympathy was shown for the imprisoned peers, in their House several of their colleagues, mostly Cavaliers or Catholics, at once applied for permission to visit them, and on 20 March 1676-7 the Presbyterian Delamere, supported by two Cavaliers—Halifax and the staunch Anglican, Clarendon—together with a Catholic, Berkshire, moved their release. However, the only result of this multi-sectarian movement was that Delamere himself narrowly escaped committal for his pains.[33]

Wharton felt unjustly treated. He noted several points: that there was no new offence to justify the closer restraint, and that many felt that questioning the four infringed the freedom of debate, and was unprecedented when so many had argued on either side. He also held that the passing over of Frescheville's first motion of censure and the long debate which followed should be taken as rejecting the motion. Finally, he pointed out that the Lords declared the charges not proved against Salisbury and Wharton, yet committed them without hearing or defence.[34] Wharton at once took legal advice on both his committal and the further restraint. He sent the same queries to [some member of] 'the Temple', and to [some lawyer living at] 'Holburne'. To the first question, whether the Lords could commit during the King's pleasure, they both answered yes. The second authority thought Wharton would be free at the end of the session; the first, only if it ended by a dissolution or a prorogation.[35]

Unfortunately, the session ended in an adjournment. Wharton had perhaps regretted his defiance as soon as it was given: not only had he not joined in the sly insolence of asking

33. Foxcroft, *Halifax*, I, 217 n 4.
34. MS Carte 79, 39.
35. Ibid 79, 55, 53, 57, 51, 35.

for private cooks, but it was said he would have asked pardon, but was not admitted.[36] When a month had passed he prepared memoranda on whether a verbal submission might suffice for his discharge, and on a petition in which perhaps all would not join, for 'to Petition alone will be liable in this case to many Reflections'. Yet he feared if there were no submission the House might inflict further censure, such as a fine. If one or two wished to petition, in honour and fairness they should inform the rest who could join if they pleased. If all were to petition, they should conceal their purpose lest things occur to alter their case before its presentation. They could very well petition, for Parliament was now acknowledged by both King and people, and they should do so before worse befell.[37] Eager for his liberty and anxious about further punishment, Wharton had little time for loyalty to his fellow-sufferers. At one stage he was even anxious as he showed in a pleading letter to Colonel Legge, to have his own release arranged before Salisbury's, as if he feared the King had only a limited fund of mercy.[38] He was without doubt the first to petition for liberty. He addressed the Lords, pleading his age, the colic he suffered most of the winter, and his moribund son-in-law. The Lords referred him to the King, to whom Wharton pointed out the advantages of making a precedent of dealing with delinquents left to him and of not making a precedent of 'tossing back' a person of quality to the Lords.[39] The King, by a letter in his own hand and an order through Northampton, allowed Wharton a month's liberty at Wooburn, his house in Buckinghamshire.[40] Charles did not answer a joint petition from the others but Salisbury, Buckingham and Shaftesbury each had a month of freedom later.[41]

Back in the Tower, Wharton continued to petition, and he, his wife and his brother all wrote asking the help of such friends and persons of influence as Ormond, Sir Ralph Verney (a

36. *Essex Papers* (Camden Society), 1913, 101.
37. MS Carte 79, 49. All in Wharton's hand.
38. *HMC Dartmouth*, I, 26.
39. *HMC 9th Report*, II, 95; MS Carte 80, 810, 808. His daughter Mary's husband was William Thomas.
40. *HMC 8th Report*, III, 7; MS Carte 80, 810.
41. *HMC Le Fleming*, 136-7; Brown, *Shaftesbury*, 244.

Buckinghamshire neighbour) and Colonel Legge.[42] On 29 July 1677, Salisbury and Wharton at last became free, and the latter even had a pleasantly jocular interview with the King. Charles told him to 'go and sin no more', a phrase Wharton had first used to Arlington when the latter was defending himself.[43] A week later, Buckingham made his peace with the King, and Shaftesbury alone of the four remained a prisoner. When Parliament met on 28 January 1677-8, there was a design to recommit Wharton, Salisbury and Buckingham. Fortunately, the last was present in the lobby and, with the help of Berkshire, at once frustrated the plot by making his submission.[44] Early in February, Salisbury and Wharton submitted to the House and, on 22 February 1677-8, Shaftesbury did the same. He had to ask pardon both for his original offence and for his aggravation of it by vainly pleading his cause before the King's Bench on a writ of Habeas Corpus.

Wharton in his autobiographical letter said little of the debates of 15 and 16 February 1676-7. It is a little surprising that he said nothing at all of that part of its sequel just dealt with, that is, his imprisonment, considering his belief in its injustice, and the intensity of his efforts to secure his freedom. Nevertheless, his silence is perhaps understandable. Not many men got themselves sent to the Tower; even fewer left it unscathed in life or fortune. Although not at that time in any great danger, Wharton would be (at a time of perhaps greater danger) as unwilling to recall so unpleasant a period as he would be unable to forget it. What he did relate to von Spaen was a sequel of quite another kind:

> On the first day of the session this opinion was debated among the peers, and I voted for it, by which I somewhat offended the late King and the present. The present King [York] stated as much to a certain friend of mine, saying among other things, that I had abandoned the late King in the above-mentioned concession of liberty to the dissenters. However, I got a friend to inform His Highness that he himself at a certain place and date had cleared my character in this respect before the King and I acknowledged the favour above-mentioned (which he

42. *HMC Le Fleming*, 137; *6th Report*, 759; *7th Report*, 496; *Dartmouth*, I, 26.
43. MS Carte 228, 92; Lady Burghclere, *George Villiers, 2nd Duke of Buckingham*, London 1903, 329.
44. MS Carte 228, 90.

had forgotten), received as granted to me from himself soon
after the return of the King. He took it in good part, allowing
me to converse with him as usual and getting his brother to do
the same. This was quite enough for me, for I did not seek
honours or preferments (being neither unprovided nor greedy)
but all I wished for was a friendly reception from them, and the
opportunity of access in the Dissenters' interest to them or the
chief ministers. My one further ambition was to have portraits
of them and their Queens (as I have had of Charles I and his
Queen) and with these they have presented me painted in full
length and from the life by the best painters in England and
perhaps in all Europe.

It is difficult to winnow grains of truthful and useful evidence
from this rigmarole, largely compounded of *suggestio falsi* and
loop-holed with *suppressio veri*. Undoubtedly he offended the
royal brothers, but his offence had been more than voting for
an opinion: he had been one of the most obstinate participants
in two concerted attempts to break the Cavalier Parliament
and bring down the King's Ministers. Whatever the Duke of
York came to believe, it is by no means clear that the King was
convinced that Wharton had not abandoned him, and it is
generally agreed that Charles II was almost as shrewd as
James II was foolish. This may be evidence that Wharton
followed Shaftesbury's example in abjuring as illegal that use
of the royal prerogative (which had failed to bring the desired
results), preparatory to attempting to bring about a favourable
result by turning a Parliamentary opposition into a dominant
party which would then attempt to alter the laws concerning
religion, against the royal position, in the manner of the Long
Parliament. No doubt Wharton did his best both to retain easy
access to the seat of government to speak for the dissenters and
also to emphasise his loyalty and gratitude to the chief royal
personages by securing their portraits, making no attempt the
while to secure personal advantages; but it is not credible that
he had no further ambitions. So long as Danby continued
successfully to unite the predominant Anglican interest in the
persistent and bloated 'Cavalier' or, now, 'Pension Parliament'
by aggravating its hostility to non-conformity (Protestant and
Catholic), so long would Wharton be bound to have political
aims: the downfall of Danby and a general election as the
necessary preliminaries to the dissenters' toleration or comprehension in the established Church.

XXII

EXCLUSION AND THE
POPISH PLOT

'...*His Highness' personal favours were not equal
to the interests of Religion and liberty.*'

SALISBURY did not appear again in the Lords until November
1678 and Buckingham was seldom present before April 1678,
but from the time they returned to the House in February
1677-8, Shaftesbury and Wharton attended regularly, and
were active on committees. The foreign policy of Danby, their
great enemy and chief target, was aimed against France. Yet
in March, when Essex demanded an immediate war with
France, he was supported not only by Clarendon and Halifax,
but also by Wharton, Holles, Buckingham and Shaftesbury.
Buckingham and especially Shaftesbury had pursued a pro-
French policy in the days of the Cabal, and Buckingham and
Holles were ready, a few weeks after the proposal of Essex, to
enter into formal engagements with the French ambassador
for mutual assistance. There is no evidence that Wharton took
part in any such treasonable trickery: it is possible that he
knew of his confederates' actions, but it seems probable that
many prominent opposition leaders were never admitted to this
secret.[1] In the sessions commencing in May and July 1678
Wharton was on all the standing committees. He and
Shaftesbury were very often on other committees, and before
the end of June they again began to use the right of protest,
though supported by only a handful of Cavaliers' sons.[2] It has
been claimed that at this period the opposition began to prepare
the minds of the nation for the exclusion from the throne of the

1. R. Lodge, *History of England, 1660-1702*, London 1910, 146-7.
2. Winchester, Essex and Carnarvon. *LJ* 13, 260.

Duke of York. A pamphlet upheld the right of Parliament to change the succession. When reproached by York, the lords who had been in the Tower merely said their hack had exceeded his instructions.[3] This may be doubted. If Shaftesbury certainly and Wharton allegedly had abandoned the Court in 1673, York had abandoned the opposition lords in 1676-7.

Before Parliament met on 21 October, 1678, the informers Oates and Tonge had begun the disclosure of what is known as the Popish Plot. Their tales were readily accepted by the mass of the nation, and created an atmosphere of vindictive panic which was fully exploited by the leaders of the opposition. Soon the secret alliance with the French King and the treachery of a disgruntled former English ambassador to that King (Ralph Montagu) gave the opposition the second weapon they needed —a lever to unseat Danby. Exclusion and the depressing of the Catholic recusants with this time the simultaneous relief of the Protestant dissenters could now be attempted by the coalition which Shaftesbury was to lead for the next three years and more. Wharton was not present when the House first sat but on 23 October he was put on the large committee to investigate the Plot. Two days later the Lords ordered the arrest of five Catholic peers denounced by the informers. For the next few days the committee heard the narratives of Oates and a similar rogue, Bedloe, examined prisoners and read their letters. Wharton kept voluminous papers, wrote out one examination in his own hand, and added marginal dates and corrections to other accounts.[4] He also apparently reported a request from the Commons to expedite a bill excluding Catholic peers.[5] Wharton noted at least five expedients offered to prevent any increase in their numbers and to suspend their right to sit, but after a check on 15 November, the bill was passed five days later, becoming the second Test Act. Some ten or twelve Catholic lords were excluded, that is, all (save the Duke of York) who were not already imprisoned. Some of the

3. J. Dalrymple, *Memoirs of Great Britain and Ireland*, Edinburgh 1771, I, 45.
4. MS Carte 81, 362-3, 365, 366-79, 413, 416, 418. Richard Gastwell's deposition, in Wharton's hand, 453.
5. Ibid 81, 382-4.

Catholics later took the Test, presumably sacrificing their religion to preserve their privileges.[6]

Wharton no doubt thoroughly approved of this Act. He was one of the eleven who voted for the Queen's removal from Whitehall, and one of the five who asked leave to protest when the Lords rejected this demand. However, only Shaftesbury, Clare and Paget did protest.[7] Yet in some ways Wharton was out of place among the triumphant group headed by Shaftesbury. Almost it seems he had more in common than he suspected with those Roman Catholic lords he helped to exclude. On 2 December, 1678, eighty-nine peers took the new Test but several, through mistakes, had to do so again another day. Wharton's name was crossed off the list because he had not kissed the Bible. He said that he thought he had taken the oath in the way appointed for all such action, 'Tactis dei Evangeliis'. He also claimed that many lords knew that he scrupled for many years in this point, yet the Journal showed him as taking various oaths. His scruples were genuine. He felt that kissing had been accepted in Scripture for an act of worship, and he intended to worship only God. He found no support for his position. He had wanted the House to ask the Judges' opinion and himself consulted some of them including Chief Justice Scroggs. He thought of petitioning for what he called his right, but in the end he 'reserved' himself to the Bishops instead, solemnly declared he did not worship the book by his act, and kissed it. Wharton's concern over this matter was characteristic of him, as his ally's joke on it was characteristic of him. Shaftesbury hoped kissing was not idolatry, lest they must forbear kissing their wives.[8]

The Plot was now the opposition's stick with which they could beat the Court. The Catholics, so long protected by the King and wooed by the opposition, were now ruthlessly abandoned by both. The leaders of the opposition planned to destroy the existing government, in different degrees and with different aims. Some no doubt moved by sheer greed and ambition wished themselves to replace Danby and the other Ministers; others probably wished to reduce the prerogative or its use and

6. Ibid 81, 480, 561-7; *LJ* 13, 526, 434; Browning, *Danby*, III, 127.
7. *HMC 12th Report*, IX, 82; MS Carte 81, 387.
8. Ibid 81, 390, 396-8; *LJ* 13, 396, 398; *HMC 7th Report*, 471.

to increase the control exercised by parliament; others, to end the Crown's protection of Catholics and the strict hereditary succession which would make a Catholic King; still others, including Wharton, would wish to gain comprehension or toleration for dissent. Most Exclusionists would believe that there was a real danger from Catholic designs, even though many of their leaders knew that the tales of Oates and his fellows were fabrications. Danby was impeached, and saved from committal by only half-a-dozen votes in the Lords. Only half of those who voted against Danby protested when their attempt failed. Wharton was among the thirteen who did so, on both 26 and 27 December 1678. As many Bishops were against Danby as for him. Perhaps they were convinced he had neglected the danger from the Plot, but they should have taken warning when the Anglican–Cavalier Minister was attacked. Already the threats aimed at recusants, reputed recusants and suspected 'Papists' were dangerously arbitrary, vague and wide. Most of the Bishops present had voted to exclude the Catholics from the House, but soon the Lords heard that a man in Worcester claimed that no more than five Bishops were Protestant.[9] Leaders of the opposition were in the pay of the most dangerous and most intolerant Catholic monarch. French money enabled them to bribe members of Parliament to join in the persecution of mostly innocent Catholics and of an anti-French Minister on the grounds of his alleged collusion with the French king, and in return the opposition had to forward Louis XIV's foreign policy. The cynicism of these proceedings can never have been surpassed, and seldom equalled. By Danby's policy Charles II had raised an army to aid Spain against France. When the Commons sent up a bill for that army's disbandment, the Lords, remembering 1642, added a proviso reserving the King's power over the militia. Against this, Wharton and twenty others protested.[10] Nevertheless, in some of these matters Wharton may have had some doubts as to the wisdom or morality of his party's policy. He copied out in his own hand the speech in which the King said he could not pay the troops (which Spain wanted kept up a little longer) and asked his Parliament's advice. Wharton

9. MS Carte 81, 358, 405; *Timberland*, 231; *LJ* 13, 399, 436, 441.
10. MS Carte 81, 455.

also kept a copy of the proviso, with several alterations, and a copy of Ossory's speech which pointed out Shaftesbury's part in making the earlier French alliance and his use of the phrase *Delenda est Carthago* in referring to Holland.[11]

On 30 December 1678, the Cavalier Parliament dispersed for the last time. In January, both Court and opposition began to campaign for a majority in the next Commons. Wharton's eldest son, Thomas, had been burgess for Wendover since 1673, and was already so high in the opposition's councils that he brought up to the Lords the impeachment of one of the five Catholic peers. On 27 January, 1678-9, Wharton wrote from London to advise his son to stand for election at Malmesbury in all events. After this he offered the Earl of Bridgwater his support to elect the Earl's heir, Lord Brackley, as Knight of the Shire for Buckinghamshire. Brackley declined the honour, and Bridgewater decided to stand neutral. Hampden (the other opposition candidate), Shaftesbury and Winchester all urged Wharton to have his son stand. Wharton sent the news to his son before the day was out.[12] To discourage the opposition, the Court changed the place of election from Aylesbury to Buckingham. This had the effect of discouraging the Hampdens. On 31 January, Wharton again wrote twice to his son, with news of those who had promised support, and advice on who could stiffen the Hampdens. Wharton tried to have the election returned to Aylesbury, and suggested 'dealing' with the Under-Sheriff, which might cost less than twenty guineas. He warned his son against rumours of a mistake in the dissolution proclamation, which were spread by the Court to make the opposition relax its efforts.[13] Thomas Wharton and the young John Hampden were elected despite the need to march their voters through rain from Aylesbury to Buckingham. The Duke of Buckingham largely helped. Wharton's son Goodwin was returned for East Grinstead, apparently by the old Goodwin interest.[14] Curiously, there is no evidence that

11. Ibid 81, 385, 403; MS Carte 80, 678.
12. MS Carte 79, 185, 188.
13. Ibid 79, 171, 173, 175-6. Carswell (*Old Cause*, 54) attributes the letter suggesting a bribe to an 'election agent', but the sum was inserted in Wharton's hand. Clearly, the letters were by Wharton's secretary.
14. MS Carte 79, 179; Carswell, *Old Cause*, 55.

Wharton took any interest in elections other than those of his own sons; the great Wharton electoral machine was to be the work of his heir Thomas, the Whig Marquess. It may be that generally only those peers who had themselves sat in the lower House felt sufficiently versed or interested in its elections to meddle freely in elections, but to any such rule Wharton's ally Buckingham would be an obvious exception.

When Parliament met on 6 March, 1678-9, Wharton was put on the standing committees and later on the committee for all information about the Plot. This committee was at first dominated by the opposition, but after a week the House remodelled it to include an equal number of Court supporters. Wharton noted its instructions to examine all who asserted the innocence of persons executed for the Plot, and also all J.P.s and others who had not expelled Catholics from London.[15] The House appointed a committee of thirteen for a bill to disable Danby, who was now in hiding. For a conference about this on the same day, Wharton alone of the thirteen was not made a manager. However, he reported the state of the impeachments depending in the House since 5 December. He also made notes of a conference in which the Commons objected to the Lords' modification of a bill summoning Danby. They had altered the penalty for not appearing from attainder to banishment. Wharton was singled out to accompany such lords as had white staves (that is, household appointments) to ask the King for a proclamation for Danby's appearance.[16]

Wharton's name now began to disappear from the shortened lists of protesting opposition lords.[17] This was the period when the King adopted (but for his own purposes, and with no sincerity) Temple's plan for a revised and revived Privy Council, in which he gave places to many of the opposition leaders. Some of these were lost permanently to their former colleagues, and all risked losing their influence with the mass of the Exclusionists. Wharton was not among the new Privy Councillors, but he may have been discouraged from protesting by their appointments. However, he was on the committee for the Habeas Corpus Bill, and it was allegedly by his 'good

15. MS Carte 79, 180; *LJ* 13, 460 ff.
16. MS Carte 81, 574, 585; *LJ* 13, 508.
17. Ibid, 502, 549.

management or pious fraud' that it passed, for he was 'much too hard in numbers' for the Court teller. Burnet attributed this cheat to another peer, shown as having a sense of humour, but as it is very possible that some peers not shown as present were in fact in the House, probably no deception was necessary.[18] Nevertheless, Wharton must have seemed a moderate or possible waverer. On 7 May 1679 the King expressed great indignation to many peers, and particularly to Wharton, about the barbarous murder in Scotland of Archbishop Sharp, which signalled a futile Covenanters' revolt.[19] No doubt Charles wished to gain support for the Bishops. At the time, their right to vote in cases of 'blood', or life and death, was under attack.

This was because Danby pleaded a royal pardon, which might be held valid if the Bishops were allowed to vote. Wharton made very full notes of the debate on 6 May. The chief 'opposition' speakers were Shaftesbury, although now President of the Privy Council, Huntingdon, Buckingham and Wharton, supported by Essex and Strafford. The Bishops of Ely, Rochester and Bath and Wells, with Chancellor Nottingham and Lord Privy Seal Anglesey, defended the Bishops' rights, supported by Northampton, Gerard, Robartes (the former puritan) and the Bishops of Lincoln, Salisbury and London. Halifax did not speak strongly against the Bishops.[20] Wharton's two contributions were as usual short, and typically legalistic and disingenuous. When Buckingham claimed that the Bishops could not vote in their own case, the Bishop of Rochester replied that recently the Catholic lords had voted on an act by which they were excluded. Wharton said this was not so, as the Catholics voted nothing 'as to themselves or any other order of Lords, but that who did not . . . swear . . . should not sit; they may yet sit . . . and . . . so some . . . have done'. His next speech is the last noted. He brought up the matter of the year book 10 Edw. IV, 'where 'tis said that upon the trial of a Peer for his life in Parliament the Lord Steward is to ask him whether he be guilty or not guilty, then

18. *Life of Thomas . . . Marquess of Wharton*, 8-9; *LJ* 13, 552; G. Davies and E. L. Klotz, 'The Habeas Corpus Act of 1679 in the House of Lords', *Huntingdon Library Quarterly*, III (1939-40) 469-70.
19. *HMC Ormonde NS*, V, 88.
20. MS Carte 81, 561-7. So far unpublished.

the Spiritual Lords are to withdraw and cannot vote in matters of death'.

From 13 to 27 May 1679, there were three protests, against the decision that Bishops could stay in court until judgement was to be pronounced, and against the repeated refusal to reconsider the matter despite the Commons' demands. The number protesting rose steadily from twenty-one to twenty-eight. Wharton, who served on one conference, was always among the protesters.[21] The experiment of bringing opposition leaders into the government had not lasted long. Shaftesbury was replaced as President of the Council by the ex-'Presbyterian' Robartes, who for his loyalty to the Court became Earl of Radnor.[22] The aims of the opposition had grown and hardened in the superficial unity of their single unanimous aim—the exclusion from the succession to the throne of the Duke of York. The fall of Danby (who spent the next few years in the Tower) and the wrecking of the King's foreign policy had been the preliminaries. Now the 'Country' party or Exclusionists openly aimed at altering the succession. Their opponents called them Whigs, from the Scots Covenanters recently in rebellion, and those of them who best deserved the reproach probably aimed consciously at altering the constitution; it is a moot point whether the altering of the succession would have done that by itself. However, the surface unity of the Exclusionists did not extend to agreement on who should replace as heir to the throne the one to be excluded. Some supported the King's bastard, Monmouth. Shaftesbury, either through ambition or because his anti-Dutch record made it impossible for him to contemplate the succession of the next Protestant heir (Mary, daughter of York and wife of William of Orange, Stadtholder of the Netherlands), favoured or at least encouraged Monmouth's pretensions. Eager for this promotion, Monmouth came under his father's disfavour, but still enjoyed the turbulent support of the London mob. Shaftesbury and Wharton alone of the nobility chose to show friendship by visiting Monmouth's house.[23] This singular and sinister prominence of Wharton belies his later account to von Spaen, which suggested a

21. Ibid 81, 583-4; *LJ* 13, 570, 587, 594.
22. MS Carte 103, 223; *Timberland*, 247.
23. *Hatton Correspondence*, I, 205.

reluctance to offend the Duke of York, and no exceptional interest in Exclusion:

> The favours thus granted me by His Highness, I, as in duty bound, have frequently acknowledged. But in the year 1678 when the Popish conspiracy against the King and religion was discovered and published abroad by decrees from the King and enactments of Parliament, when too the lower House (as the House of Commons is called) observing that the attempts of the Papists were encouraged by the Duke of York's profession of their faith, determined that he should be excluded from the succession, I, following the dictates of conscience approved the attempt, deciding that His Highness' personal favours were not equal to the interests of Religion and liberty.

Wharton's eminence in the councils of the opposition appeared in another way. To prevent the danger of a charge of conspiracy, the Whigs' informer, Dangerfield, denounced the five imprisoned Catholic lords (with some basis of truth) for preparing a false 'Presbyterian' plot, in which they would implicate Monmouth, Shaftesbury, Buckingham, Wharton, Essex, Halifax and (of all people) Radnor, the former Robartes, but now a Privy Councillor.[24] Perhaps the fear of being involved in a conspiracy, real or false, weighed overmuch with Wharton. Shaftesbury and other peers presented the King with a petition for a Parliament, an action which Wharton had been one of the first to advise. Yet he conspicuously failed to support them, apparently on Anglesey's advice. It was said that though neither his hand nor his foot was with them, his heart was: some might think his heart had failed first. For his withdrawal, some said the Court would 'remember his Christmas box'.[25] This suggestion at least (that Wharton was susceptible to bribes, or that any in high places seriously thought he was) seems—considering his behaviour at the Restoration—beneath serious consideration.

By March, 1679-80, Wharton had recovered his nerve. At his house the malcontent peers held a great meeting, which by Shaftesbury's suggestion became the first of a series held at various lords' houses.[26] In June 1680, Wharton drew up a

24. *HMC Ormonde NS*, VI, 554.
25. Ibid, 556; *HMC 7th Report*, 496.
26. *Hatton Correspondence*, I, 223.

paper on the peace treaty with France. These 'considerations' were designed to alarm the nation by showing that the King apparently sought foreign aid against his own subjects.[27] However, when Shaftesbury formally 'presented' the Duke of York as a Catholic in June 1680, Wharton was not one of the two supporting peers, although his heir, and those of two other lords, were among the numerous participating group from the Commons. Wharton was not present when the House first sat in October 1680, but he was soon added to the committee for the Plot. On 13 November the Lords expunged from the Journal the proceedings which had sent the four peers to the Tower in 1677. However, although at least one recently-promoted Court peer voted with the opposition on 15 November, the Lords then rejected, by sixty-three votes to thirty-two, the bill to exclude York from the throne. Wharton was among the many who protested.[28]

Wharton served on a committee to distinguish Protestant dissenters from Catholic recusants. This produced on its own initiative a bill which failed to pass.[29] One can readily believe that this activity was dearer to Wharton than was any other proceeding but the time was not yet ripe for it. Many, perhaps most Exclusionists were simply 'Country' Anglicans of the gentry, still suspicious of dissenters, whom they remembered as republicans and whom they had recently seen leagued with Catholics for their common ends. The most that could be obtained for puritans was the non-enforcement of the Clarendon Code, but meanwhile the depressing of Catholics could be continued. The greatest business was the attack on the five imprisoned Catholic lords. Wharton kept voluminous notes of the proceedings against Stafford, the only one of the five who was tried.[30] He was one of the Exclusionist lords who dominated the committee for considering the circumstances of the trial. They met at once 'to show their zeal'.[31] When Stafford wished to refer to the Council books for what Oates had said, Wharton made his only contribution to the trial itself by meanly pointing

27. MS Carte 81, 614.
28. Ibid 81, 654; *LJ* 13, 39 ff, 666.
29. Ibid, 709; MS Carte 81, 650.
30. Ibid 81, 678-99; 704-18.
31. *HMC Ormonde NS*, V, 506.

out that the House had resolved that no books out of court could be sent for. It was the Counsel for the Prosecution who rejoined that the book in question was in court.[32] The Lords condemned Stafford by fifty-four votes to thirty-one. Voting was not quite on party lines, and three peers normally or recently voting with the opposition gave their votes for not guilty. Wharton listed points which were not clear, questions whose answers he did not hear, names he did not know and statements he wanted to check,[33] but there is no evidence that he satisfied himself on these points before he joined in sending Stafford to his death. In fact, the trial was the usual travesty of justice; it was recognised beforehand and it was made clear to the prisoner, that only a confession would save him. The Lords had asked the King for a general pardon for the prosecution witnesses, full enough to cover perjuries. No one had yet been acquitted from a Plot trial. When a month later a prisoner was acquitted, Chief Justice Scroggs himself was impeached. The King made no effort to save Stafford, although he could have influenced enough peers to do so. If they would have voted for the King against their consciences, who can say how many voted against their consciences to condemn innocent men and to prosecute the Plot?[34]

It has been claimed that after the failure of the Exclusion Bill in November 1680, the opposition in the Lords sank into obscurity.[35] Certainly after the trial of Stafford (1-3 December 1680) the protests of the opposition failed to muster more than twenty-two peers, although Wharton listed twenty-eight.[36] Very likely more were expected to protest than had the heart to do so. Reaction was beginning to set in. The crowd which saw Stafford die did not exult, but blessed him, and responded 'We believe you' to his protestation of innocence. A wise Whig would find this change ominous. Wharton kept a copy of 'the Loyal Protestants' Association' which expressed abhorrence of the practice of petitioning for a Parliament.[37] The 'Abhorrers'

32. MS Carte 81, 678.
33. MS Carte 80, 823; Ibid 81, 672.
34. *HMC Ormonde NS*, V, 505.
35. Browning, *Danby*, III, 122.
36. *LJ* 13, 738; MS Carte 81, 656-7.
37. Ibid 81, 602.

were soon to be labelled Tories, from Irish Catholic brigands. More than a Court party, and perhaps more than a revival of the old Cavalier interests, the Tories were an Anglican Royalist reaction against revolutionary Whiggism and Exclusion, in defence of monarchic government, the hereditary succession to the throne, and the episcopal Church of England. When the King summoned his fourth and last Parliament, it was appointed to meet significantly in Oxford, the seminary of Anglicanism and the former war-capital of the Cavaliers. Shaftesbury presented a petition against this decision, claiming that there the members would be attacked by the Catholics who allegedly served in the King's guards.[38] There is no evidence that Wharton counselled, let alone supported, this insolence. Thomas Gilbert, an ejected nonconformist, arranged lodgings in Oxford which he thought would be convenient and welcome to his patron, Wharton. These would be 'directly over against' those of Shaftesbury, so that the two 'might even have looked into, and called to one another' from their rooms. Gilbert was surprised and hurt when Wharton did not accept these arrangements.[39] It would seem that Wharton himself, like those former protesters whom he vainly listed, was beginning to lose heart or grow cautious.

Parliament sat for just one week, during which Wharton made fairly full notes of its proceedings. Attendance in the House was at first fewer than fifty. The Lords spent much time on the failure of their clerk to present a bill for the repeal of 35 Eliz. c. 1, when it was ready to pass on the last day of the last Parliament. The Commons chose the same Speaker as last time, who insolently told the King that 'they were not given to change'. However, the Court was so strong in the peers that only one-third of the lords in the Plot committee were opposition, and no fewer than twelve were Bishops. A debate on granting bail for Danby was postponed, and Wharton heard that the King thought the petition ill-timed. Wharton also thought that, in a debate which was a prelude to one on the Exclusion Bill, those lords proposing expedients by which York could be King without dangerous powers were fewer than those who felt the expedients were offered merely for

38. Brown, *Shaftesbury*, 278.
39. MS Rawlinson Letters 53, 101.

delay. Apparently many were glad to take up the business of exclusion instead of the King's speech. Wharton heard a rumour, which proved false, that the guards were doubled. He noted the Commons' proceedings on the impeachment of the obscure informer, Fitzharris, which the Lords debated until 4 a.m. on 26 March 1681. The Lords refused to accept the impeachment, and the Commons voted this a denial of justice. Only eighteen Whig lords supported, by a protest, the Commons' absurd defiance. Wharton was one of them.[40]

Despite their armed followers, the Whig leaders proved helpless and even looked foolish when the King dissolved Parliament. They could not call on London mobs, and the Royal troops in Oxford were enough to prevent any disobedience of the command to disperse. Thereafter, sustained by French subsidies, the King went on to cultivate the reaction in his favour, consolidate his government and power, and administer exemplary punishment to some of the Whig leaders. Shaftesbury went on to dabble in revolt, and escaped the block only to die in exile after a futile attempt to make his peace with the Stuarts. There is no evidence that Wharton after the Oxford dissolution ever again co-operated or even corresponded with him.

On the one hand it has been stated in the Dictionary of National Biography that Wharton took little part in the prosecution of the Plot and Exclusion, and on the other by L. F. Brown that the most vigorous prosecutor of the Plot, Shaftesbury, was ably seconded by Halifax, Wharton, Grey, Essex and others.[41] A recent biographer of Wharton's son, J. Carswell, has written that Wharton followed Shaftesbury from a safe distance, dealt with him through intermediaries, pursued a cautious, contradictory policy and always kept a foot in either camp.[42] These statements cannot all be correct. The first is palpably wrong, in that Wharton served regularly on all the large, and many small, committees for the Plot, and took part in the examinations and the trials. The second is clearly correct. However, of the other lords mentioned by Professor Brown as seconding the prosecution of the Plot,

40. MS Carte 79, 164-5; *LJ* 13, 755.
41. *DNB*; Brown, *Shaftesbury*, 251.
42. Carswell, *Old Cause*, 50, 38.

Halifax became the leading opponent of Exclusion, and Grey had ceased to protest with the opposition, even on a Plot issue, by the time of the Oxford Parliament. There was no necessity for a peer to support equally the prosecution of both Plot and Exclusion, and it seems that Wharton was never as interested in the second as in the first. The third statement is demonstrably untrue. Wharton often appeared with Shaftesbury, and in company with that arch-plotter showed sympathy towards Monmouth at a time when the rest of the Whig peers obviously felt it too dangerous. There is only one reference to his using an intermediary to deal with Shaftesbury. This was in 1677, immediately after the months spent in the Tower. A certain amount of caution would be excusable in anyone at such a time. While Parliament sat, or had a date appointed for another meeting, Wharton never deserted the cause of opposition. His consistency compared very favourably with that of several other lords, including some puritans and self-appointed champions of the nonconformists. When he drew back, all legal means of opposition had come to an end, while even public opinion was veering against the Exclusionists. Only folly, violence and hopeless, lawless revolt could be attempted by those who still persisted in active opposition, and in fact most of those who suffered death in the Stuart counter-revolution were guilty of one or more of those crimes or errors. Neither Wharton nor any of his sons had joined Shaftesbury's clubs, the King's Head and the Green Ribbon.[43] Moreover, although Wharton was at some period very intimate with Algernon Sydney and others implicated in the later Whig plots,[44] it is most unlikely that this was at the time they were plotting or alleged to be plotting. There is no hint that Wharton was implicated or that he had any fear of being implicated, yet, since he had been so much suspected in 1663, he would have been, twenty years later, particularly vulnerable to suspicion. No doubt Wharton was cautious, but it is unnecessary to call his caution 'extraordinary'.[45] There were great risks in conspiracy. Russell, heir to the Earldom of Bedford, was

43. Ibid, 50.
44. *Life of Thomas . . . Marquess of Wharton*, 9.
45. Ibid.

executed, Essex escaped the block only by suicide, and Grey saved his life only by betraying his confederates.

Wharton knew that by supporting Exclusion he had greatly offended James of York. Soon he was to write for von Spaen:

> However, it has been very often told me that he took this from me very hardly. Wherefore, since the dissenters (for the last three or four years) have been suffering the greatest severity of the law whilst I, who continued to support them, not only on every public occasion, but also in the privacy of my own house, have gone untouched, I can only attribute my immunity to God's Providence in the first place, and in the next to His people's prayers and the great privileges which the nobility have from of old.

Wharton may indeed have had all the protection he details. However he was careful to impose no unnecessary strain on it for the rest of his life.

XXIII

FEAR AND TRIUMPH

*'I hope . . . I . . . may be permitted to live
in peace . . .'*

GROWING caution in his extreme old age was probably one
strong reason for the fact that there is no evidence for any
political activity by Wharton in the four years before the
accession of James II. He had shared in Shaftesbury's fortunes
in the Lords and in the Tower and shared his counsels for
some time thereafter, but he had no wish and no need to share
his fate. However, as soon as the new King summoned the first
Parliament to meet since the Oxford débacle of the Whigs,
Wharton busied himself as usual in promoting the elections
of his sons.[1] The fact that he had several sons, of whom the
eldest and ablest was also among the most able of the surviving
Whig leaders, is beyond doubt another major reason for the
decline in Wharton's own activity. He could now safely do as
his infirmities prompted, and leave matters of State more and
more to the younger generation. He could do this the more
securely since Tom Wharton (the future Earl and Marquess
of Wharton under Queen Anne) was, although an energetic
and effective Whig politician, not rash in politics though
reckless in racing and debauchery. The heir of Wharton had
been among the seven peers and peers' heirs who with eight
others formally denounced the Duke of York in June 1680 as
incapacitated by his religion from all office. By the time
York was King, one of the seven had died on the scaffold, and
three more had narrowly escaped the same fate. Tom Wharton
made no appearance among those Whigs, persistently active
at the height of Tory reaction, whose meetings led to treason

1. He offered £10 to entertain voters in Cockermouth. *HMC Le Fleming*,
403.

and its punishments. Even so, his arms were seized after several fleeing Rye House plotters had been traced to his house of Winchendon, and the government considered arresting him.[2]

When James II's Parliament met in May 1685 Lord Wharton was present, but he was put on no standing committee and after 6 June he ceased to attend. During this time Monmouth made his futile insurrection. No doubt Wharton wished neither to take part in measures against his former associate nor to draw attention to their former association by abstention, or even by his presence. His heir, Knight of the Shire for Buckinghamshire as always since 1679, sat silent in the first session among the half-hundred of utterly discouraged Whigs, outnumbered ten to one. In the second session, in November, after the King bluntly assaulted Anglican-Tory susceptibilities by declaring his intention of retaining in his forces the Catholic officers commissioned contrary to the Test Act, the Whigs could help obstruct and oppose the Court, impudently reminding the Commons of Cromwell's rule by Major-Generals and playing on the old hatred of standing armies, strongest in the Cavaliers and their heirs. In this Tom Wharton took a lead.

Lord Wharton however had by this time decided to leave the country, no doubt for the reasons he shortly after gave von Spaen:

> When, however, a person above me in rank and even in age, (whose brother was councillor to the late and the present King, and in high favour with the prelates) was not long ago cited before the ecclesiastical court, and when the bishop of the diocese in which I lived was foremost in publishing an exhortation to the civil magistracy to prosecute Dissenters with all rigour, I judged that my turn was at hand. For this reason, and because for my infirmities, physicians recommended a visit to Bourbonne les Bains, I asked the King for leave to travel, which he graciously granted, and at my farewell wished me a happy and prosperous journey.

No doubt he did believe 'he should be much safer Abroad than at Home' as Tom Wharton's biographer was to write.[3] In August 1685 he obtained a passport from Sunderland, the

---

2. Carswell, *Old Cause*, 61.
3. *Life of Thomas . . . Marquess of Wharton*, 9.

Secretary of State.[4] Poor health may have been more than
an excuse: he was (erroneously) reported dead in October.[5]
He seems to have been reluctant to take the plunge, as well he
might be, for he was now seventy-two, and he had not been
abroad for fifty-five years. He was particularly careful to be on
good terms with the King and, later, just as careful to point
out to von Spaen how successful he had been in this:

> The King on his accession allowed me to kiss his hand, (a
> favour refused to some who had committed no crime) and on
> my petition and my wife's just before the time fixed for the
> coronation remitted in my case the usual homage (though this
> also was denied to others). A few days after the meeting of
> Parliament he gave me leave of absence. All of these I accepted
> as singular favours.

The remission of homage could be further evidence of ill-health,
real or alleged. The penultimate sentence of the above quotation
is definitely misleading: it was some months after Parliament
first met, and several weeks after the second session began, that
Wharton obtained leave, on 22 December 1685.[6] He may have
been spurred on by the onset of another English winter, but
more probably by the fact that Stamford was in November
charged with complicity in Monmouth's rebellion, a danger
also hanging over Delamere.

To account to von Spaen for his presence in Germany when
allegedly his doctors had sent him to Bourbonne les Bains,
Wharton continued what was now merely an apologia:

> On my way to Aix I discovered that the proper season for taking
> the baths was over and at once put myself (as I had before
> intended) in the hands of His Serene Highness the Elector of
> Brandenburg, (of all Europe the head of the Reformed
> Religion), choosing for my abode this Duchy the honoured
> rulers of which are known to be attached to that faith. Where-
> fore I hope that I (who am no law breaker) may be permitted
> to live in peace and enjoy on occasion the just protection and
> favour of His Highness the Elector.

The words 'as I had before intended' betray more of Wharton's
disingenuity than usually appears in this letter. His manner of

4. *DNB.*
5. *HMC 7th Report*, 499.
6. MS Carte 81, 731.

reaching his goal was as tortuous as the actual route: after asking an agent to apply to the Elector for him, he expressed great surprise when permission arrived for him to stay in Rhenish territories of Brandenburg.[7] It has been claimed that Wharton 'moved mysteriously round the German principalities at about the same time as William of Orange was engaged in organising them into the League of Augsburg'.[8] But the Elector of Brandenburg did not join that league, and Wharton, so far as I know, visited the lands of no other German prince. It is true that the Elector was a secret ally of William, and his successor furnished troops for the invasion of 1688, but in 1685 William had helped his uncle and father-in-law to suppress Monmouth. William's chief contacts, and probably most of his political sympathies, were with the Tories: Danby had arranged the marriage, vital to William's ambitions, with the daughter of James. On the other hand, William was a Calvinist, as were the Elector and his deputies in Cleves. William favoured toleration for Protestant dissenters, but not political equality, for to keep and increase his Tory following he must treat as sacred the Test Act which James was attacking. After the death of Monmouth, the rival would-be usurper of the English throne, there was no impediment to the Whigs' supporting William or to William's encouragement of the Whigs. It is just possible that Lord Wharton was concerned in some secret negotiations. He may have had a watching brief for the Whigs. Burnet, now a kind of unofficial chaplain to the court of William's wife, and in fact an emissary to William from the largely Tory opposition to James's attack on the Test Act, had been a great admirer of Wharton's daughter-in-law; he had spent much time in trying to reconcile her both with her unfaithful rake of a husband and to religion.[9] It might seem that such foreign diplomacy would have been more suitably undertaken by the scapegrace heir of Wharton, but that gentleman had an important role in the House of Commons, which might be recalled at short notice.

It was not unusual to ask a distinguished stranger—by way

7. Ibid 81, 772, 740.
8. Carswell, *Old Cause*, 62.
9. Ibid, 57-8.

of compliment—to write an account of his life or of his family's
history, and perhaps Alexander, Freiherr von Spaen, President
of the Government of Cleve[s] and Mark, when he received
Wharton showed a more than perfunctory curiosity about his
travels and his desire for anonymity. To satisfy that curiosity,
Wharton wrote what has been called variously his 'political
testament', 'autobiographical letter' and 'apologia' (for it is,
in some measure, all of these) beginning it thus:

> Most Noble Lord,—As I have had the honour of conversing
> with your Lordship on my affairs and my recent withdrawal
> from England, I hope you will be able to bear with me if I give
> you a brief recital of those affairs from the time I left the
> University, and especially in reference to Charles I, Charles II,
> and the present King, for what object your Lordship's wisdom
> and friendship may decide. Since, however, it is most fitting
> for me to live a private life I would not have this letter reach
> any hands but yours; with you I can easily take an unusual
> freedom.

It is left to our wisdom as it was to von Spaen's to decide
Wharton's object in writing. In the passages quoted in the
preceding chapters, Wharton apparently gave as much of his
own version of his life as he thought prudent or necessary to
account for his presence, in such a way as might have been
intended to make the reader think that Wharton was not
dangerous to anyone, neither to James, because of his gratitude
for the King's favours past and present, nor to William, because
of his spotless record of opposition. After this abbreviated,
bowdlerized and possibly slanted autobiography, Wharton
continued his letter to explain his wish to remain inconspicuous
in terms which strongly suggest that he felt he had something
real to fear in recall to England:

> I wish to live in private because I have it on the best authority
> that this law holds in our nation—namely, if the King com-
> mand the return of any person (even with no charge made
> against him) and the command be delivered to the person
> himself by anyone authorised to do so, disobedience entails a
> heavy fine under our law. However, in default of personal
> service the command is void. For this reason I hope your
> Lordship will forgive me if I do not subscribe my name.

This seems a curious commentary on his insistence on the King's kindness to him.

Nevertheless it is just possible that Wharton had some mission from James who for most of his reign intermittently and with varying intensity tried to gain the support of his son-in-law, William of Orange, for his avowed religious policy. One of the favours which the King gave Wharton before he left England was apparently a dinner at which 'the conversation was allowed to drift round once more to vague generalities about toleration'.[10] Any Whiggish activity on the continent would have increased Wharton's danger and his fears, yet he returned to England at the end of September 1686, and was there so far from being suspected of disloyalty that a rumour was reported that he came 'to do a job towards toleration'. Moreover, Wharton was not listed by Danby as a Parliamentary opponent of the King.[11] However, the man who reported that rumour to Wharton's neighbour, Verney, could not himself believe it. It was only after the King was satisfied that the Anglican Tories, in spite of their political and religious doctrine of Non-Resistance (to the Lord's Anointed), would never consent to the destruction (by the Roman Catholic Head of the Church of England) of their monopolies, political and religious, that he attempted to revive the co-operation of Catholics and dissenters. It is still a moot point whether James really wanted only toleration and equality for all religions. The weight of opinion was and is that such equality would soon lead to the re-establishment of Roman Catholicism with a diminishing hope of toleration or even survival for other faiths. Some nonconformists were won over by James and his advocate William Penn, whose friendship for the Catholic King is the strongest evidence that he could and should have been trusted. However, a Quaker (of a sect which orthodox dissenters abhorred as much as Catholicism, and which was quite uninterested in the possibility of comprehension in the established Church) was not the best judge of the situation. There is no evidence that Wharton believed in the protestations of a King who had anticipated the repeal of the Test Act by

10. Ibid, 62.
11. *HMC 7th Report*, 500; Browning, *Danby*, III, 153.

introducing increasing numbers of Catholics into civil and military offices. Wharton had co-operated with Roman Catholics before in attempts to win the toleration which both then needed, but a condition precedent for collaboration with the hated Papists by those who hated them most was that the balance should be held by a non-Catholic King as Head of a non-Catholic Church of England. Halifax warned dissenters that the Catholics hugged them now the better to squeeze them later. The majority of dissenters seem to have agreed, and Wharton probably needed no convincing.

Virtually nothing is known of Wharton's activity in the next two years, while William of Orange and his friends consolidated the vast coalition of opposition—Whig and dissenter and republican in part, but mostly Tory and Anglican and monarchist—and skilfully spread the wide net of conspiracy, in which the more radical elements were more equally represented. However, his seat at Wooburn was visited freely by those Bertie relatives who had been such staunch allies of their other connection, Danby, and hence no friends of Wharton—but Danby and Tom Wharton were now leading spirits in the conspiracy. Young Wharton collected a large store of arms at Winchendon, and used his time in London cultivating the friendship of officers and ex-officers. Some were in James's regiments of Guards, as was Henry, the second son of Lord Wharton. Two days after William of Orange landed, Tom Wharton led a troop of sixty horse (Buckinghamshire gentry and their retainers) towards the West. His younger brother followed shortly. The Wharton brothers and their officer and ex-officer friends were the first substantial support to reach William. With them they brought the first of the King's soldiers to desert—a troop of Horse Guards.[12] But old Lord Wharton was not to stir until James had fled and the peers in or near London took over the government, which controlled little more than the capital.

Now at last Wharton could show his colours. He was one of the first to declare for the Prince. When Clarendon urged an enquiry into the birth of the King's son, Wharton said with contempt:

12. Carswell, *Old Cause*, 69. A third son, the eccentric Goodwin Wharton, was arrested. Ibid.

I did not expect at this time of day to hear anybody mention that child, who was called Prince of Wales, and I hope we shall hear no more of him.[13]

'At this time of day'—the key to much of Wharton's alternation between activity and passivity lies in that phrase. Native shrewdness, improved by long and sometimes painful experience, made him a good judge of what was safe to say or attempt to do, even at the height of a revolution whose outcome was not yet certain to most. Further than this the speech is a measure of his ruthlessness and perhaps worse. It is true that even James II's daughters managed to convince themselves that their brother was 'supposititious', and perhaps Wharton had no great difficulty in concluding that the King had been guilty of a fraud against the constitution in violating hereditary right. For all this his behaviour, in the light of his own testimony to James's favours to him, seems to be the epitome of ingratitude. In fact, in spite of all his effusions of gratitude to the three Stuart Kings whom he knew, his behaviour to them was generally as shabby as their behaviour to him seems to have been generally kind. The darkest blots on his career seem to be his callous sending of Osborne, a vociferous railer against Charles I, into that King's household in his captivity, and his contemptuous attack on the son of Charles I's son, James, who himself had been Wharton's saviour from the consequences of the earlier ill action. In truth, by 1688 Wharton's cynicism seems to have been fairly well developed. Most of the peers, after thanking the Prince of Orange for his coming, signed his Exeter 'Association', but Wharton refused. He said 'with a sarcasm which hit most of the assembly' that he had signed so many associations that he looked upon them as trifles.[14]

---

13. *Life of Thomas . . . Marquess of Wharton*, 9; *HMC Le Fleming*, 214; Henry, Earl of Clarendon, *Diary*, ed S. W. Singer, London 1828, II, 235; cf Dalrymple, *Memoirs*, 187.
14. Dalrymple, *Memoirs*, 184.

XXIV

DISILLUSION AND DEATH

*'an old and expert Parliament man . . . besides
a great friend of the Protestant Religion'*

IN the crisis of the Revolution several possible constitutional
solutions found supporters. Those whose supporters were most
numerous were not necessarily most likely to be adopted.
James could retain power as King (without any formal
limitations beyond any lesson he might have learned); he
might retain the title, while a regent—Mary or William—ruled;
or, alternatively, the Crown could be offered to Mary, or to
William. It has been claimed that no peer was more emphatic
than Wharton for the elevation of William to the throne.[1]
This seems incorrect. Almost forty peers made two protests
when the throne was not declared vacant, but Wharton was not
among them.[2] On the other hand, he considered a scheme for
considerable limitations of the prerogative, involving far-
reaching Parliamentary, electoral and administrative reforms.
The scheme apparently emanated from Wharton himself: it is
endorsed 'Proposalls Ld: Wharton', and is in the same hand as
another endorsed 'Memorandums from Lord Wharton to be
discoursed with Mr. Hampden'.[3] The scheme proposed, among
other things, that commissioners appointed by the Houses of
Parliament would control the Treasury, Chancellery and
Admiralty, and that the Houses would also appoint the Judges,
Privy Councillors and Lord Privy Seal. No borough could be
created without the consent of the Houses. Another proposal,
that no newly-created peer should sit or vote in Parliament
during his life without the consent of both Houses, not only

1. *DNB*.
2. *LJ* 14, 113, 116.
3. MS Carte 81, 766.

would have limited the prerogative, but also would have placed the House of Lords to a considerable extent in subjection to the Commons. On the other hand, Wharton apparently felt that the peers should be protected from some forms of pressure: he proposed that no King or Queen of England should be present in the House during the Lords' debates. Perhaps he had resented Charles II's lobbying.

The paper is unfortunately undated. However, there is a proposition that the elections for James II's Parliament should be considered, to see if there were any grounds for annulling its Acts, which seems to be designed to deal with a situation in which James would be still legally King, in which case it might be expedient to cancel the lavish financial provision made for him for his life. Yet the union of England, Scotland and Holland is envisaged, which is not only an anticipation of the practical union of the three in the lifetime of William, and of the constitutional union of England and Scotland a decade after Wharton's death, but also clear evidence that, to Wharton, William's rule—immediate or deferred—was assured, and that the Prince of Wales need not be considered. It seems Wharton would have liked to use the opportunity afforded by the Revolution to effect a drastic alteration in the constitution. This would be possible only if James remained King, to provide the excuse. To strip James of all power and to ensure the succession of a Calvinist, and then on pretext of the dangers experienced from the Catholic James, to strip the Crown of all its powers, would indeed have been a master-stroke for a puritan Whig. But neither the strong-willed and rather autocratic William nor the conservative Tory majority would for a moment have considered such a revolution.

By another proposal, Sheriffs, J.P.s and other officials would be released from the necessity of taking the oaths of Allegiance and Supremacy and the Anglican sacrament, taking only the transubstantiation Test. When Wharton realised (as he must soon have done) the impracticability of his wholesale scheme, he reverted to his more normal and realistic method of concentrating on what was to him the essential point, the interests of the dissenters. He put forward a proposition for their relief and employment, pointing out the need for J.P.s and for officers for the forces which would have to be raised to reconquer

Ireland, and engage Louis XIV in the Netherlands. He again proposed that only the Test be used, and urged that the Conventicle and Five Mile Acts should be repealed, and that the Houses should then proceed to bring about a comprehension which would enlarge and unite the Church of England and 'indulge' such Protestants as could not be comprehended.[4] In the Lords, Wharton did his best to forward some of these propositions, and some parts of the more radical plan. He was on a committee for explaining the abrogation of the oaths of Allegiance and Supremacy. This produced a clause removing the need to receive the Anglican sacrament in order to hold office. With a small group of former 'Presbyterian' lords, Wharton protested twice at the rejection of this clause, but there had never been any real hope for even a partial relaxation of the Test Act. William had guaranteed its integrity as the price of Tory support. The nonconformists had had the choice between simply religious toleration under a Calvinist King, or both religious toleration and political equality under a Catholic—so far as he could or would make good his aims. They had made their choice, but that did not stop them from trying to improve the price they were to be paid for their support of the Protestant champion. However, Wharton was held responsible for the substitution of a new, plain oath for the old oaths.[5]

As for comprehension, there had never been any great hope of reconciling nonconformists with a modified Church of England, most of whose lower clergy would make no concessions at all. Of the nonconformists, not a few dreaded seeing their numbers reduced by the conforming of their less strict brethren. Finally, many of those of the higher clergy who had a more conciliatory attitude became 'non-jurors', choosing to be deprived rather than to accept as lawful the change of monarchs.

Wharton still probably hankered for a constitutional change reversing the effect of the Restoration. He wanted to have Clarendon called to the Bar for describing the Civil War as a rebellion, and served on a conference, 9 February 1688-9, on amendments to the declaration for William and Mary to be

4. Ibid 81, 752.
5. *LJ* 14, 149, 157; *Life of Thomas . . . Marquess of Wharton*, 9.

King and Queen.[6] Although he accepted the office of Privy
Councillor immediately offered him by the new sovereigns, he
soon ceased to attend the House regularly. For the session
beginning in March 1689-90, Wharton was not on the sub-
committee of privileges. He protested several times in May
1690, when the Lords seemed callous to Oates or ungenerous
to the City of London, and he was soon listed by Danby as a
member of the opposition. The Duke of Bolton, Wharton's
old associate, Winchester, was expected to convert him.[7] In this
same year Wharton's heir, Thomas, now Comptroller of the
Household, wrote a bitter memorandum for the new King
about the continued use of experienced Tory Ministers.[8] No
doubt Wharton felt the same disappointment as did his son.
However, the King later managed to form a coalition government, among whose supporters in 1692 were listed Wharton,
his two sons, 'and the Whigs'.[9] Probably Wharton was proxied,
for his last noted appearance in Parliament was on 30 June 1691.

There was no particular reason for him to continue the
strain and exertion of political life. An Act of 1689 had
effectively granted toleration to the nonconformists much on
the lines he had suggested in 1661, allowing them places of
worship whose doors must be unlocked during meetings, which
had to be notified in advance. A strong King reigned, who would
not easily part with any more of the prerogative, and whose
Calvinism was so clear that no trouble could be raised against
him on the score of religion. Moreover, the heir to Wharton's
title had assumed a commanding role in politics, keeping to his
father's political principles and steadily supporting his father's
co-religionists. This is not to say that Wharton and his eldest
son always thought alike on point of tactics. Thomas Wharton
unsuccessfully introduced in the Commons a bill for the
abjuration of the titles of James II. In May 1690 a similar bill
was introduced in the Lords. Philip Wharton spoke against it,
saying:

> He was a very old man, and had taken a multitude of oaths
> in his time, and hoped God would forgive him if he had not

6. Browning, *Danby*, I, 427 n1; *LJ* 14, 122.
7. Browning, *Danby*, III, 173.
8. Carswell, *Old Cause*, 78-9.
9. Browning, *Danby*, III, 182.

kept them all; for truly they were more than he could pretend to remember; but he should be very unwilling to charge himself with more at the end of his days.[10]

This has been called 'bland effrontery',[11] but it seems of a piece with his weariness and disillusion.

Wharton had long outlived most of his contemporaries. This would have made little difference had his career been set in the following century, but in the seventeenth century profound changes had totally altered the world about him. He had not escaped unchanged himself, but basically he remained the puritan his father's teaching had made him. A puritan peer after the Restoration was a fish out of water; after the Revolution, a living anachronism. No wonder the Tories sang, with callous but cheerful impatience:

> I prithee good Lord, take old Wharton away
> That young Lord Wharton may come in his place
> To drink and to whore and a thousand tricks more
> With a damned fanatical face.[12]

Old Wharton kept them waiting a little longer, but he made no more interventions in the world's affairs. No record has survived of his last years, but if his last recorded remarks are any guide, it is unlikely that he succumbed to senility of mind before the senility of his oft-afflicted body became too great for his life to continue. It ended on 4 February 1695-6.

Wharton's monument in the parish church at Wooburn called him:

> an active supporter of the English Constitution, a loyal observer, advocate and patron of the reformed religion, a model alike of good works and of a true and living faith.

The phrase 'reformed religion' was used by and of Calvinists to describe their faith. No one can doubt the loyalty of Wharton to Calvinist puritanism, or that he was its advocate and patron to the best of his ability, but the qualification raises the question of his ability to decide what was the best policy for those Calvinists who could not conform to the restored Church of England. This in turn raises the question of the nature, and especially the strictness, of his Calvinist faith: how far could he press Calvinist ministers to conform to a Church whose government, ceremonies and services were repugnant to them? And how far could he justify or practise with any sincerity, co-operation with the hated and dreaded Papists in order to obtain toleration? Toleration would be a blessing from God for the reformed, but a gross affront to God if impiously allowed also to Roman Catholics. On the first point he seems to have practised occasional, and urged superficial conformity, while admiring those whose stiff necks would not bow in the house of Rimmon. On the second point the evidence is conflicting, but it seems possible to resolve it into the formula that while Wharton in principle opposed the slightest concession to Roman Catholics, in practice he could ignore as if non-existent any minor relief given them if this was the necessary complement of a far greater toleration for dissenters.

Shaftesbury's *Letter from a Person of Quality* called Wharton 'an old and expert Parliament man, of eminent Piety and Abilities, besides a great friend of the Protestant Religion and Interest of England.' His piety seems to have been balanced by his abilities, especially the ability to accept the possible while still agitating for what was more desirable. However, this ability did not provide an answer when Presbyterians and Independents came to open warfare: then Wharton could only stand aside. Like many of the 'Presbyterians' in Parliament he would no doubt have preferred a national Calvinist church with coercive discipline reserved to Parliament, but his soldier allies in particular were insistent that no coercion must be allowed to threaten their fellow-soldiers of the sects. This made the bitter and irreparable breach in the puritan ranks. Nor did he apparently have the ability to see that in and after 1660, toleration and comprehension were not complementary parts of the one solution, but conflicting alternative solutions to the problem of puritan Calvinism unable to conform to neo-Laudian episcopacy. On toleration itself Wharton was no more logical than most of those seventeenth-century Englishmen (a minority) who accepted it in any sense or to any degree.

Although he entertained the 'notion' of liberty of conscience, anathema to the Scots–Presbyterians, this did not necessarily imply the recognition of a right to practise a form of worship other than that one form authorised and enjoined by the State. Toleration, in his way of thinking, was hardly an ideal, though it might be a practical necessity: a necessary evil when it had to be given to those whose doctrines were repugnant to pure Calvinism; a necessary measure of simple justice if it had to be obtained for suppressed Calvinists.

In one way, Wharton's career seems to point to the future, to the supercession of monarchy by aristocracy and to the changing role of the peerage. His relations with the leaders and factions of the Commons, his increasing wealth and prestige, his increasing need to electioneer for his sons, all point the way to the development next century of the oligarchy of Whig magnates, of whom his son was perhaps the greatest. On the other hand, in his pre-occupation with the advancement of religion and his basic lack of reverence for established laws and rulers, for birth or for wealth, Wharton harks back to the age of the Protestant reformers born a century or more before him, and themselves in some ways more mediaeval than modern or Renaissance.

Wharton came into the front rank of political leadership at two points of his career. In 1640 he was the first peer to have a hand in petitioning against the acts of the King's prerogative government, and the only peer to associate with, and jointly lead the malcontent Yorkshire gentry. This was an opposition which had momentous results. Wharton was partially obscured later by other leaders, but remained close to the centre of power for nine years. At the Restoration and for some years after, Wharton was the only peer to remain in open opposition on behalf of those who were to be known as dissenters, whose natural chief he became by the default of the other puritan magnates. His attempt to organise an effective puritan party in Parliament did not achieve his immediate aims, but it was an important factor in the continuity of opposition from 1628 to 1688, and provided a solid nucleus of 'Presbyterians' for the Exclusionist opposition in the Whigs' attempted revolution.

Wharton was no man of destiny, but his actions had perceptible effects on the history of his times. He was competent and industrious, generally cautious but, when his religion was under attack, obstinate sometimes to temerity. Virtually without greed, with little vanity and no personal ambition, he did not make the impression on his contemporaries which his abilities and worth might have been expected to produce. For most of his life he played supporting roles. On the few occasions when he took the centre of a stage deserted by the star performers, his lack of brilliance in oratory and his diffidence and dislike of limelight made the fact that he was for once playing a major role pass unnoticed.

There is no more to be said about him. To borrow for the last time his (last) words to von Spaen:

> It only remains for me to beg a thousand pardons
> for all the trouble I have given you.

APPENDIX I

COUNTRY PEERS IN OPPOSITION

ONE purpose of this Appendix and its lists of peers' names is to make clear and to emphasise the extraordinary quality of Wharton's prominence among the leaders of the opposition in the House of Lords, in his close contact with a group, not of minor *country* lords like himself, but of public figures either of great repute, great skill in business, or great wealth and descent. Another purpose is to show graphically how the purely *country* elements in both the original aristocratic opposition and its expanded form in the Long Parliament tended to melt away as the leadership was openly taken by the less *country* and more 'conspiratorial' elements.

Clearly there was not in the 1630s and 40s a straight division in which all 'country' lords opposed the Court, or the King could never have had a majority in the upper House. Firth, the only historian who has offered an analysis of the opposition in the House of Lords, accepted (*House of Lords*, 75) the significance of a 1641 printed list which put the lay peers in three categories: Caroline, Jacobean, and the rest. But he then equated the Court majority with all the creations of both Stuarts, together with the Bishops; and he also accepted (page 49) a contemporary view that in 1628 'the more ancient nobility' opposed the Court, or Buckingham. However, the facts make nonsense of the pamphleteers' assertions, on which Firth's view was based. Of eleven opposition lords named in 1628, four were ennobled, three promoted and one restored by the Stuarts—a total of eight out of the eleven, and this high proportion can be maintained. Of those who could be called opposition peers before the meeting of the Long Parliament, two-thirds, and of the Parliamentarian peers when war broke out, three-quarters, had been called to the House of Lords, or promoted in the peerage by the Stuarts.

Providence Island Co.	Short Parliament	Wrote Scots	Petitioned	At Ripon	(Clarendon's) 'Managers'	Protested	Present late 1642
Say & Sele Ct(f); p.col.	Say & Sele	Say & Sele	Say & Sele*		Say & Sele	Say & Sele	Say & Sele
Mandeville sCt	Mandeville	Mandeville	Mandeville*	Mandeville	Mandeville	Mandeville	Mandeville
Brooke p.col.	Brooke	Brooke	Brooke*	Brooke	Brooke	Brooke	Brooke (killed 1643)
Warwick pr.	Warwick	Warwick	Warwick*	Warwick	Warwick	Warwick	Warwick
(Bedford) J.d.	Bedford	Bedford	Bedford*	Bedford	Bedford	(deceased)	
(connected	Essex p.s.	Essex	Essex*	Essex	Essex	Essex	Essex
through Pym)	Savile Ct(f)	Savile	Savile	Savile		(prot. R.)	(R., but not trusted)
	Wharton c		Wharton	Wharton	Wharton	Wharton	Wharton
	Howard Ct		Howard*	Howard	Howard	Howard	Howard
	Hertford c		Hertford*	Hertford		(prot. R.)	(R.)
	Paget c		Paget	Paget	Paget	Paget	(R.)
	Dunsmore c			Dunsmore		(prot. R.)	(R.)
	Rutland c		Rutland*			(deceased)	
	Willoughby of Parham		Willoughby of Parham			Willoughby of Parham	Willoughby of Parham (R. in 1648)
	Lincoln p.col.		Lincoln			Lincoln	( ) rejoined 1643
	North Ct(f)		North			North	( ) rejoined 1643
	Bolingbroke c		Bolingbroke*			Bolingbroke	Bolingbroke
	Lovelace c		Lovelace			(prot. R.)	Lovelace, but R. and to King 1643
Another director	Robartes c					Robartes	Robartes
	Nottingham Ct (p)					Nottingham	Nottingham
	Clare c					Clare	Clare (to King and back, 1643)
of the Company,	Deincourt c					(prot. R.)	(R.)
	Southampton s					(prot. R.)	(R.)
	Bath c						(R.)
less concerned with	Montagu c						(R.)
			Bristol Ct(f)	Bristol			
			Mulgrave* Ct(f)			(proxy to Essex)	(proxy to Essex)
			Exeter* c			(deceased)	Exeter (deceased 1643)
its affairs, was:			Windsor Ct(f)				

the Earl of Holland Ct (p) .. ..

* One of the twelve signing the original petition

Salisbury Ct .. .. ..
Holland .. .. ..

(The only other Ripon lords were the Privy Councillor Berkshire who, though no friend of Strafford, showed no opposition to the King, and was a Royalist in the Long Parliament and Civil War, and Lord Poulett or Paulet, a country lord who also showed no sign of opposition and became a Royalist.)

Salisbury	.. ..	Salisbury
Holland	.. ..	Holland (to King and back, 1643)
Pembroke Ct ..	..	Pembroke
Northumberland Ct	..	Northumberland (nearly to King 1643)
Grey of Wark (Ct)	..	Grey of Wark
Peterborough (Ct)	..	Peterborough (deceased 1643)
St John c?	..	St John (killed 1642)
Fielding Ct	..	Fielding
Suffolk c ..	..	) rejoined 1643
Stamford c	..	Stamford
Dacres c	..	Dacres
Bruce c ..	..	Bruce
Bedford c ..	..	Bedford (to King and back 1643)
Hunsdon c? (sCt)	..	Hunsdon
Hastings c	..	(} tried to be
Leicester Ct (prot. R. too, later)	..	(} neutral
Newport Ct	..	(R.)
Cromwell c	..	(R.)
Thanet c ..	..	(R.)
Chandos	(prot. R. later)	(R.)
Spencer c	..	(R.)
Conway Ct	..	Conway, but R. and to King 1643
Carlisle Ct	..	(R.)
(These two did not protest before the war)		Rutland, Berkeley
(prot. R. only before the war)		Portland, (but R. and to King 1643)
(another rejoined 1643)		Herbert

KEY

Ct = Courtier
(Ct) = possibly Courtier
c = country
Ct(f) = Courtier (failed)
sCt = son of a Courtier
c? = doubtfully country, or heirs to peerages summoned to the House in the lifetimes of their fathers, presumably in the Court interest
p.col. = engaged in puritan colonisation other than the Providence Island Company's
f.d. = fen drainer (on a large scale)
pr. = privateer (on a large scale)
p.s. = professional soldier
(p) = wholly or largely dependent on Royal pensions
R. = Royalist
prot. R. = protested as a Royalist (against the opposition)

But here a new question must be asked: by *which* Stuart King were the opposition peers promoted or ennobled?

In the first (1628) opposition, three out of four of the Stuart peers were Jacobean, as were four out of five of the Stuart-ennobled peers at Westminster in the first civil war—that is, more than half the Parliamentarian peers were Jacobean creations. And examination of the list printed in 1641, which counted thirty-eight Jacobean and forty-four Caroline peers, shows a similar result. Out of forty-four Caroline creations, thirty-five fought for the King to whom they owed their titles, and only half-a-dozen against him. By contrast, only ten of the thirty-eight Jacobean peers were Royalist, and sixteen Parliamentarian. This strange division existed also in the opposition during and after the Short Parliament and suggests that one cause of noble opposition could be a widespread discontent among the recipients of James's favour against a King who gave favours to others.

Firth equated the nucleus of opposition among the peers before the Long Parliament with the survivors of the twelve original petitioners for a Parliament; five of the twelve had soon died or abandoned the opposition, but to the remaining seven were gathered recruits during the sessions of the Long Parliament. Further analysis does not support this view.

The materials for an analysis of the pre-Long Parliament opposition among the peers are three groups of different sizes which appear at different times. Twenty-one peers signed various copies of the petition. Before that, twenty-five opposed the King in the Short Parliament; after the petition, sixteen 'popular' lords (none friendly, or even civil, to Strafford) negotiated at Ripon. These groups overlap considerably but (omitting two Ripon lords, who left no evidence of opposition) they total thirty-one. Present almost to a man in all three groups is a smaller group—not Firth's seven surviving petitioners but the seven lords who wrote to encourage the Scots to invade England.

None of these seven—Essex, Warwick, Say and Sele, Mandeville, Brooke, Bedford and Savile—was truly *country* by the definition given in Chapter IV. Essex was a professional soldier, who commanded the King's army in the first Scots war, and whom Clarendon considered could have been bound to the King's interest by generous treatment and employment: even after the second Scots war, he accepted office from the King. Warwick (the brother of a great courtier and favourite, Holland), Say and Sele, Mandeville and Brooke—the Providence Island Company lords—were engaged in private war, colonisation and constitution-making for the New England colonies. Bedford was connected with the Company and, in addition, the head of the vast fen-draining enterprise. Mandeville was the son of a Minister of the Crown, and had been called to the Lords in his father's lifetime as a Court peer. Say and Sele was—as well as being a 'Company' lord—a 'failed' politician, as was Savile. The former had tried to rise through Buckingham but had proved too haughty to please that favourite; the second was the bitter and disappointed rival of Strafford.

In addition to these seven, there were eighteen other lords in the Short Parliament's opposition. Fourteen or fifteen of these eighteen were *country*. Two-thirds (all but eight) of the Short Parliament's twenty-five opposition lords account for all but four of the twenty-one lords who petitioned for a Parliament, but seven of the eight who didn't petition were *country*, while of the four opposition recruits (lords who had *not* opposed the Court in the Short Parliament but who petitioned for a new Parliament) only one was *country*.

Of the sixteen 'popular' lords at Ripon, only eleven had petitioned for a Parliament, and of the ten petitioners who were not sent to Ripon, six were *country*, three were failed, elderly ex-Courtiers, and the tenth, Say and Sele, would have been sent to Ripon but for illness. To make up for their absence, the Ripon lords were made up to sixteen by the addition of only one *country* lord from the Short Parliament's opposition, one other *country* lord, and no fewer than three courtiers, Privy Councillors no less, of whom two who were Royal favourites were real recruits to the opposition.

This completes the analysis of the thirty-one peers in opposition during and after the Short Parliament. Of these thirty-one, nine were not (apparently) in opposition from the meeting of the Long Parliament, and of these nine, seven were *country*.

The opposition gained twenty-one recruits in the Long

Parliament who registered protests against votes of the Lords during the second session. Only eleven of these twenty-one were *country*. The twenty-one recruits were soon considerably reduced. Of their eleven *country* lords, four became Royalists before the war and another tried to remain neutral. Another *country* recruit temporarily deserted to the King in 1643, by which time the opposition in the Lords had lost, in all, ten out of the twenty recruits. And, in addition, the pre-Long Parliament opposition had lost by death three lords, of whom two were *country*, and to the King's interest another two *country* lords (one permanently), making in all a total loss of no fewer than twenty, of whom *country* lords were a majority.

Finally, of the small group of three lords who never petitioned or protested in the House, but who stayed at (or returned to) Westminster during the war, two were *country*.

The whole range of opposition among the pre-war nobility comprises fifty-five persons, representing only fifty-two permanent peerages, as there were two Bedfords and two Rutlands as well as both Bolingbroke and his heir, St John.

APPENDIX II

THE OSBORNE AFFAIR

THE purposes of this fuller investigation of the Osborne affair are three: first, to refute a number of inaccuracies which are almost all that history has so far related of it; secondly, to expose the full complexity of the evidence and the conflicts and contradictions within it; and, thirdly, to consider how far, and in what ways, there could have been truth in Osborne's assertions. It might be thought either that the charges made against Wharton at the end of the fourth paragraph of Chapter XII are somewhat harsh and not justified by what is (or can properly be) shown in that chapter, or that a further elaboration of an alleged plot in which no one claimed Wharton bore a leading role adds nothing to the general effect of Chapter XII. I believe that the nature of the evidence, the fore-knowledge and violent actions of Hammond and Rolph, and the circumstances surrounding the affair, show the need to accept that there was probably a good deal of dangerous truth behind Osborne's tale, and that this probability (if not certainty) must have been realised at the time by Wharton himself. This surely makes Wharton's actions more reprehensible, and justifies a strong condemnation of them. However, this Appendix is not the place for an elaboration of the connection between the Osborne affair and the relations between the two Houses and their negotiations with Charles I: that can be left for a work on which I am now engaged, dealing with the politics of the House of Lords in this period.

The publishing of Osborne's letters had on the public what Hillier calls 'a surprising effect' and the contemporary news-papers and pamphlets reflect the great stir it made until the acquittal of Rolph early in September 1648. No surprise seems called for since the affair broke during a popular reaction in the King's favour. Moreover, Hillier himself called Osborne's statements 'plausible', the tale 'well connected, and in many points capable of corroboration by contemporary authorities', and the proposition 'one to which many persons of note attached to the army were known to be favourable'.

In 1648, no doubt, men believed or disbelieved Osborne largely according to their politics. For us the matter is not, or should not be, so simple. Much more surprising than the violence of the public reaction is the fact that later historians have both minimised that reaction and the importance of the affair, and dismissed the possibility of any truth in Osborne's charges with contempt, or with disingenuousness, or with silence. Gardiner referred to the affair only in a footnote, where he accepted Hammond's version of the discovery of the escape, with no mention of any discrepancies. He was inclined 'to think with Mr. Hillier' that Osborne's accusation was 'a pure invention . . . to save himself', a very considerable misrepresentation of Hillier's opinions. Carlyle, with typical contempt for both Royalists and the truth, wrote only that:

> one Osborne, a distracted King's flunky, had written accusing Major Rolph, a soldier under Hammond, of attempting to poison Charles

contriving to get three serious inaccuracies into two lines. Rolph was accused of trying to remove the King to 'dispose of' him, after Hammond had refused to poison him. Osborne may have been malicious, but he was obviously not distracted; nor was he a flunky, but gentleman-usher in office and 'son of Thomas Osborne, Esquire, a gentleman of old family', himself probably the son of Sir John Osborne of Chicksands, Bedfordshire. Firth covers the history of April, May and June 1648 on one page on which there is no mention of the affair.

In his letter to Wharton, Osborne claimed three things: that letters to Hammond from the Army urged the removal of the King by poison or any other means; that Rolph proposed they should remove the King to a place of secrecy where they might dispose of his person as they thought fit; that Rolph said it could be done without the knowledge of Hammond, who would not agree because he would lose the profit from the allowance for the King. Hammond and Rolph concurred in denying that there was any truth in Osborne's charges; Hammond and Wharton concurred in denying that there could be any danger

to the King. But the evidence of Hammond and Rolph conflicted on several points (on some of which Rolph and Osborne
agreed) and the evidence of Wharton and Rolph conflicted
on other points.

Rolph said that Osborne after his flight hid for three days;
Osborne that he stayed three days 'or thereabouts' in the Isle;
Wharton by 1660 had servants and relatives ready to testify
that they had heard Osborne say he hid for eight days in the
Isle. Wharton had a reason for trying to prove a lengthy stay,
while Rolph had no reason to lie on this point unless to
contradict Osborne and support a political ally of the Army—
which in this matter he lamentably failed to do.

The discrepancies between the accounts of Hammond and
Rolph are curious and perhaps significant. Hammond's
earliest report stated that two of the *three* soldiers had come to
him on 28 May—the day set for the King's escape—and
divulged the plot, and that he had arrested Dowcett, John
Newland (an Islander who supplied the escape vessel) and the
third soldier 'who was the chief instrument in this design'. Only
later did he describe Osborne as the principal escape plotter
he was. Rolph in his pamphlet claimed that the plot was
revealed to him by *three* soldiers on 28 May, and that he
immediately told the Governor; that he was in his chamber all
that time he was alleged to have said he waited for the King;
that the fourth soldier named Floyd, 'true to the plot',
confessed on examination. Osborne told the Prince of Wales
that one soldier out of the three recruited by the original loyal
soldier in the plot revealed all to Hammond.

It is impossible for both the officers' accounts to be correct,
and in fact both officers lied. It is certain that Hammond and
Rolph knew of the escape plot well before 28 May, for Derby
House had long had the general terms of the scheme from
the betrayer of earlier plots—probably Lady Carlisle,
Northumberland's amoral sister. Hammond himself said he
waited 'till the plot was brought to maturity', which suggests
more than a few hours.

Osborne's evidence agreed with Rolph's to the extent that
he named *four* soldiers in the plot. He should have known and
he had no reason to lie. One of the names was *Floyd*. There
appears to be a soldier missing. A sentry who fired when the

King was getting out of the window, and who 'was afterwards accidentally shot, no person can tell how', was named Floyd. The authority for this apparently was unaware of Floyd's role in the plot, and suggested he was raising the alarm. Since Hammond was letting the plot 'come to maturity', he would want the King to emerge, and his friends approach with horses. In fact, he managed to arrest neither the King nor the horse-party (of Osborne and the Island gentleman, Worsley). Clearly the shot was not to aid the Governor: unless accidental, it was to aid the King. The descendant and biographer of Firebrace who thought the story of the sentry's shot incorrect, yet thought Floyd might well have been shot by Hammond's orders. Floyd's death at least is certain, for Hillier mentions the tombstone. Worsley related that he and Osborne were fired on as they rode off by an ambush of musketeers placed by Hammond. Hammond himself wrote that the horses came 'within musket-shot' of the works: perhaps he or Rolph or both had seen to it that it should be so.

It is perhaps significant that Floyd was at first regarded by Hammond as the 'chief instrument' of the plot. Hammond's first report claimed that all *three* of the soldiers involved were willing to swear that no one had told them the King's life was in danger. This may have been true for *three* soldiers, but not for the *fourth*. In any case, Rolph claimed that Dowcett also on first hearing of Osborne's allegations denied knowledge of and belief in any danger to the King's life. This also could be true; on the other hand, the soldiers may well have feared to say otherwise to the very officers accused of planning and permitting the regicide, and Dowcett also may have feared to speak his mind before Osborne obtained for them both a hearing from the Lords. However, Osborne claimed that when arrested Dowcett told Hammond all about Rolph's design.

According to Clarendon (who had ample opportunity to meet Osborne and other *dramatis personae*), Rolph recommended to Osborne a soldier whom the King had known before. Yet Osborne's own account to the Prince of Wales (which Clarendon kept among his papers) claimed that the King himself suggested the first soldier, of whom he (rightly, it proved) had a good opinion, merely from observation without conversation.

However, the fate of Floyd is far from clear. The Commons sent to Hammond for Dowcett and the two other prisoners, and on 21 June ordered Dowcett and Floyd to be committed to Peter House and their examinations referred to the Committee for Informations. On 30 June to a message from the Lords that 'one, being a prisoner in Peter House' was 'said to be a necessary witness', the Commons agreed to permit Dowcett to attend the House of Lords as often as necessary. Is it possible that there was by then only one prisoner (connected with the plot) in Peter House? There is also a possibility of an error of name. Since only two persons were committed to Peter House, there could have been only two sent up to London of the three sent for, and the second could have been in fact Newland rather than Floyd. There is nothing to show whether a third prisoner ever came to London, save the report of the not very accurate Royalist *Mercurius Pragmaticus* (of 20-27 June on the attempt by Rolph to *poison* the King) of a brief appearance of Dowcett 'and the rest' before a packed committee of the Commons. The fact that neither Osborne nor Dowcett mentioned Floyd's shooting or being shot proves nothing: Osborne was outside the castle (being shot at) and Dowcett, Clerk of the Kitchen, had no contact with the King's apartments where Floyd stood sentry.

Whether or not convinced merely by Osborne's account, Clarendon believed in the reality of the threat to the King, and accepted that the King also believed. Osborne said Rolph proposed to deceive the King into acquiescing in his removal by forged letters purporting to come from Cavaliers, which Clarendon (perhaps from conversation with Osborne) interpreted as warnings of danger which would make the King willing to escape, as others inspired by the Army had alarmed him into fleeing from Hampton Court. Clarendon confused two episodes in the King's attempted escapes, but may still have been justified in believing Osborne's claim that he tried to deceive Rolph and use his assistance to promote an escape (instead of the kidnapping which Rolph wanted) and that Rolph discovered the deception and thwarted it. This could explain why Osborne might show hostility against Rolph. On the other hand, if he had become a recent convert to Royalism this could have made him detest Rolph or Wharton or both for something of which he had knowledge and had become ashamed.

Whether Osborne was originally a violent opponent of the King who became at Carisbrooke a convert to the King's part, or whether he was always secretly for the King, is quite immaterial. What are significant are these facts: first, that Wharton recommended, Hammond appointed, and Rolph sought the company of a man about whom a pamphlet that was anti-Osborne and pro-Hammond said:

> No man inveighed more against the King's actings and interest than he . . . [whose] carriage and language [were] Saint-like

(an eloquent testimony to the kind of language considered Saint-like by the Army's puritans in 1648); and, second, that:

> The noble Governor [Hammond] entertained him [Osborne] with great civilities (far beyond his desert and quality).

The unwonted and exceptional courtesy of a colonel towards a young gentleman-usher of violently anti-monarchic language is worthy of note, especially when we find from another anti-Osborne, pro-Hammond newsletter that Osborne's 'usual discourse' was:

> that should the Parl[iament] command him to lock up, put in chains . . . the King . . . he would do it: nay, if to do violence to the King, he would not absolutely deny it.

This, at a time when Parliament's hacks kept emphasising that the King was cheerful and not in any real sense a prisoner, when Hammond and Wharton angrily dismissed the possibility of the King's being in danger, was the language of one who had been educated and recommended by Wharton and appointed and loaded with civilities by Hammond.

These pamphlets were intended as proof of Osborne's hypocrisy, and have been accepted as such by Gardiner and others. They are far more damning evidence of the hypocrisy of Hammond and Wharton, and of (at the very least) their culpable negligence, if not guilty intentions. Hammond himself probably was much under the influence of Rolph, his principal adviser, a notable person in the councils of the Army, and noted for speaking against the King; but I discount

Bowring's claim that he took orders from Lisle, the future regicide. Osborne told the Prince that Hammond, 'in a mischievous subtlety' concealing his knowledge of the plot, stood with Rolph, both armed, to try to catch the King in the act of escaping.

This alleged hypocrisy of Osborne is regarded by Hillier as a reason for believing him capable of fabricating the story of the murder plot. Indeed, on common sense, several of Osborne's public claims must be untrue: that, for example, he wished to ask the permission of the Derby House Committee before removing the King; that the King first asked his help; that he believed the King wished to go to his Parliament. However, for these lies his motives probably were no worse than the desire not to incriminate further the King or himself; he did not repeat them to the Prince of Wales.

It has been suggested that Osborne made his charges with the sole intention of furthering the King's wishes: that is, to effect either the removal of the King to a place whence his escape might be easier, or the replacement of Hammond and Rolph by men less alert. The only evidence adduced is a letter in which the King wrote that he told Hammond nothing concerning Rolph or Osborne because his maxim was 'never to clear one man to the prejudice of another, or of his own service.'

Hammond, and later Wharton, claimed that Osborne acted to enflame the people, and Hammond and (possibly) others claimed that, after the failure of the escape plot, Osborne met 'new Councellors', 'notorious malignants' (Cavaliers) who put ideas into his head; but the only evidence given was that Judge Jenkins, an 'exempted person' (unpardonable Royalist), was legal counsel for Osborne and Dowcett.

Osborne's letter to Wharton rightly called Rolph 'a person very intimate with the Governor, privy to all counsels and . . . very high in the esteem of the Army'. Naturally, the acquittal of (or, strictly, the dismissal of charges against) so redoubtable a spokesman of the Army, in the hour of the Army's triumph, is no evidence at all that the charges were groundless.

The presiding judge was Sjt Wilde, fresh from the hanging of Captain Burleigh for attempting to rescue the King. Wilde began Rolph's defence by reading to the grand jury (composed partly—but not, as Clarendon claims, mostly—of the jury used against Burleigh) a letter in which Cromwell announced his northern victory, saying he did so to enlist their good opinion for Rolph. The evidence of Dowcett and Osborne was taken, but as Wilde's second address began:

> Gentlemen, this is a business of great importance; take heed how you move in it; the House of Commons resent it very much, for this Major Rolph is a gallant man, and hath done great service for the state,

the jury naturally and rapidly returned an ignoramus. The legal aid of Sjt Maynard (so useful against Strafford) though available for Rolph, was not needed.

Soon after, the Commons voted Rolph £500. However, a week after Rolph's triumph, Charles I wrote to his son, the Prince of Wales, recommending Osborne as one who had got into trouble for the King's sake (not, as Gardiner would have it, to save himself).

SOURCES

This is far from being a complete bibliography of all papers and books regarded as possible sources of information and consulted in the preparation of this work. It is not even an exhaustive list of all those sources which proved to be useful for my purpose. I have here only those sources which proved to be of some importance to my work; of these, the ones which were of considerable importance I also comment on separately. The secondary sources are even more narrowly selected than the primary.

PRIMARY SOURCES

MANUSCRIPTS IN THE BODLEIAN LIBRARY
Carte MSS,* volumes 79, 80, 81, 103, 117, 72, 78, 98, 108
Rawlinson MSS Letters,* volumes 49, 50, 51, 52, 53
Wharton MSS, volume 9
Clarendon State Papers,* volumes 70, 71, 72

CONTEMPORARY OFFICIAL RECORDS
The Journals of the House of Lords,* volumes 4-14
The Journals of the House of Commons, volumes 2-4 (to some extent)

PRINTED COLLECTIONS OF CONTEMPORARY DOCUMENTS
Returns of Members of Parliament (1878)
Original Papers, ed T. Carte (1739)
Acts and Ordinances of the Interregnum 1642-1660, ed C. H. Firth and R. S. Rait (1911)
Historical Collections, J. Rushworth (1659-92)
Papers relating to the Army of the Solemn League and Covenant 1643-1647 ed C. Terry (1917)

CALENDARS
State Papers Domestic
Reports of the Historical Manuscripts Commission

MEMOIRS, DIARIES AND PRINTED CORRESPONDENCE
Letters and Journals of Robert Baillie A.M. (1841)*
Memoirs of Sir Hugh Cholmley, Knt. and Bart. (1870)*
The Writings and Speeches of Oliver Cromwell, ed W. C. Abbott (1937)*
Memorials of the Civil War: The Fairfax Correspondence, ed R. Bell (1849)
The Diary of Sir Henry Slingsby, ed D. Parsons (1836)*

CONTEMPORARY BOOKS

G. Burnet, *A History of My Own Time*, ed O. Airey (Oxford, 1900)

Edward Hyde, Earl of Clarendon, *The History of the Rebellion and Civil Wars in England begun in the year 1641*, ed W. D. Macray (Oxford, 1888)*

J. Dugdale, *A Catalogue of the nobility of England* (London 1685)

Memoirs of the Life of the Most Nobel Thomas, late Marquess of Wharton (London, Printed for J. Roberts, 1715)*

C. Walker, *The Compleat History of Independencie* (London 1661)

A. Wood, *Athenae Oxonienses*, ed P. Bliss (London 1813)

CONTEMPORARY PAMPHLETS AND NEWSPAPERS

Eight Speeches Spoken in Guild-Hall upon Thursday night Octob 27 1642 (London, Printed for G. Lindsay Octob 31 1642)

An Answer to a scandalous lying pamphlet intituled Prince Rupert his declaration, printed for G. H. (n.p., 7 December 1642)

Lord Wharton's Speech to the Petitioners for Peace on the eighth day of December at Haberdashers-hall (London, 12 December 1642)

Master Richard Osborne's Two Letters (London 1648)

Two Letters sent by Mr. Richard Osborne late Attendant on his Majesty in Carisbrook Castle touching a Design to poyson or make away his Majesty . . . With an Answer to the said Letters, and a Narrative of the whole Design (London, Printed for A. H. neere Pye-corner 1648)

The Independent's Loyalty, or the Most Barbarous Plot (to Murther his sacred Majestie) very fully Discovered, with a cleere and perfect Answer to the Lord Wharton's Evasions (London 1648)

Two Letters from the Isle of Wight (3 August 1648)

The Naked Truth (21 June 1648)

The Votes and Proceedings in Parliament (3 July 1648) and the files of *Mercurius Elencticus, Mercurius Melancholicus, Mercurius Pragmaticus* and *The Moderate Intelligencer*, especially between November 1647 and September 1648.

SECONDARY SOURCES

Rt. Hon. Geo. Bankes   *The Story of Corfe Castle, and of many who have lived there* (London 1853)

R. S. Bosher   *The Making of the Restoration Settlement 1649-1662* (London 1951)*

L. F. Brown   "The Religious Factors in the Convention Parliament" *EHR* (XXII 1907)

A. Browning   *Thomas Osborne, Earl of Danby and Duke of Leeds 1632-1712* (Glasgow 1944)

D. Brunton and D. H. Pennington   *Members of the Long Parliament* (London 1954)

G. Burton — *The Life of Sir Philip Musgrave, Bart.* (Carlisle 1840)*

J. Carswell — *The Old Cause* (London 1954)*

B. Dale — *The Good Lord Wharton* (London 1906)*

G. Davies — *The Restoration of Charles II 1658-1660* (Oxford 1955)*

E. S. De Beer — "The House of Lords in the Parliament of 1680" *BIHR* (XX 1943-1945)*

C. W. Firebrace — *Honest Harry* (London 1932)*

C. H. Firth — "A Letter from Lord Saye and Sele to Lord Wharton, 29 Dec. 1657" *EHR* (X 1895)

C. H. Firth — *The House of Lords during the Civil War* (London 1910)*

H. C. Foxcroft — *The Life and Letters of Sir Geo. Savile, Bart., First Marquis of Halifax* (London 1898)

G. E. C. — *The Complete Peerage* (London   -1898)

G. E. C. — *The Complete Peerage* ed Vicary Gibbs and others (London 1910-   )*

B. M. Gardiner — "A Secret Negociation with Charles the First, 1643-1644" ed from Tanner MSS, *Camden Miscellany, N.S.* (VIII 1883)

S. R. Gardiner — *The Personal Government of Charles I, 1628-1637* (London 1877)*

S. R. Gardiner — *The Fall of the Monarchy of Charles I, 1637-1642* (London 1882)*

S. R. Gardiner — *The Great Civil War* (London 1886)*

H. Gee — "The Derwentdale Plot, 1663" *Transactions of the Royal Historical Society* (XI 1917)*

P. H. Hardacre — *The Royalists during the Puritan Revolution* (The Hague 1956)

W. M. Hetherington — *History of the Westminster Assembly of Divines* (Edinburgh 1843)

J. H. Hexter — "The Problem of the Presbyterian Independents" *AHR* (XLIV 1938)*

J. H. Hexter — *The Reign of King Pym* (Cambridge, Mass. 1941)*

G. Hillier — *A Narrative of the attempted escapes of Charles the First from Carisbrooke Castle* (London 1852)*

M. Frear Keeler — *The Long Parliament, 1640-1641* (Philadelphia 1954)

E. W. Kirby   "The Reconcilers" *Essays in Modern English History in Honor of W. C. Abbott* (Cambridge, Mass. 1941)

A. G. Matthews   *Calamy Revised* (Oxford 1934)

A. G. Matthews   *Walker Revised* (Oxford 1948)

A. P. Newton   *The Colonising Activities of the English Puritans* (Oxford 1914)*

B. Nightingale   *The Ejected of 1662 in Cumberland and Westmorland* (Manchester 1911)

W. Notestein   "The Establishment of the Committee of Both Kingdoms" *AHR* (XVII 1911-12)

The Parliamentary or Constitutional History of England from the earliest times to the restoration of Charles II (London 1751-62) [Old Parliamentary History]

W. A. Shaw   *The History of the English Church during the Civil Wars and under the Commonwealth* (London 1900)

L. Stone   *The Crisis of the Aristocracy 1558-1641* (Oxford 1965)

A. S. Turberville   "The House of Lords under Charles II" *EHR* (XLIV, XLV, 1929-30)

D. Underdown   *Royalist Conspiracy in England, 1649-1660* (New Haven 1960)

C. V. Wedgwood   *The King's Peace 1637-1641* (London 1955)

B. Wormald   *Clarendon* (Cambridge 1951)

ON THE USE MADE OF
THE SOURCES

The Carte Manuscripts were by far the most important source for this study. They contain the vast majority of Wharton's papers, letters and notes of political significance. Some have been used, some lists have been published by Professor Browning and the notes of one debate have been published by Professor Robbins. However, many have not been made public before, in particular, the debates on Bristol's impeachment of Clarendon, and on the bishops' right to be present at capital trials; the qualifications of the peers in 1660; and the proposed sweeping constitutional changes in 1688-9. Some other hitherto unpublished papers more narrowly restricted to Wharton's career are those on the Osborne affair and on the Northern Plot of 1662-4.

The Rawlinson Letters include a great deal of Wharton's correspondence, but with few exceptions this contains nothing political.

The Clarendon State Papers are the only source of information for Wharton's attitudes and activity just before the Restoration.

The *Lords' Journals* were the second greatest single source of material. For the years when Wharton was most active, they provided the necessary context in which to study his career.

The letters, journals and memoirs of Baillie, Cholmley, Cromwell and Slingsby were invaluable for the light they threw on Wharton's activities, attitudes, importance and uniqueness over a period when otherwise his career would be fairly obscure.

Clarendon is the only full and competent contemporary historian and thus essential, although often showing prejudice.

The Life of Thomas . . . Marquess of Wharton was vital as the only contemporary or near-contemporary account of Wharton by one who knew him; it gave very little information, but what it gave was of prime importance.

Wharton's sadly few pamphlets and printed speeches were quite invaluable for the evidence they gave of the way his mind worked; contemporary replies to and comments on them were almost as useful.

Bosher's *Restoration Settlement* was invaluable for the stages of religious negotiation and legislation 1660-2.

Mr. Carswell's *Old Cause* has much interesting comment on Wharton's character.

Dale's *Good Lord Wharton* has a good factual account of Wharton's ancestry and public actions, with few inaccuracies. It is mostly concerned with his famous Bible Charity, and neither asks nor answers any questions to account for Wharton's actions.

Dr De Beer's article is a model for any attempt to analyse the seventeenth-century House of Lords.

Firebrace's *Honest Harry* was extremely useful for the Osborne affair, for which Hillier's *Narrative* was quite essential.

Firth's *House of Lords in the Civil War* was essential for that period, but often appeared to rely too much on contemporary opinion, sometimes of doubtful value, and too little on the *Lords' Journals*. It is not clear why Firth sometimes accepted and sometimes rejected Clarendon's testimony and judgements on the characters of peers. He devoted much space to a few peers and barely mentioned the rest, which can be misleading.

G. E. C.'s *Peerage* was very useful, as it often summarises or refers to accounts elsewhere of various peers.

Gardiner's is still the only full and detailed history of the puritan revolution. His works were essential, but I had to allow for bias. The greatest weakness from my point of view was the tendency to ignore the Lords except when they obstructed the Commons!

Gee's work gave the necessary background to a serious attempt to destroy Wharton.

Hexter's analytical article is the most stimulating treatment of the Long Parliament, and his book banishes confusion from one section of that parliament's history.

Newton's book was vital for understanding the 1640 opposition.

INDEX

Agas, Benjamin, 192

Albemarle, Duke of, *see* Monk

Alleine, Joseph, 212

Anglesey, Arthur Annesley, first Earl of, 153, 176, 195; protests, 218; in debate, 229, 243; dissuades Wharton, 245

Annesley, Arthur, *see* Anglesey

Antrobus, —, 106

Arlington, Earl of, *see* Bennet, Sir Henry

Armine, Sir William, 75, 95

Arminius, 21 n5

Army (New Model), 80, 93, 103, 106, 108, 112-13, 117, 119, 123, 125, 139, 153, 159; petitions for its disbanding, 107-8; its demands, 108; accuses M.P.s, 109; marches on London, 110; collapse of, 151; ex-soldiers rebel, 201

Arundell (of Wardour), Thomas, second Lord, 66

Atchison, Captain John, 205-6, 211

Atkinson, Captain Robert, 201, 206, 211

Aylesbury, Robert Bruce, first Earl of, 229

Bacon, Thomas, 179, 186

Baillie, Robert, 46 n29, 83-5, 89, 95; on Wharton, 95

Bampfield, Thomas, 176, 178-9, 184

Bankes, Sir John, letters to and from Wharton *et al.*, 47, 55-6

Barton, John, 184

Barwick, John, 161, 161 n21

Bath, Henry Bourchier, sixth Earl of, 35

Bath and Wells, Peter Mews, Bishop of, 243

Baxter, Richard, 191

Bedford, Francis Russell, fourth Earl of, 31-2, 272-4

Bedford, William Russell, fifth Earl of, 59, 163-4, 164 n27, 169

Bedloe, William, 238

Bellasis, Sir Henry, 22-3, 26

Bennet, [? Gervase], 179

Bennet, Gervase, 183

Bennet, Sir Henry, later first Earl of Arlington, 15 n7, 194-5, 207, 212, 217, 219, 223, 235; examines Wharton, 203-5

Bennet, Robert, 212

Berkeley, George, eighth Lord, 148

Berkshire, Charles Howard, second Earl of, 229, 233

Bertie, family of, *see also* Lindsey, Willoughby of Eresby, 209-10, 258

Birch, Colonel John, 178, 184, 186

Birch, Samuel, 212

Bolingbroke, Oliver St John, first Earl of, 67, 70, 274

Booth, Sir George, *see* Delamere

Bosher, R. S., 177, 287

Bowes, Lady, widow of Sir George, 16

Bowyer, Sir William, 188

Brackley, John Egerton, Lord, 241

Braithwaite, Edward, *also* Braythwaite, —, *and* Braithwaits, 206

Bramston, Sir John (the younger), 187

Brandenburg, Frederick William, Elector of, 254-5

Bridgwater, John Egerton, second Earl of, 216, 241

Bristol, Anne, Countess of, 164 n27

Bristol, John Digby, first Earl of, 56, 84, 195

Bristol, George Digby, second Earl of, 195-200, 202, 207, 229

Broghill, Roger Boyle, Lord, 136

Brooke, Catharine, Lady, 149

Brooke, Robert Greville, second Lord, 26, 32, 35, 40 n5, 59, 66-7, 67 n35, 272-3; manager of House of Lords, 31

Brooke, Francis Greville, third Lord, 149

Brown, Louise F., 249

Browne, Major-General, later Sir Richard, 176, 178

Browne, —, 188

Bruce (of Whorlton), Thomas, first Lord, 67 nn29 and 31, 70, 148, 158

Buckingham, George Villiers, second Duke of, 165, 195, 202, 217-19, 223, 232, 234-5, 237, 243, 245; forfeited estates, 148; defends Wharton, 199; possible enemy of Wharton, 206-8, 210; leagued with Wharton and Shaftesbury, 224, 226; sent to Tower, 229-35; aids Wharton, 241

Bulstrode, [? Thomas], 183

Bunce, Alderman James, 161

Bunckley, John, 184

Burleigh, Captain, 281-2

Burnet, Gilbert, Bishop of Salisbury, 243, 255; claims Wharton sentenced to death, 26

Burton, Thomas, 143

Butts, Joseph, 158

Byron, Sir John, later first Lord, 34 n16

Calamy, Edmund, 212

Capel, Arthur, first Lord, 66

Carbery, Richard Vaughan, second Earl of, 43

Carlisle, Lucy, Countess of, 277

Carlisle, Charles Howard, first Earl of, 223

Carr, William, son-in-law of Wharton, 213

Carswell, J., 4, 4 n1, 287; account of Wharton, 249

Carlyle, Thomas, 276

Case, Thomas, 63

Chandos, George Brydges, sixth Lord, 43, 63

Charles I, 15, 18, 20, 23, 31, 36, 38, 40-2, 45-6, 54, 57, 61-3, 69, 72, 84, 98-101, 104-5, 107-10, 116, 125-6, 129, 130-1, 279; summons Wharton to masques, 19; and Yorkshire petition, 24-5; warns Wharton *et al.*, 26; in Wharton's testament, 49, 128; Vote of No Addresses to, 113-14; Wharton sends Osborne to, 116; his attempted murder disclosed, 117; Wharton's culpable behaviour to, 118; evidence of attempted murder, 119, 282; recommends Osborne, 172; Wharton has portrait, 236

Charles II, 151, 153-4, 164, 172, 183, 194-7, 199-200, 212, 219-21, 223, 232, 240, 242, 247-9; expresses indignation, 8, 243; as Prince of Wales, 67, 114, 281-2; his restoration and Wharton, 152, 155-7; his taking the Covenant, 162-3; blamed by Wharton, 190, 215; and Wharton *re* Northern Plot, 203-4; converses with Wharton, 221; pleasant to Wharton, 234-5; offended by Wharton, 235-6; his lobbying, 261

Charlton, Job, 181, 184, 186

Cholmley, Sir Hugh, 22-3, 26, 41 n10

Church of England, 1-2, 5, 51-2, 85, 162, 191, 248; Erastian-Presbyterian settlement, 88;

linked with royalism, 96, 163; attempted compromise or Presbyterian settlement, 175, 182-5; Act of Uniformity, 188-91; attempt at comprehension, 262 Bishops of: 183, 188; avoid word 'reformed', 21-2; power to excommunicate King, 226; and Non-resistance Bill, 227; Protestantism impugned, 240

Claneboy, James Hamilton, second Viscount (first Earl of Clanbrassil), 141

Claneboy, Anne, Lady (Countess of Clanbrassil), 141

Clare, John Holles, second Earl of, 164 n27

Clare, Gilbert Holles, third Earl of, 218, 239

Clarendon, Edward Hyde, first Earl of, as statesman, 154, 162 n22, 172, 182-3, 191, 193, 217, 222; and Wharton's pardon, 155 n10, 156-7; attacked by Bristol, 195-200; and Wharton, 207, 210; as historian, 29, 35 n24, 52, 210, 272-3, 288; on Bristol's attack, 200; on Osborne affair, 279, 282

Clarendon, Henry Hyde, second Earl of, 225, 233, 237, 258

Clark, Samuel, 212

Clark, Colonel —, 183

Clifford, Henry, Lord, later fifth Earl of Cumberland, 33, 41 n8

Clifford (of Chudleigh), Thomas, first Lord, 217-18, 223

Clifton, Sir Gervase, 32 n10

Cole, William, 192, 212

Committee of Both Kingdoms, 78-114, *passim* esp. 78, 80, 87, 98-100

Conway, Edward, second Viscount, 46 n28

Cornwallis, Charles, third Lord, 229

Cottington, Francis, first Lord, 17, 43

Covenant, first, 76; Solemn League and, 76, 110, 162, 193, 227

Cresset, Francis, 116

Cromwell, Henry, 140

Cromwell, Mary, 140

Cromwell, Mrs, 118

Cromwell, Oliver, 4, 9, 85, 87, 92-3, 107, 109, 125-8, 139, 142, 150, 282; writes from Wharton's house, 113; letters to Wharton, 115, 129, 133-7, 140, 146; son's proposed marriage, 140; grants Wharton's requests, 141; Wharton's opinion of, 141-3; summons Wharton to Upper House, 143

Cromwell, Richard, 151, 155 n7

Dacres, Francis Lennard, fourteenth Lord, 67 nn28 and 31; 95, 105, 130, 148

Dalton, John, 192

Danby, Thomas Osborne, first Earl of, 9, 202, 224, 236, 238-40, 242-4, 248, 257-8, 263; possible enemy of Wharton, 209-10; Non-resistance Bill, 225-7; punishment of Wharton *et al.*, 229-31

Dangerfield, Thomas, 245

Danvers, Sir John, 32 n10

Darcy, Conyers, eighth Lord, 225

Darcy, James, 178, 204, 212

Darley, Henry, 33, 56, 72

Delamere, George Booth, first Lord, 176, 178, 218, 225, 233, 254; supports Wharton *et al.*, 230

de la Warr (Delaware), Charles West, fifth Lord, 67 n30, 130, 148, 158, 169

Dell, —, 212

Denbigh, Basil Feilding, second Earl of, 67 n37, 70, 116, 131,

Denbigh—*continued*
147, 151, 158 n17, 218; and
Wharton and Waller-Tompkins
Plot, 72; letters to, from Wharton, 107-8; alleged attempt to
save King, 130; inveighs against
'young lords', 158; Restoration
depends on, 160; supports
Wharton, 215

Denton, family of, 18

D'Ewes, Sir Simonds, 43

Dodds, John, 212

Dodson, Thomas, 192

Dorchester, Henry Pierrepoint,
first Marquess of, 229

Dorset, Richard Sackville, fifth
Earl of, 158-9

Dowcett, Abraham, 116, 119, 124,
155, 167, 172, 277-9, 281-2

Downing, George, later Sir George,
178, 186

Ellis, —, 179

Ely, Peter Gunning, Bishop of, 243

Essex, Arthur Capel, first Earl of,
218, 237, 243, 245, 251

Essex, Robert Devereux, third
Earl of, 31-2, 35, 40 n5, 43,
46-7, 58, 60-4, 71-3, 75, 77,
91-2, 272-3; orders to Wharton,
61-2; praises Wharton, 65;
and governorship of Portsmouth, 74; and Committee of
Both Kingdoms, 78, 80-1, 93

Eure, George, sixth Lord, 147, 218

Exeter, David Cecil, third Earl of,
67 n31

Fairfax, Ferdinando, first Lord,
22 n22, 41 n10, 64-5

Fairfax, Sir Thomas, later second Lord, 93, 118, 125, 165,
201-2; defies House of Lords,
106; in arms in Yorkshire, 152

Falkland, Henry Carey, fourth
Lord, 179

Fauconberg, Thomas Belasyse,
second Viscount, 142, 147, 215,
223, 229-30

Feilding (of Newnham Paddocks),
Basil, Lord, *see* Denbigh

Fiennes, James, 178

Fiennes, Nathaniel, 53, 145

Firebrace, Henry, 116, 172

Firth, Sir Charles, 102, 130, 140,
158 n17, 269, 272, 276, 288

Fitzharris, Edward, 249

Fleetwood, family of, 18

Fleetwood, General Charles, 141

Floyd, —, 277-9

Foley, Thomas, 178

Frescheville, John, first Lord, 229,
233

Gale, Theophilus, 212

Gardiner, S. R., 29, 35 n26, 100,
107 n9, 130-1, 190, 276, 282,
288

Gastwell, Richard, 238 n4

Gerard, Digby, fifth Lord, 243

Gerrard, Sir Gilbert, 153, 156,
176, 179

Gilbert, Thomas, 212, 226 n11,
248

Glynn, John, 176, 179, 186

Goodwin, Arthur, 18, 43, 60,
74-5, 148; letters to Lady
Wharton, 6, 36, 54, 71-3

Goodwin, Robert, 95, 179

Goodwin, Thomas, 83-4

Gower, E., 175 n13

Gower, Sir Thomas, 202

Grey (of Groby), Thomas, Lord,
167

Grey (of Rolleston), Charles North,
first Lord, 226

Grey (of Wark), William, first
Lord, 67, 67 n36, 80 n4, 148,
160

Grey (of Wark), Ford, third Lord,
249-51

Grey (of Wilton), Arthur, fourteenth Lord, 148

Grimston, Sir Harbottle, 176,
178-9

Gunter, Humphrey, 212

Gunter, John, 206-7, 209, 211

Hale, Matthew, 164, 178

Halifax, George Savile, first Marquess of, 9, 202, 218, 225, 229, 237, 243, 245, 249-50, 258; and his 'guardian' Wharton, 166-7; possible enemy of Wharton, 208-10; activity on Wharton's behalf, 231, 233

Hammond, Colonel Robert, 116, 122, 125, 127, 129, 142, 275-81; urged to murder Charles I, 117; letters to Wharton, 119, 126

Hampden, John (I), 9, 18 n16, 21, 32, 52, 63, 66; cousin and ally of A. Goodwin, 18; and Twelve Peers' Petition, 29 n2

Hampden, John (II), 241, 260

Harley, Edward, 176, 178-9

Haselrig, Sir Arthur, 9, 94 n13, 155

Hatcher, Thomas, 95, 179

Henrietta Maria, Queen Consort of Charles I, 38, 38 n42, 40, 54, 72

Herbert (of Chirbury), Edward, first Lord, 47

Heron, A., 33 n14

Hertford, William Seymour, first Marquess of, 43, 56, 59

Hieron, Samuel, 212

Higginson, Francis, 192, 206

Hill, Matthew, 183

Hillesly, —, 183

Hillier, G., 126, 275-6, 278, 281, 288

Hinson, William, 179

Holland, Henry Rich, first Earl of, 40, 46 n28, 47 n30, 56, 58, 70, 116, 142

Holland, Sir John, 178

Holles, Denzil, first Lord, 9, 55-6, 153, 156, 176, 218, 223, 226, 226 n11, 237; 'leader of Presbyterians', 224

Hotham, Sir John (I), 22, 26

Hotham, Sir John (II), 202

House of Commons, *passim* esp. 10, 39, 42-3, 73, 85, 88, 103, 107, 110, 129, 217, 248-9; Wharton's party, 177-82; struggle over religion, 182-6

House of Lords, 1, 10, 36-7, 39, 44, 47, 92, 94, 146, 153, 164, 188-91, 193, 218, 238, 248-9, 263; effect of mob on Strafford's attainder, 35 n25; revival of protests, 37; 'Opposition' Speakers, 45; declining importance, 81, 103; fluctuating 'Presbyterian' control, 104-9; 'secession' to Army, 110-12; control by 'Presbyterians' favours King, 114, 117, 119, 123-4, 128-30; abolished, 130; groups in, 130; Say and Sele's view of, 144; views of 'Independents' on, 146; plot to exclude 'young lords', 156-61; Bristol attacks Clarendon, 195-200; Wharton plans obstruction, 214; debates, 215-16; opposition grows, 225-8; Bishops and blood debate, 243-4; trial of Stafford, 246-7; limitations proposed by Wharton, 260-1

Committees and committee activity (especially Wharton's), 34-7, 40-2, 45, 48, 72, 81, 93-4, 98-9, 105-9, 112-14, 123, 118-19

Howard (of Escrick), Edward, first Lord, 41, 67, 67 n29, 71, 76, 80, 147; allegedly sentenced to death, 26; with Wharton meeting Scots, 75

Howe, John, 212

Howes, —, 34

Hunsdon, John Carey, Lord (Viscount Rochford by courtesy; later second Earl of Dover), 67 n28, 109, 114 n34, 130, 148, 157-8, 218; as Speaker examines Rolph, 123; possible witness for Wharton, 169

Huntingdon, Theophilus Hastings, seventh Earl of, 243

Hyde, Edward, *see* Clarendon

Inchiquin, Murrough O'Brien, first Earl of, 114

Independents, 9, 84, 106; and Ogle Plot, 79; in Westminster Assembly, 82, 86-7; Proposals at Restoration, 183; 'Independents', 82, 100, 104, 111; 'Independent' lords, 88; in the Convention, 185-6

Ingoldsby, Colonel (later Sir) Richard, 178

Irby, Sir Anthony, 184

Jackson, Christopher, 212

James I, 15

James II, *see* York, Duke of

Jenkins, Judge, 281

Jones, Colonel Philip, 203

Jones, Walter, 203

Joyce, Cornet, 109

Knightley, Richard, 178, 184

Knox, John, 16

Lascelles, Francis, 160

Laud, William, Archbishop of Canterbury, 21-2, 51-2, 135

Lauderdale, John Maitland, second Earl and first Duke of, 94, 227

Lawrence, Henry, 136, 139

Lawson, Sir Wilfred, 178, 184

Legge, George, later first Lord Dartmouth, 164 n27, 234-5

Leicester, Robert Sydney, second Earl of, 45

Lenthall, William, 110-11, 117-18, 122, 122 n10

Leslie, David, 96

Leven, Alexander Leslie, first Earl of, 64-5, 94

Lever, —, 188

Lever, Henry, 212

Lewis, Sir William, 156, 176, 178, 184

Lincoln, Thomas Barlow, Bishop of, 243

Lincoln, Theophilus Clinton, fourth Earl of, 67, 67 n31, 80 n4, 99, 130, 148, 157; excluded from Lords, 227

Lindsey, Montagu Bertie, second Earl of, 149, 169, 215

Littleton (Lyttelton), Edward, first Lord, 37 n36, 43

London, Henry Compton, Bishop of, 243

Loudoun, John Campbell, first Earl of, 76

Love, Christopher, 136

Lovelace, John, second Lord, 79

Lucas, John, first Lord, 198-200, 215, 218

Macaulay, Thomas, first Lord, 220

Manchester, Henry Montagu, first Earl of, 29, 37 n36

Manchester, Edward Montagu, second Earl of, (by courtesy Viscount Mandeville till his father's death), 19 n20, 32, 40 n5, 64-5, 67, 67 n37, 80, 82, 84, 91-3, 130, 147, 197, 199, 201-2, 215, 218, 272-3; manager of House of Lords, 31; listed with Wharton, 40; leads 'secession' to Army, 109-11; and Osborne affair, 117, 122 n10, 123; intrigues before Restoration, 148, 151, 153-6, 161; prays with Wharton, 161-2; and religious settlement, 162, 182, 191

Mandeville, *see* Manchester

Mansfield, Charles Cavendish, Viscount, 187

Marten, Henry, 76

Mary, Princess (later Mary II), 244, 259-60, 262-3

Massey, Colonel (later Sir) Edward, 178

Masy, Henry, 86, 106

Matther, Increase, 212

Maynard, William, second Lord, 67 nn30 and 32, 148, 157

Maynard, Sjt. John, 178, 282

Meers (Meres), Thomas, later Sir Thomas, 179

Middlesex, James Cranfield, second Earl of, 67 n30, 130

Middlesex, Lionel Cranfield, third Earl of, 158-9

Mildmay, Sir Henry, 134; his attack on Wharton, 73-6

Mohun, Charles, third Lord, 225, 228

Monk, General George, later first Duke of Albemarle, 136, 152-3, 164, 176, 202; and exclusion of 'young lords', 158-61, 163 n26

Monmouth, James Scott, first Duke of, 50, 244-5, 250, 253-5

Monmouth, Robert Carey, first Earl of, 16

Monmouth, Henry Carey, second Earl of, 141

Montagu (of Boughton), Edward, first Lord, 41, 54

Montagu (of Boughton), Edward, second Lord, 67 n30, 102, 130, 148, 158, 218

Montagu, Edward, later first Earl of Sandwich, 136, 155 n9, 195

Montagu, Ralph, later Duke of, 238

Montagu, William, 41

Montrose, James Graham, first Marquess of, 95, 97

Mordaunt, John, first Viscount, 154 n5, 159, 163 n26, 255; visited by Wharton, 155; letter concerning Wharton, 156-7, 157 n12; possible deception of Wharton, 162-3, 163 n25

Mordaunt, Elizabeth, Lady, letters concerning Wharton, 155-7, 155 n10, 157 n13

Mosely, Colonel —, 79

Mulgrave, Edmund Sheffield, second Earl of, 67 n30, 147

Murray, —, Lord, 74-5

Musgrave, Sir Edward, 166

Musgrave, Sir Philip, 141-2, 166, 169, 188, 204-6, 212

Neal, Sir Paul, 26 n22

New Model, *see* Army

Newcastle, William Cavendish, first Earl, Marquess and Duke of, 59, 224

Newland, John, 277, 279

Newport, Mountjoy Blount, first Earl of, 37, 47

North, Dudley, third Lord, 67 n31, 130, 148, 158

Northampton, Spencer Compton, second Earl of, 66

Northampton, James Compton, third Earl of, 155, 158, 243; conversation with Wharton, 157, 162-3; supports Wharton, 215; order for Wharton's release, 234

Northcoat, Sir John, 184

Northumberland, Algernon Percy, fourteenth Earl of, 58, 67 n29, 70, 80, 92-3, 95, 130-1, 147-8, 158, 164; beliefs and aims, 55; Firth's estimate of, 102; willing to serve crowned Cromwell, 146; intrigues at Restoration, 154, 156-8, 160-2, 162 n22, 163 n26

Norton, Colonel Richard, 136

Nottingham, Charles Howard, third Earl of, 67 nn28 and 32, 70, 148, 158, 227 n15; Wharton's fellow-commissioner, 110 n19, 111

Nottingham, Heneage Finch, first Earl of, 227, 243; as Chancellor, 230-2

Nye, Philip, 82-4, 139, 183

Oates, Titus, 238, 263

Ogle, Henry Cavendish, Earl of, 224

Ogle, —, 79, 84

Onslow, Sir Richard, 167-8, 178-9, 184, 186, 202

Ormond, James Butler, first Duke of, 108, 154, 212, 229; asked to aid Wharton, 234

Osborne, Sir Edward, 24

Osborne, Sir John, 276

Osborne, Richard, 120, 122-6, 155, 167, 172, 210, 275-82; educated and recommended by Wharton, 116; letters to Wharton and Speakers, 117; Wharton's attack on, 118; on Wharton's behaviour, 127

Osborne, Sir Thomas, *see* Danby

Osborne, Thomas, Esq., 276

Ossory, Thomas Butler, Earl of, 241

Owen, Dr John, 141-2, 212

Oxford, Aubrey de Vere, twentieth Earl of, 155, 159, 163 n26

Paget, William, sixth Lord, 31, 48, 225

Paget, William, seventh Lord, 239

Peace Party, 39, 69, 70, 72-3, 78, 80

Pembroke, Philip Herbert, fourth Earl of, 32 n10, 47 n30, 58, 67, 80 n4, 116, 131, 147

Pembroke, Philip Herbert, fifth Earl of, 157

Penn, William, 257

Peterborough, John Mordaunt, first Earl of, 43

Petre, William, fourth Lord, 159

Petty, Edmund, 178, 184, 186, 188

Phineas, 135

Pickard, Thomas, 212

Pierrepoint (Pierrepont), William, 154, 156, 176, 178-9

Plots, 3; (first) Army Plot, 35; (second) Army Plot, 40; Waller-Tompkins Plot, 71-2; Ogle's Plot, 79, 83-4; for King's escape, 116; Cobham Plot, 148; Derwentdale Plot, 201-11; Popish Plot, 238 *et seq.*; (false) Presbyterian Plot, 245; Whig plots, 249-53; Rye House plotters, 253

Portland, Jerome Weston, second Earl of, 47

Potts, Sir John, 178-9

Poyntz, Major-General Sydenham, 100

Presbyterians, 79, 84-5, 103, 106; at Restoration, 154, 162-3, 174-5, 182-3, 185
  pseudo-Presbyterians: 222-4, 245; in the Convention, 182-6

'Presbyterians', 109; definition, 82; in House of Lords, 104, 114, 123; and Restoration, 174

Pride, Colonel Thomas, 129, 168

Proctor, Anthony, 212

Protests, 42, 54; 'revival' or innovation, 37, 37 n37; by Royalists, 39, 40 n3, 42, 47; by 'Presbyterians', 81, 99, 107; by 'Independents', 92, 108-9; against second Conventicle Act, 218; threat to right of protest, 226-7; resumption of, 227 n13; by Country Party or Whigs, 227, 239-40, 242, 244, 246-7, 249; last by Wharton, 263

Providence Island Company, 21, 31-3, 70

Prynne, William, 176-9, 184, 186

Puritans, puritanism, 1-3, 5-6, 9, 16, 18, 21; insoluble political dilemma, 10; in Parliament, 52-4, 70, 78; split, 82-7, 186, 265; ejected at Restoration, 190-3; attempts at toleration for dissenters, 194-6, 219, 221, 235-6, 257-8, 261-3; persecution of dissenters, 214-15, 218, 225, 251

Pym, John, 9, 21, 29, 29 n2, 32, 38, 74-5; threatened, 40, 54; attitude to church and religion, 52; policies, 70-2; disbelieves accusation against Wharton, 73

Rawlett, John, 212
Raynsford, Richard, later Sir Richard, 179
Rich, Robert, Lord, 47
Rigby, Alexander, 43
Riley, —, 79
Rivers, Thomas Savage, third Earl, 159
Robartes, John, second Lord, later Earl of Radnor, 35, 40 n5, 80, 142, 148, 158 n16, 243-5; terms for Restoration, 151; bill supporting toleration, 194-5
Roberts, Sir William, 183
Rochester, John Dolben, Bishop of, 226, 243
Rogers, John, 212
Rolph (Rolfe), Captain (Major) Edmund, 118, 124, 127, 129, 167-8, 172, 275-82; proposes regicide, 117; attempts regicide, 119; importance, 123, 125; trial of, 126
Rosewall, Thomas, 212
Rudyerd, Sir Benjamin, 52
Rupert, Prince, 64, 71; opposed by Wharton, 62; jeers at Wharton, 65; challenged by Wharton, 65-6
Rushworth, John, 178
Russell, William, Lord, 250-1
Rutland, John Manners, eighth Earl of, 67 n31, 94, 148, 158

St John, Oliver, 9, 29 n2, 79, 82, 87, 91, 100, 153
St John, Oliver, Lord, 155-6, 156 n11, 274
Salisbury, William Cecil, second Earl of, 47 n30, 80 n4, 131, 147
Salisbury, James Cecil, third Earl of, 223, 237; co-operates with Wharton *et al.*, 224-5, 229-35
Sambourne, *alias* Slingsby, Sir Robert, 154-5, 154 n5, 164 n27
Sandwich, Earl of, *see* Montagu, Edward

Savile, Thomas, second Lord, 31-2, 47-8, 56, 93, 272-3
Savile, Sir George, *see* Halifax
Savile, Sir William, 95
Say and Sele, William Fiennes, first Viscount, 9, 26, 31-2, 34-5, 40 n5, 71, 76, 78, 80, 92-3, 104, 118, 123, 129-30, 158, 161, 272-3; letter to Bankes, 55; defends Wharton, 74; in Westminster Assembly, 82-3, 87; and Osborne affair, 117, 122; motives and attitudes, 131-2; advice to Wharton, 143-5; demands for Restoration, 151
Say and Sele, James Fiennes, second Viscount, 218
Scot, Thomas, 160
Scots, 87, 98-100, 105; Wharton and, 75-6; treat with Wharton *et al.*, 96-7
    In Westminster Assembly, 81-2, 85-6
    Scots Kirk, 85
    Scots Army (of second Bishops' War), 23, 25, 36-7
        (of first Civil War), 84-5, 89-91, 94, 96-7, 99-100, 104-5
Scroggs, Chief Justice Sir William, 239, 247
Seaman, Lazarus, 212
Shaftesbury, Anthony Ashley Cooper, first Earl of, 9, 30, 136, 156, 176, 195, 218-19, 223-4, 228, 230-5, 237, 239, 241, 243-6, 248-50; supports toleration, 194, 217; defends Wharton, 199; wrongly identified, 215; his 'Letter from a Person of Quality', 225, 265
Sharp, James, Archbishop of St. Andrews, 8, 243
Sheldon, Gilbert, Bishop of London, later Archbishop of Canterbury, 191, 193, 215
Skippon, Major-General Philip, 122-3, 148

Slingsby, *see* Sambourne

Southampton, Thomas Wriothesley, fourth Earl of, 198-9, 215

Spaen, Alexander, Freiherr von, 11, 254, 256
See also Wharton, Philip, fourth Lord, Autobiographical letter to

Spencer, Henry, third Lord, 43

Stafford, William Howard, first Viscount, 246-7

Stamford, Henry Grey, first Earl of, 59, 62, 64, 67 n36, 76, 94, 148; aids Wharton, 167-8

Stamford, Thomas Grey, second Earl of, 254, 255

Stanhope, Charles, second Lord, 225

Stapleton, Sir Philip, 38, 41, 74-5, 109

Stedman, Rowland, 212

Stephens, Edward, 184

Stevens, —, 188

Stone, Captain John, 183

Stone, Professor L., 57 n25

Strafford, Thomas Wentworth, first Earl of, 22, 34, 135; indignant against Yorkshire petition, 24; takes second petition to Wharton, 25

Strafford, William Wentworth, second Earl of, 155, 159, 243

Strange, James Stanley, Lord, later seventh Earl of Derby, 42-4, 59; letter to Wharton, 43-4

Strode, William, 63-4, 75; praises Wharton, 65

Stukely, Lewis, 212

Suffolk, James Howard, third Earl of, 67 n31, 148, 157, 169

Sunderland, Robert Spencer, second Earl of, 253

Swinfen (Swynfen), John, M.P., 176, 178-9, 184

Swynfen, John, 212

Sydney, Algernon, 9, 141-3, 250

Taylor, William, 106, 106 n7, 212

Temple, Sir Richard, 178, 184, 186

Temple, Sir William, 242

Thurland, Edward, later Sir Edward, 184

Thurloe, John, 155 n9, 179, 183, 195

Todd, Cornelius, 212

Toleration, attempts to obtain, 83-4, 109, 194-6, 217-23, 240, 246, 257-8, 261-3

Tonge, Israel, 238

Trevor, Sir John, 179

Trevor-Roper, Professor H. R., 29-30, 143

Van Druske, Colonel, 100 n25

Vane, Sir Henry (the elder), 95

Vane, Sir Henry (the younger), 9, 75-6, 78-9, 82-4, 86-7, 91, 148, 176

Verney, Sir Ralph, 234, 257

Wales, Samuel, 16, 16 n11

Waller, Richard, 211

Waller, Sir William, 73-4, 91, 153, 178

Walters, —, 205, 211

Wandesford, Sir Rowland, 17, 33 n14

Warwick, Robert Rich, second Earl of, 19 n20, 31-2, 35, 40 n5, 73, 80, 92, 100, 109-10, 142, 147-8, 272-3; replaces Wharton, 108; and Osborne affair, 117

Wenman, Thomas, second Viscount, 179

Wentworth, Thomas, Lord, 66

Westminster Assembly, 79, 81, 82, 85-6, 88-9; effect on Wharton, 83

Westrowe, Thomas, 136

Wharton, Anne, Lady, widow of Admiral Popham and third wife of fourth Lord Wharton, 213

Wharton, Anne, daughter of fourth Lord Wharton, 213

Wharton, Elizabeth, Lady, née Wandesford, first wife of fourth Lord Wharton, 17, 18

Wharton, Elizabeth, daughter of fourth Lord Wharton, 140, 149, 167

Wharton, Henry, son of fourth Lord Wharton, 258

Wharton, Humphrey, 15, 17

Wharton, Jane, Lady, née Goodwin, second wife of fourth Lord Wharton, 6, 18, 36, 54, 71-3, 166, 171

Wharton, Margaret, daughter of third Lord Wharton, 15

Wharton, Philip, third Lord, 14-15

Wharton, Philip, fourth Lord, *passim*

    Autobiographical letter to von Spaen: 11; untruths or false implications in, 194, 220, 244; quoted, 11-12, 19, 28, 49, 50, 128, 138, 152, 166, 168, 172, 189, 190, 191, 214, 215, 216, 219, 220, 221, 228, 235-6, 245, 251, 253, 254, 256, 267; omissions from, 68, 102, 171, 174, 201

    character: courage, 64-5, 69-70, 155-7, 245, 248-50, 256

    honesty 6, 8, 118-22, 127, 167-71, 216-17, 242-3, 280

    humanity 7-8, 246-7, 258-9, 280

    loyalty 7-8, 73-6, 211, 233-4, 245, 248-50, 259

    politics: democratic views, 9-10, 129-33, 260-1

    relations with and attitudes to monarchs, 10, 129 *et seq.*, 141, 190, 216, 221, 235-6, 251, 258-9, 280

    religion: 5-7, 10, 17, 50, 56, 79, 82, 86-7, 134-7, 161-3, 186, 239

    views on, and work for, toleration: 9-10, 86-7, 186, 188-91, 193, 212-13, 219-21, 236, 257, 262, 265-6

    wealth: 8-9, 17, 18, 20-1, 58, 102

    (committee activity: *see* House of Lords

    protests, *see* Protests)

Wharton, Thomas, first Lord, 13-14

Wharton, Thomas, second Lord, 14

Wharton, Thomas, later fifth Lord and first Marquess of, 4, 242, 252-3, 255, 258, 263; hypocrisy, 6; debauchery and sacrilege, 7; letters to, from fourth Lord Wharton, 241

Wharton, Sir George, elder son of third Lord Wharton, 15

Wharton, Goodwin, son of fourth Lord Wharton, 6-7, 241, 258 n12

Wharton, Sir Thomas, father of fourth Lord Wharton, 16

Wharton, Sir Thomas, brother of fourth Lord Wharton, 17-18, 59, 142, 169, 171; chosen by Strafford, 34-5; negotiates with Ormond, 108; letter to Ormond, 154; in favour, 170; party manager, 178; correspondence *re* Derwentdale Plot, 201-12

Widdrington, Sir Thomas, 110 n18, 178-9, 181, 186

Wilde, Sjt. —, 281-2

William of Orange, later William III, 244, 255-63

Willoughby of Eresby, Robert Bertie, Lord, 149, 155, 169

Willoughby (of Parham), Francis, fifth Lord, 59, 67, 67 n36, 99

Willoughby (of Parham), William, sixth Lord, 218

Winchester, George Morley, Bishop of, 193, 199

Winchester, Charles Paulet, sixth Marquess of, 225-6, 229, 237 n2, 241; to convert Wharton, 263

Wing, Charles, 139, 170

Wolseley, Sir Charles, 178

Worcester, Henry Somerset, fifth Earl of, 59

Worsley (of Gatcomb), —, 278

Wotton, Edward, first Lord, 15

York, James Stuart, Duke of (later James II), 169, 198-9, 223, 225, 237-8, 244, 246, 252-3, 257-9; saves Wharton, 168; possible motive, 182; affability to Wharton, 221, 236, 254; in opposition, 226-7; urged by Wharton, 229; offended by Wharton, 235, 251; Wharton's attitude to, 260-1